DESPERATE SEED

The Cowboy

Jim Gray

DESPERATE
SEED

*Ellsworth, Kansas
on the Violent Frontier*

Jim Gray

ISBN # 978-0-9822741-0-1

Printed in the U.S.A.

Cover Design by Dee Warren

Quotes are printed with grammar and misspelling left in place without the normal recognition of (sic). If words are misspelled they are that way in the cited document.

CONTENTS

ACKNOWLEDGEMENTS

Much of the information for Desperate Seed was initially collected for publication in the *Kansas Cowboy* newspaper, published by Linda Kohls and myself since 1996. Linda has been my ally and judicious critic through many years.

Thanks to Rod Beemer, author of *The Deadliest Woman in the West*, for his invaluable advice and encouragement. Rod spent many long hours schooling me concerning the mysteries of accurate composition. It takes one to know one and Rod handled my shortcomings like a seasoned cowboy.

My sincere thanks to everyone who has kindly helped in the collection of material for this book: Georgia Smith and Evelyn Arensman, Ellsworth County Historical Society; Linda Homolka, Colleen Sippel, Carol Searles, Luetta Havlik, and Betty Kepka, Robbins Memorial Library, Ellsworth, Kansas; Patty Booher and Angela Mueller, Ellsworth City Office; Janice Sneath and Sue Arensman, Ellsworth County Register of Deeds; Jan Andrews and Ona Crawford, Ellsworth County Clerk's Office. An extra special thank you goes out to Rebecca Seeman, Saline County Register of Deeds, for going out of her way to provide me with copies of the plat maps of the original town of Ellsworth.

I have been fortunate to have friends and family with wonderful creative talent. They knew me well enough to offer suggestions that have made this book better than I had hoped. Thanks from the bottom of my heart to Cody & Kristin Gray. A special thank you to Dee Warren for taking a few ideas and coming up with a cover that was better than I imagined. Thank you to Kim and Dee Warren for opening up your house and to Kim for providing your professional expertise. Thanks to Andrew Kohls for all your suggestions and spending countless midnight hours getting the final draft ready for printing. And finally, a big thank you to John & Gerry Curry for your words of encouragement, your inspiration, and for always keeping your eyes open for books that helped in my research.

Lastly I want to offer a hearty Cowboy thanks to all the readers of the *Kansas Cowboy* who have encouraged The Cowboy to publish this book.

Jim Gray

PREFACE

The evolution of Ellsworth is far from typical. From a town platted along a narrow stretch of hostile river bottom along the Smoky Hill, to that of an enterprising rural community, Ellsworth's history is like no other in Kansas. The story is not a typical one and deserves an atypical title.

As the reader will soon recognize, Ellsworth was established in unrelenting times and as a seed sown in unprepared soil, Ellsworth struggled desperately to survive and thrive. Desperate Seed is an uncommon history set in the violent atmosphere that was pervasive following the great American Civil War. It is my hope that in these pages not only a history can be found but also a recognition of the intensity of life won and lost.

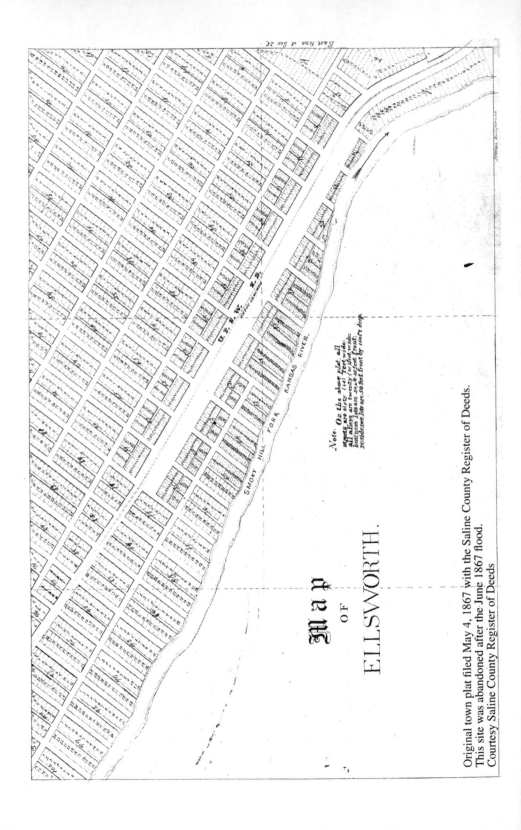

Map of ELLSWORTH.

Original town plat filed May 4, 1867 with the Saline County Register of Deeds.
This site was abandoned after the June 1867 flood.
Courtesy Saline County Register of Deeds

INTRODUCTION

Set in the valley of the Smoky Hill River, Ellsworth, Kansas, is as pleasant a community as one could hope to find. The town lies at the crossroads of Kansas Highways 14, 140 and 156. Driving through downtown Ellsworth reveals an atmosphere that quietly touches one's heart. There is something special here, something subtle yet inexplicably striking at its core.

Early Americans certainly recognized something exceptional. The Smoky Hill River was heart and soul to a people whose very existence relied upon the cycle of nature. The course of human existence on the vast plain that came to be known as central Kansas could be charted along that very river. Generations passed along an ancient route we know as the Smoky Hill Trail.

The river formed a boundary between earth-lodge people to the north and grass-lodge people to the south. Spanish Conquistadors explored. French Voyagers discovered. The Smoky Hills were a land of wonder.

A young country with the greatest of expectations dared to call itself the United States of America as adventurous explorers mapped the limitless horizons and made known the virtually unknown. For the next several decades the prairie would be a place to cross. Only the perceptive recognized the Smoky Hill River valley for the treasures that it held dear. Fleeing civilization the pioneers recognized and preferred the natural existence of man to the smoke and conflict of the "civilization" they had left behind.

Civilization would not linger long. Kansas officially came into being with the creation of the Kansas-Nebraska Act of 1854. A military trail was soon surveyed to connect the newly established Fort Riley to the Santa Fe Trail and the great southwest. The Fort Riley Road crossed the Smoky Hill River, turning southwest toward the Arkansas River valley.

Discovery of gold in the foot-hills of the Rocky Mountains in 1858 brought a frenzy of travelers onto the plains in search of that illusive strike that would make them rich. The catchphrase was on everyone's lips, "Pikes Peak or Bust!" Both the Santa Fe Trail to the south and the Oregon Trail to the north jammed with travelers. But one trail, The Smoky Hill Trail, held off all but the most intrepid, or perhaps most foolish gold seekers. Turning northwest at the Smoky Hill Crossing of the Fort Riley Road the wild adventurers passed from an identifiable route into a land known only to the plains Indian and the rare enduring frontiersman.

That point in time marked the first noticeable appearance of today's Highway 156. The modern highway parallels the Fort Riley Road to the southwest. To the west the Smoky Hill Trail foreshadowed today's Highway 140. Travel brought commerce and soon "ranches" were established along the trail to serve those who

1

traveled. The Kansas Stage Company established regular stage travel from Kansas City to Santa Fe in 1862. The progression of civilization had caused but slight alarm among the prairie people who knew the Smoky Hills as if it were their own backyard. Reality struck home as the men who had gone to the mountains to retrieve the yellow metal did not return to their homes in the east. Instead, more and more of them surged across the ancient sacred lands between the Arkansas and the Platte Rivers.

A general uprising by all the plains tribes brought travel to a standstill in May of 1864. Supplies could not reach the great settlement of Denver City, Colorado. Something had to be done. Government troops were sent to re-open the Fort Riley Road. At the Smoky Hill Crossing 2nd Lt. Alen Ellsworth, in command of a troop of Seventh Iowa Volunteer Cavalry bivouacked 40 men in June. The camp was designated Fort Ellsworth in July of 1864.

Despite the great "Indian War of 1864," Denver City's population continued to multiply. A young grocery man by the name of David Butterfield recognized Denver's supply dilemma. His answer was the Smoky Hill Trail. The shortest, most direct route to Denver held the promise for a grand transportation company that was branded "Butterfield's Overland Despatch," known far and wide as the B. O. D.

The route was surveyed during the summer of 1865. The survey crew witnessed a great herd of buffalo standing in the Smoky Hill River just below their camp very near the intersection of Ellsworth's Douglas Avenue and 8th Street. The water there was described as being, "… so strong of the buffalo urine that the men got pretty thirsty before they could use it, and then we were obliged to boil it and make as strong coffee as possible."

Great wagon trains of freight began crossing the plains on David Butterfield's new Smoky Hill route as early as August of 1865. Butterfield's stage stations were in place by September. Fort Ellsworth was utilized in the system as one of the all-important eating stations. The fort was the last vestige of civilization for travelers as they pointed wagons and coaches west to cross the immense sea of grass.

The first stage to leave Fort Ellsworth on the B. O. D. route set out September 16, 1865. Seven days later David Butterfield triumphantly arrived at Denver City. As stage and freight service developed along the trail, Indian attacks became prevalent. The federal government responded by establishing additional military posts west of Fort Ellsworth to protect Butterfield's business.

Indian troubles escalated, bankrupting the B. O. D. Ben Holladay purchased the line but also found it unprofitable. Holladay sold out to Wells Fargo.

By the fall of 1866, a new venture brought a whole new set of entrepreneurs to the plains. The Union Pacific, Eastern Division proposed to build a railroad along the Smoky Hill route to the Rocky Mountains. The prairie tribes were being asked to give up the sacred Smoky Hill River. They were told that they must move to a permanent home south of the Arkansas River. At Fort Ellsworth, Cheyenne warrior Roman Nose declared that before he would give up the Smoky Hills he would "fight forever." Peace talks broke down.

The new commander of the Department of the Missouri, General Winfield Scott Hancock, believed that the Cheyenne and all plains people needed to understand

2

that the United States was something greater than themselves. General Hancock conceived the plan to defend the frontier with a series of modern military posts manned with regular United States troops fresh from the recently concluded American Civil War.

Fort Ellsworth was renamed Fort Harker, moved to a more expansive location and fitted as the anchor of supply for Hancock's campaign against the Indians. The posts to the west were upgraded as well, providing a dependable chain of military readiness across the state of Kansas.

As the winter of 1866 progressed into the spring of 1867, Kansans held their breath in anticipation of the coming war. The Kansas frontier was the picture of a powder keg filled to the brim with a short fuse to boot. From this boiling cauldron the newborn village of Ellsworth was delivered. Born of strife, Ellsworth's beginnings were far from ordinary. Civilization with all of its discord and conflict had arrived on the banks of the Smoky. The desperate seed had sprung to life and its name was Ellsworth, Kansas.

Ellsworth was described as a "tough little hole" when it sprang to life in 1867. Alexander Gardner Photograph. Courtesy Ellsworth County Historical Society.

Chapter One

A TOUGH LITTLE HOLE

Whether the birth of a child, the birth of a village, or the birth of a nation, the origin of life is customarily recognized by its emergence upon the scene of daily activity. But for each instance, its history actually begins when an idea evolves into tangible action. Ellsworth's conception began on the busy streets of Junction City, a town built to serve the soldiers of Fort Riley, Kansas.

Fort Riley had been established following the opening of Kansas Territory in 1854. Four years later Junction City was platted just beyond the military reservation. From its inception Junction City was a military town founded both to serve and to harvest the soldiers employed by the United States.

The Union Pacific Railway Company, Eastern Division, (U.P.E.D.) promised to bring prosperity beyond anything previously imagined for the men and women who depended upon the proceeds of the federal payroll. The railroad began building into Kansas on October 30, 1865. As the first passenger train pulled into the state capital at Topeka Monday, January 1, 1866, expectations heightened in Junction City. Within the year they would have their railroad. (1)

The Kansas City and Santa Fe Stage Company moved stock and coaches to the expected "end of track" at Junction City. The move required a new route for the company utilizing the Fort Riley Military Road to the southwest. The road crossed the Smoky Hill River at Fort Ellsworth.

J. M. Coombs was dispatched west to inspect the road and establish a stage station. Fort Ellsworth was nearly 80 miles west of Junction City. Just west of the military reservation Coombs located the stage station along the bank of a small spring-fed tributary of the Smoky Hill River. Trees growing along the river bottom provided the logs used to construct the station.

"The mail station was completed by the month of July (1866) and it became one of the most important on the western half of the route, for then landseekers commenced pouring into the country and the mail station was the only place to put up in the country …" (2)

The rails of the U.P.E.D. reached Junction City by the first of November, 1866. A special excursion train from Leavenworth toured the new route November 6th. Tourists were greeted at the Fort Riley stop by the "Boy General", Bvt. Major

General George A. Custer of the newly formed Seventh U. S. Cavalry and Bvt. Major General John W. Davidson of the Tenth U. S. Cavalry.

Junction City, with its close proximity to Fort Riley, took on an appearance of boom towns that had sprouted overnight during the California and Colorado gold rushes. The streets were filled with activity as people swarmed to the end of the track, each seeking his own fortune. (3)

The Plains Indians who still roamed the land of their ancestors obviously posed a problem for the planned expansion. The government's answer was military action. Politicians and capitalists proposed that the uncivilized tribes should be forced to accept the confiscation of their ancestral lands.

Existing military posts were slated for upgrades in preparation for the military campaign to crush Indian resistance. Fort Ellsworth was officially renamed Fort Harker on November 11, 1866. Fort Harker would be the base of supply. To allow for expansion of the post a new site was surveyed one mile to the northeast of the Smoky Hill River. (4)

The rousing activity at Fort Harker did not go unnoticed by a group of enterprising men in Junction City. During the waning days of 1866 a gleam in those entrepreneurs' eyes transformed thought into the concept as plans were initiated to build a town west of Fort Harker. Junction City produced a descendant in its own image. The envisioned village was named Ellsworth.

A corporation was formed to create the Ellsworth Town Company on January 15, 1867. The town of Ellsworth was laid out on January 23, 1867, beyond the Fort Harker military reservation and just southwest of the Kansas City and Santa Fe Stage station. (5)

Ellsworth soon became the focus of wealthy and powerful forces at the state capital. The close of the Civil War brought great herds of Texas cattle streaming into eastern Kansas in search of good prices but some of the cattle brought devastating disease. Texas Cattle Fever carried by the coastal Texas Longhorn cattle was known to kill domestic cattle raised in the north. There had been many confrontations along the Missouri-Kansas border. An earlier law forbidding Texas cattle to be driven through Kansas during the summer months was being challenged and with that challenge a new law allowing the cattle to be driven into the unsettled parts of southwestern Kansas was being proposed. The final bill set the quarantine line at Ellsworth. No Texas cattle were to be driven east of that line. Governor Samuel Crawford signed the bill into law February 26, 1867.

Interestingly enough the very next day the Topeka Live Stock Company was incorporated with former Kansas Governor Thomas Carney and other influential political leaders as stockholders. Flyers were sent to Texas newspapers and to known Texas cattlemen announcing that a new trail was being marked to enter Kansas west of the 6th principle meridian. The proposed trail was very near what would someday be known as the Chisholm Trail. The flyers announced that the Union Pacific was laying tracks to an undisclosed location west of the settlements and that the company would build stockyards at that location. Agents for the Topeka Live Stock Company were to be posted at the Kansas line to lead trail herds to the new cattle depot. From recent actions by the state legislature it was obvious that Ellsworth was slated to become the first cattle terminal on the Union Pacific Railroad. (6)

6

Settling the Indian question was an important element to establishing a successful cattle depot beyond the settlements. If drovers were to be induced to drive cattle to Ellsworth the route would have to be free of hostile Indians. By late March the entire Kansas frontier was in a stir with rumors of a coming Indian war. Troops at Fort Harker busied themselves in preparation for the "much-talked-of Indian Expedition."

The expedition became a reality March 27, 1867, when General Winfield S. Hancock rode out of Fort Riley at the head of a command of cavalry, infantry, and artillery. The expedition reached Fort Harker on April 1, 1867, going immediately into camp on the river bottom southwest of the post. Fourteen hundred men were assembled at Fort Harker. The men were rested, re-supplied, and moving again by April 3, 1867. Hancock's destination was Fort Larned. The General planned to confront Cheyenne and other tribal leaders with the powerful presence of the United States Army, thereby causing the would-be renegades to submit to the authority of the United States government. (7)

News of the progression of the Hancock expedition no doubt contributed to an optimistic gathering in Junction City, April 4, 1867. The stockholders of the Ellsworth Town Company met to complete the organization of the company. William McGrath and Colonel Greenwood were authorized to survey the tract of land that had been staked for the Ellsworth town site. H. J. Latshaw was elected president with several military men also participating in the company. (8)

However optimistic the new town builders may have been, optimism alone was not enough to carry the day as two cultures suddenly collided on the plains of southwest Kansas. General Hancock's expedition failed its expectations miserably. His grand army of one thousand four hundred troops actually provoked the Indians to war.

Western Kansas stage stations along the Smoky Hill Trail were aflame. Instead of peace, the general brought war which perhaps drove the first nail in the coffin for the Topeka Live Stock Company's grand plan to establish a cattle depot at Ellsworth. Cattlemen who had fought Missouri toughs and Kansas Jayhawkers in 1866 were not about to fight Indians in 1867. (9)

The Union Pacific tracks reached Salina with trains running to the town by April 29, 1867. In spite of the failed military action against the Indians people were flocking to Ellsworth, thirty-five miles west of Salina even before the town was officially recorded.

The plat for the town of Ellsworth was finally recorded at the Register of Deeds office in Salina, Kansas, on May 4, 1867. E. W. Kingsbury built the first structure, a combination store and hotel. The log accommodation was known as the "Stockade". Within two weeks the town seemed to take root from the prairie sod as buildings, "… were springing up like magic". Others, "… cut holes into the banks and low bluffs and covered them with tin, hides, and lumber, anything that would keep the elements out and would give them shelter for a season."

The lively activity at Ellsworth soon gave rise to the possibility of town-building by others. Bill Cody wrote that while employed as a courier for the U. S. Army he met a man who owned a plot of land near Fort Hays.

7

William F. Cody worked as a courier and scout for the army out of Fort Ellsworth and Fort Harker. Ellsworth was the inspiration for the new town of Rome that Cody helped establish near Fort Hays. There he became famous as "Buffalo Bill."
Author's Collection.

At the town of Ellsworth, which I visited one day while carrying dispatches to Fort Harker, I met William Rose, who had a contract for trading on the right-of-way of the Union Pacific near Fort Hays. His stock had been stolen by the Indians, and he had come to Ellsworth to buy more.

Rose was enthusiastic about a project for laying out a town site on the west side of Big Creek, a mile from the fort, where the railroad was to cross. When, in response to a request for my opinion, I told him I thought the scheme a big one, he invited me to come in as a partner. He suggested that after the town was laid out and opened to the public we establish a store and saloon.

I thought it would be a grand thing to become half owner of a town, and at once accepted the proposition. We hired a railroad engineer to survey the town site and stake it into lots. Also we ordered a big stock of the goods usually kept in a general merchandise store on the frontier. This done, we gave the town the ancient and historical name of Rome.

In spite of the grand appellation Rome was destined to failure. The competing town site of Hays City proved to be a more successful enterprise. Cody, however, rode into the pages of legend at Hays City as the celebrated Buffalo Bill.

Ellsworth was well on the way to becoming legendary in its own right as the town filled with characters of every description. Frank Melville, a painter by profession, erected a tent by a plumb thicket near the Smoky Hill River. A drunkard by habit, Melville's tent was the center of lively revelry and gambling through all hours. For the most part those who were attempting to establish legitimate businesses built away from that area. Melville attracted the lower class of society, creating an area near the river that became known as "Scragtown". (10)

Fanny Kelly and her husband, Josiah were among those looking to Ellsworth for a new beginning. Fanny had received national notoriety as a captive of the Sioux in Wyoming Territory in 1864. Upon her reunion with her husband the couple returned to her former home of Geneva, Kansas. The prospect of good fortune led them to relocate in Shawneetown, Kansas, where they prospered, but "... better prospects offering farther west, we went to Ellsworth, a new town just staked out on the western line of Kansas. I was the first woman located there. We lived in our wagon for a time, then built a hotel, and were prospering," Prosperity would soon turn to destitution and anguish.

Indians remained a constant threat to frontier Ellsworth and with the failure of the Hancock expedition everyone was on heightened alert. Fanny Kelly recalled her own unbearable torment during those days; the result of her previous captivity. "... A terrible dread of again falling into their hands intensified my apprehensions for our safety. The scouts, Jack Harvey and 'Wild Bill,' were constantly on the lookout, and eagerly would we look toward the hills for any one who could give us news and gather around them, when they came from the front, with anxious faces and listening ears." (11)

The spring of 1867 was unusually wet. Continued rains kept the Smoky running near bank full. The Kansas City and Santa Fe Stage Company experienced great difficulty fording the swollen river prompting station agent, J. M. Coombs to build a boat to ferry his stages over the river. (12)

The narrow strip of river bottom selected for the town site suddenly rose to ragged bluffs before leading to an irregular prairie that spread beyond a seemingly endless horizon. Estimates place the population at one to two thousand people.

Clouds loomed dark on the horizon the evening of June 5th. A new storm front settled in and torrential rains further to the west brought a heavy deluge. June 8th witnessed a sudden surge of water in the already swollen Smoky Hill River. J. F. Brennan reported to the Junction City *Union* that Ellsworth "... experienced the heaviest rain and hail storm he ever saw. Hail stones were picked up that weighed an ounce each. About 4 o'clock on Friday evening the water began coming up over the town site, and having filled a large bottom on the opposite side, which was some five or six feet lower. In two hours' time the water covered the counters in the stores. During Saturday the water was over a man's head in the buildings."

At the time Charles Raber worked as a freighter on the big wagon trains out of Fort Harker. He later recalled that the flood had carried away about half of Ellsworth. (13)

9

Nevertheless the denizens of Scragtown were not to be denied their celebrations. The July 6, 1867, Junction City *Union* reported that the residents of the lower portion of the city were "compelled by the recent flood to find a more secure place to ply their vocation. They accordingly pitch their tents on the top of the hill, or as a narrator called it, a 'beautiful plateau.' What would be known as 'nymphs du pave,' in Manhattan or Leavenworth but at Ellsworth 'nymphs du prairie,' were the innocent cause of a melee in which two stage drivers lost their lives at the hands of a gang who claimed prior possession of the premises." Several more had been wounded, giving rise to a wild rumor that Ellsworth had been the victim of yet another Indian attack. (14)

But as the waters returned to the river banks Indians attacked and killed men west of town. The attack was followed by a bold raid on some horses being grazed just outside the town. Consequently a local militia of men kept watch in regular relief.

Fanny Kelly spoke of the danger and terror.

> …The population of Ellsworth had rapidly increased, and military companies were formed for protection. Thus we lived in a continual state of alarm, until at last one night the signal was given that the Indians were approaching, when every man flew to his post, and the women and children fled to the places of refuge that had been prepared for them, an iron-clad house and a 'dug out,' or place under ground. I fled to the latter place, where about fifty altogether had congregated, and among them were three young men who were the sole survivors of a large family-father, mother, and two sisters-murdered and horribly mutilated in the Minnesota massacres. The Indians were repulsed, but they continued to harass us and threaten the town, so that it became necessary to apply for military protection. (15)

Raids resumed on railroad workers June 14th just west of Ellsworth. U.P.E.D. Superintendent Shoemaker called on Governor Crawford to provide Kansas Militia for the protection of the men. On June 24th workers were again driven from the roadbed for a stretch of twenty miles. Shoemaker sent an urgent message for help. "Unless you send us protection our work must be abandoned."

The president of the rail line, John D. Perry followed Shoemaker's plea with a pronouncement that one thousand laborers along seventy-five miles of road were about to be driven from the line. The relentless attacks continued west of Ellsworth. Anxious for relief Superintendent Shoemaker wired the Governor on June 28th stating that, "… unless the roads were promptly protected all the workers would be driven off and all the citizens would be forced to leave the region." (16)

June 28th was also the date that the tracks finally reached Fort Harker. That same day a beef contractor suddenly died of cholera. The weekend of June 29th and 30th brought several soldiers exhibiting symptoms of cholera. Fear gripped the town as healthy men and women succumbed to the fast moving disease.

Captain George Armes of the 10th Cavalry experienced the shock of the fast moving disease first hand. His younger brother, William had come to Fort Harker for a visit to the frontier before returning east to begin classes at West Point. Captain Armes took to the field with his troopers on a typical summer morning.

On his return later that day Armes was filled with the anticipation of seeing his brother one last time before he returned to West Point. The expected farewell turned to grief as General A. J. Smith broke the news to the Captain that William had succumbed to cholera.

Armes thought back to his last encounter with his brother saying that William had been, "… in the best of spirits and apparently in the best of health. He was taken with cholera and died before three o'clock that afternoon." Armes continued, "I reached his camp just in time to see his dear face again before they took him to his grave, but was unable to see him buried, being overcome with grief and completely prostrated." (17)

Cholera quickly spread from Fort Harker to Ellsworth. Everyone who could get away from the disease fled the town and military post as quickly as possible. Ellsworth fell into silence. The population of one thousand or more quickly dropped to a mere forty citizens by the middle of July. Work came to a standstill. Long trains stood quietly on the siding with no one to unload the railcars. Bodies of the dead were laid out in the open with no one to prepare them for burial. The Roman Catholic Church at Leavenworth sent several Sisters of Mercy and two Priests to tend to the cholera victims.

Early day settler Mrs. W. E. Sheriff later recalled the disagreeable conditions resulting from the June 8th flood waters, "so many fish were left on the land by the high water that an unbearable stench pervaded the town." The unclean conditions did little for the general health of the public and may well have contributed to the rapid spread of cholera. (18)

The hardy souls that persisted and survived moved Ellsworth to a new site that had not flooded. A mile west of the original town the prairie rose above the river valley, providing safe refuge from the inundated Smoky.

While cholera and Indian raids continued, a handful of Ellsworth citizens clung valiantly to the idea that their city would one day take its place as a serene and peaceful prairie village.

Railroad construction resumed when the first train entered Ellsworth on July 5th, 1867. County commissioners held their first meeting on July 9th, formally recognizing the county as Ellsworth. The United States Postal Service bestowed an official post office on Ellsworth July 17, 1867. Popularly referred to as the "Addition", the plat for the new town site was filed July 18, 1867 and soon the town was surging with activity. As the railroad reached the town its "end of track" reputation soared. (19)

General Custer probably paid little attention to the new town of Ellsworth as he and his troops passed quickly by on the trail just north of the city. Custer had been in the field searching for Indians. Upon his return to Fort Wallace he learned of the cholera epidemic. Fearing for the safety of his wife, Libby, Custer left Fort Wallace with one hundred troops on July 12, 1867. He arrived at Fort Harker seven days later on July 19th at two o'clock in the morning. Finding that she was not at Fort Harker, Custer boarded a train, which swiftly took him to Fort Riley and the arms of his beloved Libby.

It is perhaps the most famous of western love stories, but it cost Custer dearly. On his return to Fort Harker, July 28, 1867, he was arrested and held for court marshal on the charge of deserting his command without permission. (20)

Fanny Kelly and her husband Josiah were two of the hardy souls who remained in Ellsworth throughout the plague. Fanny described the dreadful destruction of cholera as it spread through the citizens, creating a "terrible panic". Speaking of Josiah, Fanny Kelly wrote, "On the 28th day of July, 1867, a violent attack of this disease carried him off." The desperate nature of the surroundings defies description. Strangers ransacked Josiah's body for valuables. The five hundred dollars he was known to be carrying was missing. (21)

Louisa Sternberg, the wife of the post surgeon at Fort Harker also fell victim to the disease. Her husband, Dr. George Sternberg was devastated. As post surgeon his primary responsibility was health and sanitation and in the end Dr. Sternberg was helpless to protect that which was most dear. The evening following Mrs. Sternberg's death, Bridget, Mrs. Sternberg's cook, visited the only remaining officer's wife on the post, Mrs. Frank D. Baldwin. The next morning Mrs. Baldwin walked out on the verandah of her quarters, "… and glanced over at the next set of quarters. I saw a row of something under a canvas covering, and one of them was poor Bridget, the cook! There they all lay, waiting to be interred in the lonely little makeshift cemetery. All were well and in their usual health only the night before."

Mrs. Baldwin recalled seeing the Priests and Sisters of Mercy tirelessly tending to the labor at hand. "With tenderest care and attention, regardless of creed or creedless, they took care of and nursed the sick and dying, day and night, until the scourge had lessened and passed." A sergeant and his wife fell victim to the disease, leaving four small children alone. The Sisters took the children to Leavenworth where they were provided for.

Father Martyn often traveled from Fort Harker to Ellsworth tending to cholera victims. With so few people left in the county the road to Ellsworth was nearly deserted, and so it was that a soldier came upon Father Martyn's body lying in the road midway between Ellsworth and Fort Harker. His mule was grazing nearby. He undoubtedly was overcome by cholera where no one could relieve the suffering of one who had done so much to ease the torment of others. (22)

Another casualty of the series of disasters that had plagued Ellsworth was the Topeka Live Stock Company. Perhaps due to the uncertain future of the town the company failed to establish the promised stockyards. No agents were sent to meet oncoming drovers. Joseph McCoy, an enterprising young Illinois cattle buyer picked up the idea and through the summer actively worked to make Abilene, Kansas, just what the Topeka Live Stock Company had boasted they would accomplish in Ellsworth. (23)

In the midst of those days of turmoil, few could imagine children on the untamed streets of Ellsworth. But in the summer of 1867 Miguel Antonio Otero was only seven years old. His father, Don Miguel Antonio Otero I had joined with John Perry Sellar in the wholesale commission business. Their first warehouse was established at Fort Harker in 1866. With the opening of Ellsworth, Otero & Sellar joined dozens of businesses poised to make great profits from freighting merchandise to Santa Fe, New Mexico. Seven year-old Miguel and his brother were rewarded with a summer vacation away from the boarding school they were attending in Leavenworth. Ellsworth's dangerous streets became the children's playground and provided an education like no other imaginable. Miguel Antonio Otero was destined to become governor of New Mexico.

Ellsworth was a "tough little hole". Otero described the town as "almost wholly a town of tents and small, rough, frame buildings, but as busy a place as can be imagined." To a young wide-eyed youth the town must have fueled the wildest of imagination. "It seemed as if nearly every other house in the town was a drinking place, while gambling rooms and dance halls and other questionable resorts were most common. Shooting scrapes were every-day occurrences, and the nights were frequently made hideous by drunken men firing off pistols promiscuously and shouting like bands of wild Comanches."

Buffalo and antelope could be seen in all directions from town, but to venture beyond the little frontier city was risky business in the Indian infested countryside. "They skulked about the settlement practically all the time, and frequently killed and scalped herders who went out only a mile or so to hunt buffalo or antelope. I have often seen these hunters coming back in a cloud of dust, with Indians pursuing them hotly almost into the town." Railroad construction crews were almost daily attacked by Indians even though the military posted guards from Fort Harker to protect the workers. (24)

Two of the most popular scouts at Fort Harker were Wild Bill Hickok and Captain Jack Harvey. People never tired of telling tales of their daring adventures. Perhaps it was because they truly lived as though there were no tomorrow.

Correspondent Henry M. Stanley who later became famous for his quest to find Dr. Livingstone wrote of the exploits of the frontier scouts in his accounts to an eastern audience.

> You should know that the daring express rider, who faithfully conveys in his saddle bags the plethoric and important official document, bears also the letter from the newspaper correspondent across the burning plains, and desert wastes, alone, dashing through black night and the chilling storm of sleet and rain, with such an enduring spirit, that the very tempest itself might pause and admire. While performing this errand two days ago the scout Atkins was chased by Indians for about five or six miles. One bold savage overtook Atkins (Tom Adkins), and raising a sabre, manifested an intention to cut short his career by decapitation, but, taught by long experience to be wary, Atkins presented a long dragoon revolver so suddenly before the Indian's triumphant face, as to cause in him an immediate revulsion from hatred to amity.
>
> The Indian informed Atkins, in 'pigeon English' that he had no cause of quarrel with him, but that on the prairies every one was bound to be on his guard. Atkins, as a matter of course, laughed at him, and strange to say, forgave him. Touched by 'the magnanimity of his white foe,' the Indian warned off his comrades. Atkins continued his gallop, and thus our letter from Fort Hayes reached you.
>
> 'Wild Bill,' who is an inveterate hater of the Indians, was also chased by six Indians lately, and had quite a little adventure with them. It is his

custom to be always armed with a brace of ivory-handled revolvers, with which weapons he is remarkably dextrous; but when bound on a long and lonely ride across the plains, he goes armed to the teeth. He was on one of these lonely missions, due to his profession as scout, when he was seen by a group of the red men, who immediately gave chase. They soon discovered that they were pursuing one of the most famous men of the prairie, and commenced to retrace their steps, but two of them were shot, after which Wild Bill was left to ride on his way. The little adventure is verified by a scout named Kincaid, who, while bearing despatches for General Custer, was also obliged to use his weapons freely. The lives of these Indian scouts are made up of these little experiences.

The reputations of men like Wild Bill and Captain Jack Harvey were carried far and wide but everyday life on the frontier was far from ordinary. Wild Bill was known to have an affection for watches. As the story goes, he one day proudly showed off his brand new gold pocket watch to Captain Jack. That watch had an unusually large ring over the winding mechanism. Jack was so certain of his shooting abilities that he bet Wild Bill he could safely shoot a lead ball through the ring. Bill bet Jack ten dollars that he couldn't; took the watch by the end of the chain and dangled the watch giving Jack a clear shot at the wide open ring at the top. One pistol shot later Wild Bill's watch was shattered. Bill coolly put the gold chain in his pocket along with Jack's ten dollars. Bill's only comment was that for the next month Jack was his property and subject to do what ever Wild Bill demanded.

The next day Wild Bill saw Captain Jack walking across the parade grounds at Fort Harker. Wild Bill called out for Jack to hold his hat over his head. As Jack lifted his hat Wild Bill pulled his pistol and fired, leaving a "long furrow" through Jack's hair. With that Captain Jack calmly replaced his hat, turned and, "walked away as though nothing had happened." (25)

Ellsworth County held its first election on August 10, 1867. Wild Bill was a candidate for sheriff. Never one to do things in the usual way Hickok attempted to garner votes based upon his horsemanship. Dressed in buckskins and looking every bit the part of a frontier hero Wild Bill saddled up and raced a train from Fort Harker to Ellsworth. He outran the train, "... in a feat of horsemanship that aroused the admiration of all." Even so the man who had erected the log "Stockade" in the first Ellsworth, E. W. Kingsbury was elected county sheriff. A young man from Michigan by the name of Chauncey Whitney was chosen as undersheriff. The town had not yet qualified as a first class city which meant that Ellsworth had no marshal. Two men serving as township constables resigned a month later. In addition to his duties as undersheriff Chauncey Whitney was appointed constable of Ellsworth Township. (26)

The Leavenworth *Daily Conservative* observed that in Ellsworth no "fouler birds ever congregated around the putrid carcass of a departed ox than those which frequent and tenant the brimstone scented dens of this modern Sodom." The same editor noted that in two days, four men had been killed. The tent that the city council erected for a "guardhouse" did little to curb the violence. The word was out that "Ellsworth has a man for breakfast every morning." Holding the lid on

Wild Bill Hickok, one of the most famous men on the plains, called Ellsworth home during its most dangerous years.

Ellsworth would prove to be difficult for any lawman.

A gang of "... roughs and cutthroats ... undertook to run the town, and who, by their desperado deeds, sought to rule the people by establishing a 'reign of terror.'..." The new lawmen were powerless to control such a group. However, these were post-Civil War times. The merchant on the street may have appeared to be harmless, even meek, but nearly every storekeeper had been tested on the field of battle. A vigilance committee was formed and on Oct. 3rd, the two ringleaders of the gang, George Craig and a man named Johnson, were seized by the citizens, taken to the banks of the Smoky Hill River and hung from the branches of a cottonwood tree.

A sign was posted on the hanging bodies warning all such men of their fate, which created "... quite a panic among the thieves, rowdies, gamblers, and other flash characters of Ellsworth." (27)

Eight days after the hangings the Ellsworth County Commissioners authorized Chauncey Whitney to purchase lumber and materials to prepare the H. D. Blake house for use as a jail. (28)

Gunmen in the Old West are often portrayed as lawmen, gamblers or drifting shootists with reputations to uphold. Rare indeed are soldiers recognized for

15

their shooting skills. Mrs. Custer wrote of the exploits of a man she refers to as Sergeant Andrews. The sergeant had a reputation as a fearless man and an expert marksman. During Custer's earlier search for Indians in northwest Kansas and southwest Nebraska, Sergeant Andrews tracked down and captured nine deserters single handedly. At Fort Harker he again tracked a deserter into Lincoln County, just north of the fort.

Sergeant Andrews once again captured his man. As they were returning to Fort Harker the men passed through Ellsworth. The attraction of civilization brought a plea from the prisoner to stop for something to eat before reaching the post. Andrews agreed and took his prisoner to an eating house. While standing at the counter, the prisoner took the cover from a box of red pepper. Suddenly the sergeant's vision failed him as the prisoner threw the contents of the red pepper box in his face. "Though groaning with agony, he lost none of his self-possession. Listening for the footfall as the deserter started for the door, he fired in the direction and the man fell dead." (29)

The author of Moses Milner's biography, *California Joe, Noted Scout & Indian Fighter,* was Milner's grandson Joe E. Milner. He put to paper the stories of California Joe that had been handed down through the family. One such story was the shooting of a gambler "… at Newton, Kansas, then a trail-end Cowtown …"

Most likely, the shooting occurred in Ellsworth. The clues are found in "the rest of the story".

California Joe awoke from a drunken stupor to find that he had been robbed. A little talk with the bartender confirmed his suspicions that a gambler he had associated with the night before had set him up in a crooked game. Joe searched the saloons. When he finally found the man the gambler ran for the door. Joe knew that calling for him to "Stop!" would do no good.

Joe realized that the man was about to outrun him. There was only one thing to do. Joe fired five shots in rapid succession. The gambler dropped dead in the street as Joe quickly reloaded, thinking the dead man's friends would be interested in revenge. Men poured from the saloons to see what the shooting was all about and as they gathered over the gambler's lifeless body, Joe called out, pistol in hand, "If any of yo' fellows are friends of that dead thief, just step up an' we'll shoot it out."

The crowd didn't move. No one was prepared to take on California Joe. One man stood out, towering over the rest. His hair fell below his shoulders and he was laughing as though the whole scene was a comical play on a stage for his own personal entertainment.

"Yo' big long-hair, if yo' want to laugh at me step out here and we'll shoot it out," Joe roared.

But the big fellow just laughed all the more and without a word turned and walked away.

Joe was informed that the man was Wild Bill Hickok. California Joe knew of Hickok and Hickok had surely heard of Joe. They would meet again.

California Joe entered one of the saloons and soon was engaged in a game of cards at a table surrounded by soldiers. A stranger entered the room and walked straight to California Joe, informing him that Wild Bill would like to see him, "in his camp at the edge of town,"

California Joe replied, "You tell Wild Bill to go to hell; I'm playing cards now." The stranger turned and left the saloon.

As the story goes, Wild Bill walked through the saloon doors a couple of hours later. California Joe was standing at the bar as Hickok approached and amiably offered to "buy a drink". A couple of drinks later, the two were on the way to becoming fast friends. Years later the August 26, 1876, Cheyenne (Wyoming) *Daily Leader* published words attributed to Wild Bill Hickok in which he stated, "… I have two trusty friends, one is my six-shooter and the other is California Joe."

The interesting part of the story is that if this was the first meeting between Wild Bill and California Joe it could not have occurred in Newton, Kansas, as California Joe's biographer claimed. Newton did not exist until 1871 and both Wild Bill and California Joe were employed out of Fort Harker from the fall of 1867 until the spring of 1868. While Ellsworth had not yet become the famous end-of-trail town that it would become, that reputation was later a fundamental part of the Ellsworth reputation. The story seems to have realistically occurred in Ellsworth. (30)

Wild Bill certainly made his mark on Ellsworth. His reputation as spy and scout for the Union during the Civil War had done much to spread his name across the west. When he arrived in Kansas from Springfield, Missouri, he was accompanied by Anna Wilson. While not named, she was reported as Hickok's wife by the Leavenworth *Daily Bulletin*, "… recently arrived from the FAR West with trains loaded with furs, peltries and buffalo robes, Wild Bill brings his wife along …" The little woman would come to be known as Indian Annie and as Wild Bill's wife was recognized with a certain notoriety on the streets of Ellsworth. However it was a man's world and women were seldom mentioned by correspondents on the edge of the frontier. (31)

J. H. Beadle traveled "the far west" for seven years and visited Ellsworth in October of 1867. He spoke of meeting Wild Bill. "Those were the days of your 'Wild Bills'… and 'Long Steves,' your 'Dad Smith', 'Rake Jake' and Tom Smith of Bear River." Beadle repeated Ellsworth's most famous question, "'Shall we have a man for breakfast?' was the ordinary morning salutation; and usually it was found that somebody had answered the question affirmatively during the night. 'A short life and a merry one,' was the motto of these roysterers."

The Ellsworth County prosecutor was a fellow by the name of J. H. Runkle. He was the "Rake Jake" referred to by J. H. Beadle. In conversation as to the character of the little end of track town over which he presided, Rake Jake informed Mr. Beadle that, "for ninety-three days there was a homicide every day in the town or the vicinity." Beadle noted that in the year 1867, Ellsworth, "was the terminus of the (rail) road – also the terminus of at least a hundred lives." (32)

The railroad terminus was a fleeting designation as construction continued westward. The tracks reached Hays City in late October, 1867. Notorious Ellsworth badman, Jim Curry, was engineer of the first train to enter the town. By November, trains were running regularly into Hays. Much of the tent city that followed railroad construction disappeared from view at Ellsworth as a great migration was begun to the new end of the track. False fronted buildins lined the streets housing hotels, saloons, restaurants, and all the attending agencies of commerce on the frontier.

Hoping to retain the vibrant "end of track" railroad business the Ellsworth Town Company obtained a charter for the Ellsworth & Pacific Railroad. The road was to turn southwest from Ellsworth, following the freighting trail to Santa Fe and from there to the west coast. The company then petitioned Congress to withdraw support for the extension of the Union Pacific, Eastern Division to Denver and to support the Ellsworth & Pacific. The new railroad failed to gain the desired support even with Governor Samuel Crawford as a charter shareholder. (33)

Military activities at Fort Harker brought new excitement in October as the government again sent a large force southwest to meet with Indians. This time the Indian Peace Commission had taken the time to prepare the Indians through extensive planning. Agents and interpreters met with the various tribes over the preceding summer months. All of the troublesome Southern plains tribes gathered together for one grand peace conference on Medicine Lodge Creek in the fall of 1867. The conference succeeded in gaining the signatures of the leading peace chiefs, giving the U.S. government rights to the Smoky Hill country between the Arkansas River in southern Kansas and the Platte River in Nebraska. (34)

The lively atmosphere of Ellsworth certainly would have been attractive to the newspaper business. E. F. Campbell was drawn from Iowa to the lusty streets of Ellsworth in late December, 1867. The Ellsworth *Tri-Weekly Advertiser* was born Christmas day, December 25, 1867. Campbell's first observations only confirmed the extraordinary character of a town that was already becoming a legend. "Last Wednesday was a windy, disagreeable day, but we were determined, if there was pluck enough in Ellsworth, to get our press upstairs which was then lying in the street. Capt. Seavers and Wild Bill proved pluck doesn't go begging here. These two gentlemen doffed their 'good clothes', rolled up their sleeves and gathered hold of our Wells Power Press as if it were but a toy. To these two gentlemen we are under many obligations." Alas, the Ellsworth *Tri-Weekly Advertiser* was soon discontinued. (36)

If the good citizens of Ellsworth were thinking that a new end-of-the-track would cure Ellsworth's wicked ways they must have soon realized that peaceful calm would not come so easily. Ellsworth's lawmen earned their pay on a regular basis. Although not an elected lawman in Ellsworth City or County, Wild Bill Hickok had obtained a commission as a Deputy United States Marshal. His exploits were often reported in the papers, however one unreported story that has persisted throughout the years was of Wild Bill coming to the aid of Ellsworth lawmen during the winter of 1867-68. A band of drunken toughs were carousing and hurrahing the town one winter's eve. Hickok, Sheriff E.W. Kingsbury and Under Sheriff Chauncey Whitney corralled the gang. Rather than jail the rowdies the lawmen tied them to posts to cool off. (35)

Ellsworth was indeed a "tough little hole". Its shaky beginning stiffened the resolve of its founders to make something of the little town on the banks of the Smoky. The next several years would test their mettle many times over.

Chapter Two

PRINT THE LEGEND

Ellsworth remained the division headquarters for the Union Pacific as the end-of-the-track crews moved to Hays City in 1868. Despite the move west, many railroad employees continued to call Ellsworth home, allowing its saloons to continue operating at a lively pace.

Two stage companies operated out of Ellsworth. The United States Express Company through a contract with Wells Fargo carried mail all the way to California on the trail first surveyed for Butterfield's Overland Despatch. Barlow & Sanderson's coaches ran southwest from Ellsworth three times a week on the Santa Fe Trail. Their destinations included, "Bent's Fort in southeast Colorado and Fort Union, Taos, Santa Fe and all points in Arizona and New Mexico." (1)

Fort Harker remained the major economic engine for Ellsworth as the post was the main designated supply post for all military activity to the west and southwest. All government freight would be unloaded from railcars for storage in government warehouses at Harker. Supplies were then delivered west and southwest by wagon train. The great wagon trains required a large workforce to support delivery to the western posts.

At one of those western posts a young army hospital steward with Ellsworth connections witnessed one of the West's legendary events. According to his personal account David B. Long nearly missed becoming a long-time resident of Ellsworth. The story reflects an image of frontier conflict as it was frequently played out along the Smoky Hill route.

H.P. Wyatt quarreled with the well-known U. S. Army scout Medicine Bill Comstock in the sutler's store at Fort Wallace. Hospital Steward David Long knew both men. Long recalled that the men were arguing over money.

Wyatt got up and was leaving the store and Comstock pulled out his six-shooter and shot Wyatt twice in the back. Wyatt ran out of the store and fell dead. During the trouble, as Comstock was shooting, I stepped up and tried to prevent Comstock from killing Wyatt, and he turned on me and said, 'You keep your your hands off or I will kill you.' ... Comstock was arrested and taken to the Hays City for trial ... There was raised among

19

the rough element $500.00 to clear Comstock. The Justice of the Peace, Joyce, an Irishman from Leavenworth who was there to make more money, when (post sutler) Mr. Todd, the principal witness was put on the stand and swore that he saw Comstock shoot and kill Wyatt. Joyce asked the witness, 'did he do the shooting with felonious intent?' 'I do not know what his intentions were but I did see Comstock shoot Wyatt and Wyatt ran out of the store and fell dead.' said Mr. Todd. Joyce said, 'If the shooting was not done with felonious intent and there is no proof that it was, the prisoner is discharged for the want of said proof.

Scouts of the plains provided abundant fodder to eastern writers looking for adventure in the Wild West. From left to right: Medicine Bill Comstock, Ed Guerrier, Thomas Adkins, and California Joe Milner. They were all subjects of popular narration in the 1860's.
Courtesy the Fort Wallace Museum, Wallace, Kansas.

Another version of the court proceedings portrayed Comstock as a confessor. When arraigned before the court, and asked by Judge M. S. Joyce how he would plead, Bill answered, "Guilty, sir." The Judge asked him if he did not wish to alter his plea. The scout replied, "No, sir." The Judge immediately exclaimed, "Ye are a damned fool for tellin' it. I discharge ye for want of ividence." The second story certainly adds local flavor but lacks credibility.

Whatever version one wants to believe, Comstock was released. However, the Ellis County Attorney hoped to save his case by calling David Long to support sutler Todd's testimony on the witness stand. Comstock should have been rearrested but was already on the road back to Fort Wallace. Long was detailed to go to Hays City by stage. Comstock learned of Long's passage by stage and positioned himself in a barn at one of the stage stations. Long surprised Comstock by not getting off the stage to stretch his legs. A few minutes later the stage pulled away with its passengers safely on board. Long learned later that Comstock was waiting to kill him. Long's trip to Hays City turned out to be unnecessary. Comstock was never returned to Hays City.

David Long was soon discharged from service. He returned east, established a ranch west of Sternberg's Cottonwood Ranch south of Fort Harker and began a dairy for the manufacture of cheese. (2)

William Sternberg related a story of being chased by Indians south of Fort Harker. The Sternberg family maintained the Cottonwood Ranch along the Smoky Hill River selling produce and stock to the fort.

Ed Ellison, one of the men at the ranch, was my beau ideal of a man; he had been long on the frontier; had been a poney-express rider, and had experienced some wonderful adventures; every evening I sought him out and begged for a story – we became great friends.

Ash creek empties into the Smoky Hill a mile west of our ranch; it was well timbered along its banks with oak, hackberry, ash and elm; contractors were cutting this wood for fuel for the Post. Ellison, and a man by the name of McDermott, got one of these contracts and established a camp five miles up from the mouth of the creek.

We had a band of young colts that were allowed to range at will, for they never strayed far from the ranch. In the spring of eighteen hundred and sixty eight, Indian rumors being frequent, I was sent to hunt up and drive home the colts and herd and corral them with the cattle nights. I soon got trace of them on Ash creek.

I found the colts near Ellison and McDermott's camp, so went over for a visit with Ed. Just as I was starting down the creek, I saw about seventy five horsemen riding two by two in double column; they were several miles away near the head of the creek, coming our way and traveling the old Fort Grierson trail. I supposed them to be a company of Cavalry on their way to Fort Harker, for it was not customary for Indians to ride in regular formation. It never entered my head they were Indians.

When half way to the mouth of the creek I heard heavy firing at Ellison's camp; I then realized the men I had seen were hostile Indians. I was mounted on a good horse, and soon had the colts going for home at a fast pace. I put my saddle rope in trail, and if a colt allowed me to get within thirty feet of him, he got a slap on the ribs that raised a painful welt. All cowboys know how to snap a trailing rope with great accuracy, but the punishment is so severe it is rarely practiced.

It took but a few minutes to reach the wood-choppers at the mouth of the creek. As soon as I came within sight and hearing I yelled 'Indians,' 'Indians!' They were quick to act, almost by the time I reached their camp, they had thrown the wood from the racks, had clambered on, and were lambasting the mules into a mad run for the Post, nearly three miles away.

We had scarcely crossed the river when some of the Indians appeared on the opposite bank and commenced firing at us; the distance, however, was too great and no damage was done; had they crossed the river and continued the chase they would surely have killed some of us for none were armed.

As the wagons went tearing across the prairie they were soon observed, and "Boots and Saddles" rang out, and a company under command of Col. Benteen, turned out and came at full gallop to meet them; they pursued the Indians clear to the Sand Hills of the Arkansas, but were unable to overtake them. (3)

Ellsworth continued to maintain a vibrant economy along with a nasty reputation. Early in March, 1868, a Mexican freighter by the name of Chaves announced to an Ellsworth barroom crowd that Americans did not like Mexicans. In a flash he drew his pistol and shot one man in the arm, but the wounded man's pistol found

William Sternberg lived the life of a cowboy before becoming an attorney.

Courtesy Ellsworth County Historical Society.

22

its mark, leaving Chaves dead on the floor. (4)

For many months Wild Bill Hickok and Captain Jack Harvey were often seen together on the streets of Ellsworth. They were employed as government detectives on the plains. As Deputy United States Marshals they roamed as far west as the Colorado border. The two had been comrades during the Civil War and also served together as scouts during General Hancock's campaign in 1867. But the wild life was about to catch up with Jack Harvey. He died of consumption March 13, 1868, in Ellsworth. The Leavenworth *Daily Conservative* pronounced him, "Brave. Cool in the hour of danger, and one of the best shots on the western border, Jack was always ready for a bold ride or a fight with the enemy. He was as generous and true-hearted as he was brave, and no man hereabouts had more friends." (5)

An editor by the name of P. H. Hubbell arrived in the spring of 1868 with intentions of commencing a newspaper. In spite of the earlier *Tri-Weekly Advertiser's* failure, Ellsworth was certainly fertile ground for news. The Ellsworth *Advocate* was born in April but as its predecessor had done, languished only to survive six months. (6)

The frolic rolled on and the whiskey poured forth. Peter Robidoux recalled a frontier scene of soldiers, dames, gamblers, Indian scouts, teamsters, bull whackers, "and citizens of all sorts" at the U. S. House Saloon. The proprietor, Rowdy Joe Lowe sold Peter a room for the night for seventy-five cents. Joe led him away to "drunkards heaven" where at least 50 drunken men slept on cots. Wondering what he had gotten himself into Roubidoux recalled, "I lay there with fear and trembling until daylight, then got out quickly by the outside stairway, thanking God I was spared once more."

Today's Douglas Avenue was known as Walnut Street. Businesses lined Walnut Street from South Main Street to the Smoky Hill River. Many of those visiting Ellsworth traveled Walnut Street on their way to the freighting trail that led to Santa Fe. Coe's dancehall was a popular Walnut Street dive.

Pistols and knives were as much a part of a man's outfit as were hats and boots. Fights erupted at a moments notice. One such incident involved saloonkeeper Charley Johnson and a wagonmaster by the name of Sweringer. Bad blood already flowed between them when they met in Coe's doorway. Pistols flashed and two more ruffians were dead.

Charley Johnson and his brother Frank owned a saloon together. It was called the Halfway House and was located east of town near the old stage station. When Sweringer's friend, Charley Allen learned of the shooting, Allen swore revenge even though the men had killed each other.

Allen's friends warned him not to go to the Halfway House. Word was sent to Charley Johnson's brother, Frank, to meet Allen on the Plaza for a duel.

The Plaza was a public gathering place consisting of a wide open stretch of ground along the railroad tracks. North and South Main Streets bordered the Plaza. Allen was informed that Frank Johnson had received his challenge. Each man walked slowly across the open territory until they were only a few feet apart. Words were spoken but only the two men heard them. Pistols were drawn and hammers blazed as each man emptied lead into the other. Charlie Allen died in a pool of blood. Frank Johnson survived with slight wounds.

South Douglas Avenue was known as Walnut Street but was platted as F Street in 1867. The bull train in the street would ford the river at the location of today's Smoky Hill River bridge. The dark building on the left is the Marshall House Hotel.
Alexander Gardner Photograph. Courtesy Ellsworth County Historical Society.

But that was not the last for Frank. He had been warned to mend his ways, to which he merely replied, "Go to Hell!" Finally the vigilantes had had enough. Frank Johnson was taken from his Halfway House and hung to a cottonwood tree. (7)

Two strangers came to Ellsworth that summer of 1868. Like so many of the early Ellsworth tales, the details have been lost to time. One of the men lay down on a billiard table and went to sleep. The other man took offense and proceeded to tap the sleeping man on the head with his pistol. Waking from his sleep the man was understandably startled to see a pistol waving in his face. He jumped up and ran for the door, but just as he passed through the doorway a shot rang out. The fleeing stranger was dead. The next morning, his killer was found hanging from one of the cottonwood trees down by the river. When Ellsworth cottonwoods bore fruit the banks of the Smoky received a new tenant. (8)

A new end-of-track town was established in June of 1868, in far western Kansas. Phil Sheridan, Kansas, known by most simply as Sheridan, was the headquarters for the grading crews bringing the Union Pacific Eastern Division nearer to the western Kansas border. Sheridan was filled with men who had earlier known Junction City, Ellsworth, and Hays City, as each village took its place as an end-of-track town. (9)

Following the 1867 Medicine Lodge peace treaty, the Indians remained relatively quiet through the first half of 1868. The calm was broken when an old feud between the Kaw Indians at Council Grove and the wild Cheyenne of the western plains suddenly caught settlers in eastern Kansas by surprise. Folks in that part of the state had grown used to the Kaw who resided peacefully on their reservation. The Cheyenne threatened that sense of security in early June, 1868.

Although the farms and ranches of that area were not the intended target of the wild tribe, the Indians were not fully aware of the alarm they were producing. The Cheyenne were only seeking revenge on their old enemies, the Kaw. Joined by war societies of Arapaho, Kiowa and Comanche, the total war party was estimated at four hundred to five hundred warriors, but may well have been only half that many. At even half, the number triggered alarm throughout eastern Kansas.

The approach of the war party did not go unnoticed by the Kaw. Just outside Council Grove on June 3rd the reservation tribe devised an ambush and caught the Cheyenne as they advanced on the reservation. A battle raged for several hours, resulting in very few injuries. Little Robe demanded that scalps taken by the Kaw in an earlier conflict be returned to the Cheyenne. The Kaw refused. The fight had come to a standoff. Frustrated and with little success to show for his efforts Little Robe threatened to return with more warriors from Black Kettle's band. With nothing left to be gained the war party turned and began its return journey to the plains.

On the journey west, several eastern Kansas settlers' homes were raided for beef cattle, chickens and turkeys. The raid unfortunately stirred the settlers, creating a generally bad impression of the Cheyenne people across the settled parts of Kansas. Little Robe and his people passed through Ellsworth County on their return to buffalo country. At Fort Harker Little Robe explained that the tribe had only taken enough food from settlers to feed themselves. A passing Texas herd obliged the Indians with meat when the returning war party happened onto the herd. The trail boss cut out four head of cattle for them to butcher. He felt the Indians posed no particular problem. (10)

By 1868, buffalo were rarely found east of Ellsworth, contributing to the Cheyenne's inability to live off the land in eastern Kansas. Buffalo were still plentiful west of Ellsworth. Herds were often seen within sight of town. Captured buffalo calves were often staked out around the town. Calves were quite a novelty and were in great demand in the east where they were easily sold as "Wild West" curiosities.

One would have thought that the site of buffalo would have become commonplace on the plains, but even among Ellsworth's rough and tumble denizen's buffalo could create quite a stir. J. H. Hughs recalled an exciting summer day in 1868 when buffalo were reported to be grazing on a hill just west of town. He and three friends, James Edgar, Jim Erwin, and Titus Buckbee quickly armed themselves with "a brace of holster pistols each". Running to the livery stable they were soon mounted on swift ponies and racing for the open prairie.

"We circled the hill on the north in order to gain the west side of the herd, while making the circuit one of the party, Jim Edgar, suggested that if we succeeded in gaining the desired vantage, it would be a huge joke to chase the herd down the railroad track, into and through the town."

The four young men soon accomplished their plan. With a mad dash they rode directly into the herd from the west. Down went the buffalo heads as they stampeded away, following the slope and into town. "We followed in hot pursuit, shouting, hollering and firing our pistols in the air, (it was not our aim to kill any of them)." The buffalo were soon running through the town.

> Such a surprise had not been sprung on that unsuspecting town before - nor since. The citizens at fever heat in their excitement, thinking perhaps the Indians were upon them, but our hasty appearance on the scene reassured them. Wagons and teams, horsemen and footmen all scattered in their eagerness to give us the road, and before we had gone much further, every man who could secure a horse or mule, with or without a saddle, did so, all had the contagion of the hunter's fire as we raced hotly on.

With all government supplies being unloaded from rail cars at Fort Harker, both the military post and the city of Ellsworth were the gathering places for the many wagon trains delivering supplies to the western forts. As the herd of buffalo stampeded through the Plaza the Mexicans freighters took up the chase. Hughs recalled that they quickly mounted their mules bareback, "not forgetting to take their lassos," Once the herd had passed through town the chase continued for several hours. Five buffalo were killed by the hunters while seven calves were captured by the Mexicans. The hunters were not quite "Buffalo Bills", but the day was thrilling just the same. (11)

In August of 1868, the Cheyenne again set out to raid another old enemy. This time it was the Pawnee on the Platte River in Nebraska. Whatever their intentions, the war party suddenly turned their attention to the settlements just north of Ellsworth in Lincoln County. Beginning the attack at Spillman Creek, the raid continued north as far as the North Fork of the Solomon River. At that point they were turned away by a large party of armed settlers. The Indians succeeded in avoiding a direct battle by attacking outlying houses. Several people were killed and two little girls taken captive. Eighteen-year-old Sarah White was captured west of Concordia, Kansas, on August 13th. In the settlements the raid was known as the "Solomon Massacre".

The war party returned to Lincoln County, attacking a military blockhouse near the Schermerhorn trading ranch. Lon Schermerhorn watched the attack from inside his barricaded ranch house. The situation looked grim. As his wife prepared to give birth he told her and a midwife not to worry, he would kill them before allowing the Indians to take them captive. Colonel Benteen of the 7th Cavalry arrived just in time. The troopers surprised the Cheyenne and chased them with enough strength to cause the warriors to leave the two little captive girls behind on the prairie. (12)

War had returned to Kansas. Ellsworth was once again alerted and on guard. Ellsworth County Undersheriff Chauncey Whitney was in Hays City when news of the Indian attacks resulted in the formation of the "First Independent Kansas State Militia" August 18, 1868. Another Ellsworth man, Deputy U.S. Marshal John Park was designated captain of the militia. Chauncey Whitney and Matthew Bouton were appointed lieutenants. (13)

Adolph Roenigk worked on a section crew for the Union Pacific Company Eastern Division out of Fossil Station (Russell, KS). Speaking of the construction crew, Shoemaker, Miller & Company, Roenigk recalled that he and others recognized trouble.

Titus Buckbee was one of Ellsworth's favorite fellows. The buffalo chase of 1868 was only the beginning of his exploits. He had been a prisoner of war in a Confederate camp, but despite a delicate physical condition he was always ready for action.
Courtesy Ellsworth County Historical Society.

To us workers at that time things did not look very favorable. The road bed was thrown up very cheaply, culverts and abuttments of bridges were built rather temporary, the tracks were the old fashioned light iron chair rails. The line in this part of the state was very crooked, running as it did on the divide between the Saline and Smoky Hill Rivers. It was intended to avoid all heavy cuts and fills so as to build cheaply…it appeared as if Shoemaker, Miller & Company were more bent on building as many miles of road with the least expense, and in that way profit by obtaining more of the bonus (the sixteen thousand dollars per mile) than following a more direct line to connect with the Central Pacific. (14)

The railroad ground to a halt September 5, 1868, at Sheridan, Kansas. The Union Pacific Railway Company Eastern Division was out of money. Additional subsidy from the Federal government would not be available until the next meeting of Congress. (15)

Meanwhile the Indian conflict grew worse. A series of attacks on wagon trains and outlying road ranches began to occur along the Santa Fe Trail in southwestern Kansas. General Sheridan traveled by train to Fort Harker to investigate the events

27

of the initial Lincoln County raid for himself. The Indians retreated to the isolated regions of the Solomon River in western Kansas using hit and run tactics to harass the frontier.

Sheridan soon learned that conventional troops were no match against illusive warriors who could strike and disappear without warning. To deal with the situation, Sheridan conceived of an elite fighting force that could meet the Indians on their own terms. The force he envisioned would move swiftly, without supply wagon support, living with limited supply from pack animals while foraging from the land. Brevet Colonel George A. Forsyth was ordered to recruit fifty men to be known as Forsyth's Scouts. The Scouts would answer directly to General Sheridan.

Forsyth found his initial recruits from the frontiersmen who had suffered the devastating "Solomon Massacre." Thirty men were recruited at Fort Harker and an additional twenty men at Fort Hays. Eight of the First Independent Kansas State Militia, including A.J. Pliley and Chauncey Whitney joined Forsyth's Scouts at Hays City. Lieutenant Beecher was appointed second in command. The Scouts rode north and west of Fort Hays, searching for signs of Indian movement. After completing a large arc without discovering any Indians the band of Indian fighters arrived at Fort Wallace on the western border. An attack on a freighting caravan near Sheridan, Kansas, brought the Scouts into action. They trailed the war party northward into the wilds of northwest Kansas.

The First Kansas Frontier Battalion was formed at Hays City September 17, 1868. Capt. John Park's First Independent State Militia was incorporated into its ranks. The battalion consisted of four hundred thirty men who were placed on a line from Lake Sibley (present-day Concordia), at the northern edge of the Solomon Valley raids, to Camp Davidson near the mouth of the Little Arkansas River (present-day Wichita). The citizens of Ellsworth no doubt applauded the military action knowing that continued pressure on the Indians kept them at bay and away from Ellsworth's door.

The same day that the frontier battalion was formed, September 17th, 1868, far to the northwest, across the state line in Colorado, Forsyth's Scouts were pinned down on an island in the middle of the shallow Arikaree River.

Approximately six hundred Cheyenne warriors attacked the men in camp in the early morning hours. The Scouts endured several charges throughout the first day. Roman Nose, who had vowed to fight forever, was killed in one of the charges. Forsyth's band of Indian fighters held their ground for eight days, sending messengers for help two at a time by foot to Fort Wallace some seventy miles away. Seven days after the initial attack, Ellsworth's intrepid lawman, Chauncey Whitney recorded in his diary doubts of survival, "My God! Have you deserted us?" One day later "the little band of heroes" was rescued when Colonel Carpenter rode into the midst of Forsyth's Scouts with his Tenth U.S. Cavalry Buffalo Soldiers on September 25th. The Cheyenne had pulled out leaving the stranded Scouts to survive on rotten horse meat.

September 26, Whitney wrote, "Tomorrow we are to start for Fort Wallace, where I shall bid good-bye to our brave band of scouts to prepare to return east, where I will try to forget in a peaceful home the scenes of the past two years." (16)

Two wives had gone before him in death. A third adoring lover awaited his return from the frontier, holding dear the promise of marriage faithfully given at their heartfelt parting. Chauncey Whitney had seen enough blood and chaos. His heart yearned for home. But Whitney's "peaceful home in the east" was not Ellsworth. His thoughts were of Aurelius, Michigan, and the girl he left behind. He was twenty nine years of age. In the aftermath of the horrendous fight with the wild Cheyenne on an island in the middle of nowhere he determined to turn thirty in the midst of Michigan's familiar surroundings. (17)

General Sheridan's campaign to drive the offending tribes from Kansas was proving to be unexpectedly discouraging. Sheridan wasted little time adjusting his strategy. On word of the fate of Forsyth's Scouts, General Sheridan fired off a telegram to his exiled field commander Brevet Major General George A. Custer. Custer had been suspended from rank and pay for abandoning his post in July of 1867. He was residing in a peaceful home with his family not far from Chauncey Whitney's hoped for desire in Monroe, Michigan.

Meanwhile General Sheridan was about to initiate a winter campaign against the Indians. The plan was conceived and worked out in Quartermaster Major Henry Inman's quarters at Fort Harker. Sheridan would take the fight to the families and homes of the Cheyenne while they quietly rested on the reservation. All supplies would be handled by Major Inman. Sheridan would take no chances with the winter campaign. Even though Custer's sentence required him to remain away from service for two more months, General Sheridan requested, "Can you come at once. Eleven companies of your regiment will move about the 1st of October against the hostile Indians ..." (18)

The boldness of the Indians startled even the toughest of frontiersmen. Indians were reported near Ellsworth on October 12, 1868. One man was killed and several were missing. A new series of raids commenced October 13, 1868, north of Salina in the counties of Ottawa, Mitchell, and Cloud. In the Ottawa County raid, Anna Morgan was away from home searching for her missing husband when she was surprised by Indians. In her desperate attempt to ride for safety a Sioux warrior overtook her. Horses hurtled over the prairie as the warrior pulled near and struck Anna with a war club, slamming her hard to the ground. When she recovered she had been placed on an Indian pony, supported by a warrior on each side.

Word of the raid spread through the settlements like wildfire. Excitement ran high all along the frontier. The Indians kept up a constant harassment of unguarded places. Train workers were killed. Rails were torn up. Travel was far more dangerous than ever.

The frontier trembled at the news that Army Scout Medicine Bill Comstock had been killed by warriors from the camp of a Cheyenne chief known as Turkey Leg. His companion, Abner Sharp Grover survived the attack by hiding in the grass and walking to the railroad grade approximately seven miles east of Monument. His story was soon spread across the state. (19)

Train officials adjusted schedules for the safety of travelers and crew. The last train of the day arrived in Ellsworth each evening at 8 o'clock. Passengers were "booked for the night." Rudolph Keim was just such a passenger. "Leaving the train and walking a few hundred feet across an open space covered with boxes, broken barrels, tin cans, and every other variety of rubbish, we reached the 'first class' hotel, known as the Anderson House…The hotel was a frame structure about forty feet front and two stories in height…Those who could not be accommodated at the hotel were taken in tow by a seedy African and escorted to some neighboring house or tent to be provided for.

Being the first to reach the hotel I had the first chance of accommodation and was accordingly assigned to room No. 1.

After a supper on buffalo steak, antelope ham, soggy bread, and a cup of warm water, flavored with a grain of coffee or a leaf of tea, the passengers gathered in the hotel office, a small room eight by ten and furnished with a counter and several dilapidated chairs. The proprietor presided. Seating himself on a three-legged chair and cocking his feet on the stove he entertained himself spinning yarns laudatory of his own prominent career, throwing in occasionally a bit of history connected with the laying out and subsequent growth of the town of Ellsworth.

The proprietor continued his description of Ellsworth's "early days" which in fact were only months previous.

The population consisted of rather a miscellaneous assortment of human beings. Nor was the order of the place any better. Shooting at each other upon trivial grounds was an expected and ordinary occurrence. Drinking shops and gambling dens were the only profitable places of public amusement. Since the railroad had been pushed further west, the town had become quite orderly and the population had at the same time suffered material diminution.

Several times during the night Mr. Keim reported that they found their attention distracted from the host by "violent yells…salvos of uproarious oaths" and "demonstrations of the scientific use of the fist…as no one was killed the reputation of the place was not effected, and the parties were allowed plenty of room to finish it out in true frontier style."

"By three o'clock the next morning the passengers were rallied at the hotel … All bills had been settled in 'advance'." The cooks had overslept. There would be no breakfast before departing for the train. "… with a parting benediction on the landlord's head most of the passengers retired to an adjacent 'rum mill' and 'stowed away' a 'slug' or two of 'mountain dew' to keep their spirits up." With that, the train was boarded. "The locomotive whistled 'up breaks' and away we started westward." Keim was traveling west to Fort Hays to cover the Indian War as a war correspondent for the New York *Herald*.

Defense of the frontier was on everyone's mind. 1,300 men volunteered for the newly organized 19th Kansas Militia. Kansas Governor Crawford resigned from office to personally take command of the 19th. (20)

In the midst of all the Indian excitement Ellsworth was incorporated as a village. J. H. Edwards presided over a council of five. Charles C. Duncan, a twenty-four-year-old grocer, served as the Ellsworth Congressman to the Kansas House of Representatives. (21)

General Sheridan's winter campaign was begun November 5th as the 19th Kansas marched along Topeka's Kansas Avenue. Each platoon filled the street from curb to curb with Samuel Crawford at its head.

The 3rd Cavalry marched east from Fort Bascom, New Mexico. The 5th Cavalry rode southeast out of Fort Lyon, Colorado. The main force of 7th Cavalry, two companies of the 19th Kansas, Pepoon's Scouts and five companies of infantry marched from Forts Hays and Dodge. District Quartermaster, Major Henry Inman coordinated supply out of Fort Harker.

The 19th Kansas advanced into Indian Territory with Apache Bill Seamans and Jack Stillwell as scouts. Apache Bill claimed to know the country and referred to his route as the Dutch Henry Trail.

A winter storm set in with a blinding rage. Soon Apache Bill and the 19th Kansas were forced to wander through the breaks of the Cimarron River rather than take a direct route. Horses and mules died from exposure. The men suffered but were able to subsist on fresh buffalo meat. On the 27th of November they finally reached Camp Supply, Indian Territory, having endured nine days of cold and misery.

Custer did not wait for the arrival of the 19th Kansas. Black Kettle's camp on the Washita River, was attacked November 27, 1868. The village was overrun and completely subdued within ten minutes. One hundred Indians were killed. The central Cheyenne chief, Black Kettle was among the dead. Fifty women and children were taken captive. Sheridan had his victory. The discovery of over two thousand warriors camped further downstream convinced Custer to retreat to Camp Supply. His attack on Black Kettle's camp was a success. The campaign would continue sporadically throughout the winter. (22)

In Ellsworth, Sheriff Ezra Wolcott Kingsbury continued to have his hands full maintaining some semblance of law and order. It was said, "One sip of Ellsworth whiskey will make a man burn his wife's dress." How many wives could attest to the ill fame is unknown, but it was certain that whiskey flowed freely throughout the town. That whiskey was the cause of so much danger could hardly be denied. "Men kept their hands on their pistols."

Word went out that Old Bill Smith, proprietor of the New York House had gotten an early start or perhaps he had never taken an intermission from the previous night's drinking. Whatever the case, Old Bill had consumed way too much of his own whiskey. At 10 o'clock in the morning Bill stood in the doorway of the New York House. Spying movement in the street he cocked his pistols and began promiscuously firing away. Sheriff Kingsbury was certainly no stranger to danger. He had served as Captain of Company I of the 2nd Colorado Cavalry. The outfit had seen action from Westport to Newtonia, Missouri, during the Civil War. Kingsbury had been wounded twice and had suffered from an attack of smallpox. Following Newtonia, the 2nd Colorado was sent to Fort Riley for Indian service. Now, he was in Ellsworth and Old Bill was sending lead in all directions.

Kingsbury cautiously made his way close enough to the New York House to hail the drunken saloon keeper. "Bill stop your damn fooling before you kill somebody."

"All right, Cap." Smith smiled and put his guns away, but he kept right on drinking. Smith was also a former cavalryman. Old Bill was no spring chicken but at sixty-five he could still handle a horse. He knew the back of a horse better than he knew his own inebriated soul. It was to the back of a horse that Old Bill finally stationed himself.

With pistols at the ready Old Bill guided his trusted war horse into the street with his knees. Kingsbury stepped into the street, revolver in hand, hoping to talk Bill out of the saddle. Bill rode a circle around the sheriff, flailing his guns in the air, announcing his dominion over all who would challenge him. Sheriff Kingsbury ignored the shots that churned the dusty street at his feet.

A sudden cue to his mighty steed sent Old Bill's war horse hurtling up the street as the aged cavalryman fired at anything and anyone that moved. With his pistols empty Old Bill returned to the sheriff, "sitting his horse straight like a veteran dragoon."

His skill had not forsaken him. Bill had either exchanged his empty pistols for loaded ones or he had reloaded on the fly. Either way it was done with such brilliance not even the Sheriff was aware that his pistols were loaded.

Sheriff Kingsbury stepped forward to put a halt to Old Bill's mischief. Bill warned him back, but thinking the guns were empty, Kingsbury came on. Suddenly the air exploded with lead and smoke as Old Bill sprayed the ground at the sheriff's feet, one shot after another. Kingsbury raised his own pistol, firing over Old Bill's head. The shootout was described as an "absurd duel ... the smoke from the guns met and mingled in friendly fashion, spectators howled with delight."

A shot finally hit Sheriff Kingsbury in the foot. His boot filled with blood. That was it! The fun was over. Kingsbury rushed Old Bill, pulling him from his horse. Sheriff Kingsbury was cheered by one and all for his coolness on the job. Old Bill would live to drink his own whiskey yet another day. (22)

Some may say that the Old West has become an exaggeration. Shootouts in the street and daily killings were unusual. Perhaps that was true of the majority of towns but Ellsworth came by its legendary reputation of excess because of men like Old Bill and Sheriff Kingsbury. Ellsworth was a town that viewed men like Wild Bill Hickok and Captain Jack Harvey as perhaps first-rate, but in many ways not out of the ordinary.

A certain amount of controlled mayhem emerged as the order of the day. As the frontier spread west, the name of Ellsworth was spoken as though it had materialized from the distant mists of a long lost age; another time and another place.

In our modern times we often think of tourism as something new, but frontier Kansas brought the curious to see for themselves the exciting life reported by eastern newspapers.

An excursion train scheduled for a trip to the end of the track provided a relatively safe way for tourists to experience the frontier for themselves. An example was the August 5, 1868, item in the Topeka *Daily Kansas State Record.*

The Topeka Excursionists will leave the Depot on Thursday morning the 6th inst., at six o'clock SHARP, and run to the end of the track. Everybody is expected to take along their own eatables, and occupy as small a space for the same as possible, as the baggage car will not accommodate large boxes or trunks. Mr. Pape will furnish the refreshments, consisting of Ice

Cream, Lemonade, Sherry Cobbler, Mint Julips, Wines, etc. A general good time is expected. All are expected to provide their own mode of conveyance to the Depot.

The notice attracted two hundred excursionists for three days of excitement on the wild Kansas plains. John H. Putnam recorded his adventures in a letter dated August 22, 1868.

> Our route is through the country of the Smoky. The road however here cuts across a great bend and after a seventy five miles ride through a rough, uninhabited, and almost uninhabitable country, which shows many signs of volcanic action, we again strike the Smoky at Ellsworth-one hundred and sixty five miles from Topeka.
>
> We are now, ... *in the West*. Here is *life*. The fine spun theories, the moon-eyed inventions, the old time manners, and obsolete customs of the East are unknown. The houses here are alternately Beer Houses, Whiskey Shops, Gambling houses, Dance houses and Restaurants. There is little difference however as the Beer houses sell whiskey, and the whiskey houses retail beer, while the Club rooms and Restaurants all dispense the lightning (here sweetly called 'Tarantula juice'). The dance houses combine the worship of Bacchus with terpsichorean amusements of a very high order. They used to 'have a man for breakfast here every morning' as they pleasantly spoke when chronicling the nightly murders in the town, but, as they pensively admit, 'business is very dull now.' From Ellsworth to Hays City is nearly a hundred miles. This is part of the 'Plains,' what on the old maps is called 'The Great American Desert.' There are no signs of human life except at the wood and water stations of the rail road, where are generally one or two little sod houses, and a few negro soldiers loafing about. (24)

Walt Whitman, famed American poet and essayist, traveled across Kansas by train in 1879. He referred to his trip as "*The Long Jaunt West*". In describing the trip he notes that Ellsworth County is in the "centre of the State-where I must stop a moment to tell a characteristic story of early days-scene the very spot where I am passing-time 1868."

> In a scrimmage at some public gathering in the town. A. had shot B. quite badly, but had not kill'd him. The sober men of Ellsworth conferr'd with one another and decided that A. deserv'd punishment. As they wished to set a good example and establish their reputation the reverse of a Lynching town, they open an informal court and bring both men before them for deliberate trial. Soon as this trial begins the wounded man is led forward to give his testimony. Seeing his enemy in durance and unarm'd, B. walks suddenly up in a fury and shoots A. through the head — shoots him dead. The court is instantly adjourn'd, and its unanimous members, without a word of debate, walk the murderer B. out, wounded as he is, and hang him.

The legend of Ellsworth had touched even the famous Walt Whitman. (25)

In the celebrated western movie, *The Man Who Shot Liberty Valence*, aspiring attorney Ransom Stoddard questions newspaper editor Maxwell Scott. "You're not going to use the story Mr. Scott? To which Scott replies, "No, sir. This is the West, sir. When the legend becomes fact, print the legend."

Legend will forever be a part of the Ellsworth story. What confounds most historians is the confounding reality that where Ellsworth is concerned fact has become legend.

Chapter Three

A TOWN AHEAD OF ITS TIME

Ellsworth witnessed many great men in the few short years of its infancy. By 1869 the names already read like a who's who of the Old West: Sheridan, Custer, Hickok, Cody, and Comstock were but a few. Many more were yet to come. Volumes could be filled with the narratives of these storied men. Each legendary life made a contribution to the chronicle of Ellsworth, yet one man carried a spirit that would identify him more closely with Ellsworth than any other. In time Chauncey Whitney's life would personify the very heart and soul of Ellsworth, a frontier town struggling to make sense of the madness.

Chauncey Whitney returned to civilian status December 31, 1868. While many of his comrades were on the frozen plains of Indian Territory, Whitney was making good on his pledge to return to Michigan and the arms of his betrothed, Dorm Nichols. Citizens of Ellsworth naturally expected him to return to his duties as constable and undersheriff. To their surprise he quickly packed his bags. Before leaving he paid a visit to an old soldier whom he had come to admire as a father, Marcius Henry.

The two had much in common. Both had served in Michigan units during the Civil War. Whitney had suffered from dysentery during the war. Henry had also suffered greatly from drinking "bad water" while stationed at Fort Leavenworth. He was still suffering. The chronic stomach cramps and dysentery had progressed to a degree that left him virtually home-bound. Whitney's visits were a way to put the insanity of frontier life out of his mind during the moments he spent in the Henry home. There were many hours of good-humored conversation in a relatively normal family setting.

Henry's wife and daughter had become Whitney's adopted family. When eleven-year-old Nellie's health was threatened with the ague in the spring of 1867, Nellie recalled that Whitney came to the house often. "I had Ague and had shaken myself nearly to death. Could not walk and when he came he would take me off the bed and carry me out of doors to rest."

On his last visit with the Henry family Whitney related his pledge to return to Michigan. He bid his adopted family good-bye and boarded the train for Kansas City.

The visit with the Henry's opened feelings that perhaps he had hidden even from himself. At Kansas City he rested, not certain of his decision. His thoughts lingered not on his betrothed Miss Nichols of Aurelius, Michigan, but on Nellie Henry of Ellsworth, Kansas. He later told Nellie that, "… the thought of leaving me, only a child perhaps fourteen or less – was more than he could do. So he wrote her (Dorm Nichols) breaking the engagement and in a week was back in Ellsworth."

Only he knew the reason for his return. He simply stood back and watched Nellie grow to become a woman. (1)

The residents on the frontier were no different than anyone today. They were interested in current events and looked forward to the delivery of eastern newspapers at the U.P.E.D. depot. *Harper's New Monthly Magazine* was a popular publication of the time and often reported on frontier activities. Its January, 1869, edition ran an extensive article by Theodore Davis entitled, "The Buffalo Range". Davis described the already popular tourist attraction of hunting buffalo from the passenger cars along the Smoky Hill Route of the Union Pacific Eastern Division Rail Way.

On several occasions the buffalo were sufficiently close to the train to be killed by shots from the car windows and platforms; the engineer being accommodating enough to slow the locomotive sufficiently to keep pace with the buffalo, which were seemingly engaged in a race with the iron horse. When buffalo were killed the train was stopped, the game secured being granted a free ride in the baggage-car. It would seem to be hardly possible to imagine a more novel sight than a small band of buffalo loping along within a few hundred feet of a railroad train in rapid motion, while the passengers are engaged in shooting, from every available window with rifles, carbines and revolvers. An American scene certainly. (2)

Apache Bill Seamans was well known on the frontier. His reputation as a frontiersman gained him the position of Chief of Scouts for the 19th Kansas during Sheridan's winter campaign. But fate intervened to tarnish Apache Bill's reputation when he lost his way and the 19th Kansas was forced to wander in a snow storm south of the Kansas border. General Sheridan filed a highly critical report implying that the 19th Kansas had performed in an unprofessional manner. The blame for the delay was placed squarely on Apache Bill leading to his release from duty. In defense of the Kansas militia Governor Crawford filed his report.

On the march from Wichita to Camp Supply, there was no road; not even an Indian trail. It was simply a southwest course through an uninhabited country from one point to another, with only the sun and the compass as guides. There was nothing from which to get lost. There were no roads nor cross-roads to mislead us; and at the time General Sheridan understood that fact. We made the march in twelve days, and if, as he says, we had been subsisting on buffalo meat for 'eight or nine days,' it simply shows that we marched the greater part of the distance without rations or forage. The truth is that General Sheridan, knowing nothing of the country over which we marched, was laboring under a misapprehension of facts. He had been misinformed by his scouts and others, whose reputations and wages depended largely on their skill as liars.

Apache Bill returned to Kansas where he continued to find more trouble than he had counted on. At Fort Hays he and a man by the name of Alexander Boyd were accused of stealing four mules late in December, 1868. Apache Bill was arrested at Fort Harker on January 6, and Alexander Boyd was arrested at the same place January 7, 1869. (3)

While Sheridan's Winter Campaign continued pressing the Indians on reservation lands Ellsworth was dealing with it own pressing concerns. Even though Ezra Kingsbury had been one of the original founders of the Ellsworth Town Company, as Ellsworth County Sheriff he had evidently had enough of the town. Kingsbury left the state. When it was evident that he wasn't returning, the Board of County Commissioners declared his bonds insufficient and his office vacant on February 11, 1869. Constable Chauncey Whitney was appointed acting Sheriff in Kingsbury's absence.

Since the job of Ellsworth County Sheriff was an elected position Whitney could not officially be recognized as Sheriff without the governor's approval. Letters of recommendation were forwarded to Governor James M. Harvey extolling the virtues of Chauncey Whitney. He was the natural choice of the Ellsworth County Commissioners. Ellsworth County Superintendent of Public Instruction Lorenzo Westover noted that Whitney already served as undersheriff of the county and that he was "well versed in the business & will discharge the duties the best of any man ..."

Others disagreed but had no one to recommend who would go along with taking the job. Former Probate Judge James Miller evidently felt that Whitney was not the best man for the job. He requested Governor Harvey to withhold the commission of Ellsworth County Sheriff as they waited for "... developments that will occur soon."

The present Probate Judge George Geiger was more specific in his opposition, referring to Whitney as "... far from the proper person for sheriff and we will write to you again on this subject and recommend some suitable person if we can get such a one to take it."

The opposition must have worked vigorously to persuade county officials to support another candidate for sheriff. They finally found their man, Edgar A. Kesler. During the Civil War Kesler, another Michigan man, had suffered a severe head wound while in pursuit of Brigadier General John Hunt Morgan at the Battle of Buffington Island, Ohio, July 19, 1863. He was in a federal hospital at Covington, Kentucky for six months before being discharged from service in December, 1863. The wound disfigured Kesler's face giving him a rather imposing look. Lorenzo Westover dropped his support for Whitney and telegraphed Governor Harvey. "Appoint E. A. Kesler sheriff of Ellsworth county."

Kesler was issued commission No. 84 for Sheriff of Ellsworth County on March 1, 1869. (4)

The Kansas legislature of 1869 was the first to convene in the new state house building at Topeka. During the session, bond issues were passed to deal with the state debt of seventy-five thousand dollars, "incurred for military purposes for the year 1869". Another one hundred thousand dollars was tagged for a military contingent fund "to be used in protecting the frontier of the state." Fourteen thousand dollars was allotted "for the purpose of paying the expense of organizing the Nineteenth regiment of Kansas volunteer cavalry."

Parts of Kansas were once again suffering from drought. The sum of fifteen thousand dollars, "or so much thereof as shall be necessary," was appropriated "to purchase 6,500 bushels of good, spring wheat, to be distributed by an agent appointed by the governor among the destitute citizens on the western frontier."

Ellsworth was considered the western most part of settled Kansas. The provisions of the act allowed for one thousand bushels to be distributed at Ellsworth for Lincoln, Mitchell, and Ellsworth counties; two thousand bushels at Salina for Saline, McPherson, and Ottawa counties; two thousand bushels at Junction City for Marion, Clay, and Cloud counties; and fifteen hundred bushels at Waterville for the counties of Jewell, Washington, and Republic. (5)

In far western Kansas the failing Union Pacific Railway Company Eastern Division underwent reorganization and on March 2, 1869, became known as the Kansas Pacific Railway Company. The paper change allowed the "new" company to seek additional government funding to continue construction of rails from Sheridan to Denver. Changing the name to Kansas Pacific seemed to give the railroad a new sense of adventure and romance associated with the new frontier. Tourists poured forth in ever greater numbers to ride to the end-of-the-track expecting excitement at every turn. For the most part they were not disappointed.

Pawnee Indians normally had good relations with Kansas settlers. They were enemies of the Cheyenne and Sioux and could often be found working as scouts for the army. To everyone's surprise a band of Pawnee suddenly began to run rampant. They were reportedly stealing property and terrorizing civilians in outlying areas around Ellsworth. Some had been arrested and held at the Fort Harker Guardhouse. U. S. Marshal Charles C. Whiting was present in Ellsworth and telegraphed Fort Harker with an urgent message on March 9, 1869. "Twenty (20) Indians are in town send squad of soldiers." Chauncey Whitney's old friend M. H. Henry also sent a telegraph apprising military officials that "they are not arrested and are making themselves generally free."

Pawnees returned on March 12th. Deputy U.S. Marshal John S. Park and Constable Chauncey Whitney, who had fought at the Battle of Beecher's Island, confronted the Indians, informing the chief he was under arrest. When he made a threatening move with his bow and arrow the officers drew weapons and began firing and chasing the Indians while a number of Ellsworth citizens followed in pursuit. Two Pawnees were killed, including the chief. Wagonmaster Thomas A. Atkins was enraged. In a letter to the Secretary of War he called the shooting of the Pawnee a "harable outrage."

Atkins was a well known frontiersman with a reputation nearly as large as Wild Bill Hickok. Correspondent Henry M. Stanley found Atkins a thrilling subject.

A spirited collection of adventurers gather for a rare photograph in front of a warehouse at Fort Harker. The imposing fellow on the far left is Wild Bill Hickok. Major Henry Inman stands near the middle, wearing a military cap called a kepi.
Alexander Gardner Photograph. Courtesy Ellsworth County Historical Society.

Tom Atkins has ... been proved in many a skirmish with the rebels and Indians. In 1861 he took command of a train for Santa Fe. He had twenty-nine men with him. When about half way his train was attacked by a mounted band of seven hundred Indians, mostly Comanches and Apaches. After a fight of four hours, during which many an Indian bit the dust, the Indians retreated, leaving Atkins' little band masters of the situation.

The train consisted of twenty-seven wagons, which were filled with costly merchandise. Three days after the fight the teamsters went in a body to Captain Atkins, and informed him that they had determined to drive the train to Texas. 'Well, boys,' said he, 'that was just the thing I was thinking of, so you will have to take me along; but I want to make a speech to you first, and tell you of a plan better than that.' His men gathered about, and were impatient to hear his plan. 'Sit down, boys, and let us discuss things sociably.' They all ranged themselves before him on the grass. When all were seated he drew his revolvers, and presenting them at the trembling party, informed them that he would most certainly blow out the brains of the first man who should attempt to rise. Not one dared to move. Then calling his assistant waggon-master, he sent him off with a despatch to Fort Garland for a squad of soldiers to arrest his men, who had mutinied. His waggon-master saddled the best horse in the train, and galloped full speed to the fort, and returned with a strong detachment which took the whole party prisoners. During the time that intervened between the departure of his wagon-master and the arrival of the soldiery, which was fully four hours, Tom Atkins kept guard over twenty-eight men, until they were marched off to Fort Garland. Atkins was then obliged to employ Mexicans, and in due time delivered his freight safely at Santa Fe. (7)

While Ellsworth was fighting it out with "friendly" Indians the Winter Campaign continued south of the Kansas state line. Custer was able to gain the release of two white captives. They were eighteen-year-old Sarah White who had been taken captive west of Concordia on August 13, 1868, and twenty-four-year-old Mrs. Anna Morgan who was taken captive October 13, 1868, in Ottawa County. As officers and soldiers gathered around the newly released captives, Custer described the event. "Men whom I have seen face death without quailing found their eyes filled with tears, unable to restrain the deep emotion produced by this joyful event."

The Cheyenne were ordered to return to Camp Supply, ending General Sheridan's Winter Campaign. The soldiers left the next day for Camp Inman, a supply depot that had been set up on the Washita River by District Quartermaster Major Henry Inman. They continued their march from Camp Inman to Fort Hays to mark the end of General Sheridan's famous Winter Campaign April 7, 1869. (8)

Colonel Nelson A. Miles was appointed commander of the 5th U. S. Infantry in March of 1869. He later wrote of his first introduction to the plains.

My first impression of the plains country was obtained after leaving Fort Leavenworth, in the spring of 1869, as we passed out through the fertile valleys of Kansas to what was then the terminus of the western railway system, Ellsworth. There we took a construction train, which was carrying rails and material, a short distance further to the westward to what was then known as Fort Hays, where I found the headquarters of my regiment, the Fifth United States Infantry. The plains were then a wild, weird waste of rolling prairie and valley. Along the lowlands and river courses were occasionally trees and tall grass, with here and there a grove or small forest, but generally speaking, the face of the upland country was covered with a close mat or carpet of buffalo grass not more than one or two inches in height, while on the hillsides sage brush and bunch grass were found ... Here I watched the tremendous strides that were making in the construction of railroads and the extension of channels of communication and commerce, and the steady westward march of settlements as the long trains of cars came laden with immigrants, not only from the East, but from all parts of Europe, and established hamlet after hamlet, and village after village, farther and still farther toward the western horizon. (9)

For all of its beauty and grandeur, Miles had already missed the natural prairie. His vision was one of transition from the primordial past to the progressive future. Nothing would ever be the same again.

The founders of Ellsworth had witnessed the change. They had contributed to it. But from the town's formation things had remained the same; violent. Tensions continued to intensify in Ellsworth. Thomas Atkins, who had been critical of the killing of friendly Pawnees at Ellsworth, had threatened several men while Atkins himself was threatened by supporters of Deputy U.S. Marshal Park and Constable Whitney. A feud developed between saloon-keeper Joe Brennan and Atkins. April 6, 1869, the two men argued. Atkins pulled his pistol and cocked the hammer, but was wrestled to the floor by a bystander. While Atkins was pinned to the floor Brennan drew his own pistol, jumped over the bar and squeezed the trigger. The pistol misfired and Brennan was also wrestled down. Constable Whitney stepped in and took control of the guns. The two men were separated and nothing more was done.

Atkins soon was making the rounds of several saloons, asking for someone to give him a gun, but no one came to his aid. Late that night while Atkins was standing at the bar in a place called the St. Louis Rest, Joe Brennan rushed in the front door, his six-gun belching smoke and fire. Atkins dived over the bar, using the bartender as shield. But Brennan just ran behind the end of the bar and continued shooting. Akins crouched in the corner, wounded from one of the shots as Brennan fired one more time. By that time Constable Whitney had arrived. He rushed Brennan and wrestled him up against the wall. As Whitney dragged Brennan toward the door two soldiers went to Atkins. He was carried from behind the bar and placed on a table. One of the soldiers removed his blouse and placed it under Atkins' head. By this time a crowd of fifty or so men and women had gathered. A doctor arrived and began to probe Atkins' groin for the bullet. Thomas Atkins was eventually taken to his room where he lingered in agony for a few days, eventually coming to his death in bed at the Marshall House.

There is no record of a verdict. It is assumed that Joseph Brennan was acquitted on the evidence brought before the court during the trial. He continued in the saloon business for many years. (10)

At the State Capital in Topeka the Kansas State Legislature created a commission to examine claims of destroyed property and stolen stock from Indian raids during the years of 1867 and 1868. The governor was authorized to appoint a commission of three disinterested citizens to investigate the claims.

Immediately after the passage of the act, Gov. Harvey appointed as Commissioners Z. Jackson, of Ellsworth; Edson Baxter, of Salina; and James F. Tallman, of Washington, Kansas. The commissioners met and organized soon after their appointment, and on May 7 reported that they had audited and allowed claims amounting to just over forty-three thousand dollars. (11)

While commissioners were scrutinizing depredation files the reorganized Kansas Pacific Railway Company prepared to resume building tracks toward Denver, Colorado. The decision to build to Denver had been ratified by the stockholders on April 5th. The first leg of construction targeted Big Springs, Colorado, one hundred and thirty-three miles west of Sheridan. Construction would not get underway until fall.

Sheridan had been an end-of-track town for eleven months and would remain so for several more months. No formal law enforcement had been established at Sheridan, leaving justice in the hands of vigilantes. (12)

May 12, 1869, proved eventful in Ellsworth. A man named Fitzpatrick had just lately come from Sheridan. Vigilantes had given him fair warning to get out of town.

Fitzpatrick found a job at one of Ellsworth's many saloons, but evidently consumed too much of the merchandise. The evening of May 11, he stepped into the street and began firing his pistol indiscriminately. Anyone foolish enough to remain on the street found Fitzpatrick's pistol pressed against them, accompanied by an oath proclaimed to all who could hear that he would "shoot!" Each victim was released with his life and most certainly more oaths as to their character. The east-bound train made for perfect sport as Fitzpatrick fired through the cars.

Returning to the saloon the drunken gunman found a man asleep in a back room. Infuriated, Fitzpatrick shook the man awake and angrily asked how he got in the room. William Bryson was in the habit of sleeping there, evidently on the sly. He told Fitzpatrick that he had crawled in through the window. Fitzpatrick then proceeded to pistol whip Bryson. In the mix-up Bryson broke loose but Fitzpatrick's trigger was faster. The shot to Bryson's groin dropped him like a bag of rocks. He lingered through the rest of the night, taking his last breath about eight o'clock in the morning.

A coroner's jury was quickly called. The pronouncement was "guilty in the first degree". Ira W. Phelps, Ellsworth grocer and former member of Jennison's Jayhawks wrote an account of the event to the Junction City *Union*.

According to Phelps, Fitzpatrick was taken from jail by a mob of Ellsworth citizens and marched to the banks of the Smoky Hill River. There before a strong Cottonwood branch he confessed that he had stabbed, "a great many men." Within moments Fitzpatrick was dancing into eternity at the end of a rope.

Phelps was quick to point out that Ellsworth had the assurance of the Texas cattle trade and that citizens there were determined to have law and order, "if they have to fight it out on this line all summer." (13)

The turmoil in Ellsworth and other railroad towns was making leaders at the state level nervous to say the least. Ellsworth's earlier killing of Pawnee Indians in March had far reaching consequences at the highest level of Federal law enforcement. United States Marshal for the State of Kansas, Charles C. Whiting, was found responsible for his deputy's actions while dealing with the Pawnee, a supposed military ally on the plains. Whiting was suspended from his position on May 13, 1869, succeeded by David W. Houston. Houston would soon remove most of the deputies under his authority from service. Wild Bill was one of the few that retained his badge. (14)

Determined Ellsworth promoters were fighting a stiff battle to civilize their town but they would not be discouraged. Construction of new stockyards began in May. William Sigerson & Company began not only stockyards but, "a structure to hold the requisite banking facilities." The Kansas Pacific was more than happy to provide a siding to load cattle and present Joseph McCoy at Abilene, Kansas, with competition. McCoy was having trouble holding the railroad to its obligations. With potential railheads all along the line the Kansas Pacific used the competition to get out of paying McCoy a just compensation for his efforts to establish a cattle depot at Abilene.

Instead of the railway company co-operating with Abilene, as they had engaged to do, and as any one would naturally suppose they would have done, to make it the shipping depot; the cattle point; and by such concentrated effort build up a permanent cattle market on the line of the road; instead of this, they began to intrigue, and devise plans to divert as much of the cattle trade to other points on the road as possible ... and gave lower rates of freight per car, per mile, than was given from Abilene.

McCoy even tried to induce the Kansas Pacific to support a permanent cattle trail in the form of a "... national highway on or about the sixth principal meridian, over which the cattle commerce of Texas could and would have flowed on to the line of their road for many years, undisturbed by State legislature. But no such enlightened and intelligent policy found favor with the railway company. Theirs was one of narrow selfishness, such as induced them to hazard the loss of the cattle trade, by dividing and diverting it to points where they owned, a part at least, of the town site."

Ellsworth had coveted the Texas cattle trade from its very beginnings in 1867. Circulars and posters were printed and sent to Texas and on May 31, 1869, agents for the new venture left for Texas, intent on guiding great herds of Texas cattle to Ellsworth. Excitement ran high as businessmen prepared for the coming throng of cattle and Texans. (15)

With the Cheyenne subdued, military leaders believed there would be no more trouble from Indians in Kansas. Ellsworth was certain of the new cattle trade from Texas. The continual push westward seemed inevitable.

Seeming inevitability may have laid the groundwork for a clumsy false sense of security. General Carr was ordered to shift his 5th Cavalry to the Department of the Platte in Nebraska. The military soon realized they had made a serious blunder. Carr should have recognized the mistake when his troops accidentally ran into approximately three hundred Dog Soldiers on Beaver Creek in northwest Kansas, May 13, 1869. The unexpected fight cost Carr four men while he counted twenty-five dead warriors. The General noted that his Chief of Scouts Buffalo Bill Cody, "deserves great credit for his fighting ... his marksmanship being very conspicuous ... I hope to be able to retain him as long as I am engaged in this duty."

Carr's efforts only served to drive the Dog Soldiers south. Raids continued harassing workers laying down the iron rails of the Kansas Pacific. At Fossil Station (Russell, Kansas) Adol ph Roenigk was among the men of a section crew working on the tracks west of the station. The Indians spotted the seven workers from a distance and worked their way toward the crew from a ravine just to their west. As the Indians charged from the ravine, bullets flew all about the railroad workers. The men jumped on a handcar and began to race for their lives. According to Roenigk, "The Indians seemed to be more excited than we were, for all the miserable marksmanship I ever saw in my life this was the worst. Many shots were fired at us and we had gotten nearly half a mile before anyone was struck." The speed of the car allowed the men to outrace the mounted Dog Soldiers. Once safely inside the station each man found that he was wounded.

The next day, May 29, four buffalo hunters were attacked on a tributary of the South Fork of the Solomon River. May 30th brought yet another raid along Spillman Creek in Lincoln County. Four men, one woman and four children were killed. Mrs. Susanna Alderdice and her four children were captured. The three oldest children were killed. Susanna and her baby daughter, Alice, were hoisted on the back of a mustang pony and spirited away over the prairie.

At the same time Susanna was being taken, George and Maria Weichel and a family friend, Fred Meigerhoff were discovered on the open prairie. The two men were killed. Maria was thrown on the back of a horse and carried away as the Solomon Valley raid of 1869 came to a close. The settlers were devastated.

The number of troops stationed at Fort Harker was critically low. The army was in no position to respond to such a large force of Indians. Realizing the error of leaving the Kansas frontier unguarded, the military ordered General Carr to return to Kansas from Fort McPherson, Nebraska, on June 9, 1869. Carr's force consisted of eight companies of the 5th U.S. Cavalry and four companies of Major Frank North's Pawnee Scouts. (16)

A correspondent noted the enthusiasm for the future that he found at Ellsworth in early June. Several merchandising firms served the community. There were four hotels, a drugstore, four taverns, a school house, and an Episcopal church. He evidently had made a quick study of the town for there were probably three times as many taverns as he reported.

In southern Kansas, the new village of Wichita consisted of only a few houses while the near-by post, Camp Beecher appeared to have outlived its usefulness. The Leavenworth *Times and Conservative* of June 3, 1869, reported an order issued by General Schofield, the commanding officer of the Department of the Missouri: "The Seventh cavalry, now at Camp Beecher, will at once move northward towards the big bend of Smoky Hill, scouring the country between the Arkansas and Smoky Hill. If no Indians are discovered they will go to Fort Harker." A dispatch from Ellsworth to the *Times and Conservative*, under the date of June 15, 1869, reported that: "Company 'K' of the Seventh United States cavalry, Brevet Major Hale commanding, arrived yesterday at Fort Harker, from Camp Beecher ..." (17)

Near Ellsworth, stockmen were discovering one of the reasons the Indians were fighting so hard to hold on to their ancestral Smoky Hills. The grasslands along the Smoky Hill River were as close to heaven on earth as a rancher could get.

Elijah W. Halford recognized the value of the seemingly endless prairie. He wrote of it in June of 1869.

> From Ellsworth to Hays the country is the plains. There is a boundless scene of prairie, covered with a short grass, withered and parched. After Ellsworth came no more settlements, only here and there a lonely hut, not a living human being or inhabitant to be seen, the feeling of solitude prevailing.
>
> Here is a virgin country. We are beyond the reach of plows and reapers, no sod has ever been turned, no kiss has as yet pressed the fallow earth save that of the sun which since creation has saluted this solitude with its daily breath. Here, with the vastness of creation before you, you realize

how insignificant is man and all his works.

The scene at night, with the moon and stars twinkling overhead, is one which compels the mind to acknowledge a God of the universe (and Mother Nature at her finest in creativity). (18)

Freighters did not need to be convinced of its worth. The large numbers of oxen required to handle the extensive freighting business also required a good understanding of grazing those same animals for health and profit. David W. Powers knew from his freighting experiences the perfect nutrition found in the prairie grasses of the Smoky Hills. Powers started his career as a purchasing agent for other freighters. Eventually he acquired enough capital of his own to invest in three teams complete with wagons and all the necessary outfitting. By 1869 he had developed a promising career traversing the plains with great bull trains to Denver and Salt Lake City.

Freighters found that the central Kansas prairies not only fed their passing teams well but were also ideal for wintering over herds of oxen in preparation for the coming season. D. W. Powers followed suit. In 1869 he and two nephews, James W. and David B. Powers established a ranch with headquarters at the mouth of Bluff Creek in southeast Ellsworth County. As Texas cattle began to pour into the area, D. W. put his experience to good use. He began to deal in the rangy cattle, fattening thin Texas Longhorns for the spring market. The Powers' Bluff Creek Ranch became one of the first large operations established near Ellsworth. (19)

Soon enough cattle would completely replace the buffalo and ranchers followed by farmers would call the sacred hunting lands of the Cheyenne and Sioux home. The Dog Soldier Society had valiantly fought against overwhelming odds. The tide had turned against them as they retreated to the isolated regions of northeast Colorado. General Carr's scouts eventually discovered a trail of lodge poles that led him to a location that has come to be known as Summit Springs. Buffalo Bill discovered the camp.

Major North's Pawnee Scouts stripped to the waist to prepare for battle. At two o'clock on a hot, windy afternoon the charge was sounded. The wind was so strong that it covered the sound of the attack but a young brave who was herding horses on the open prairie warned the village.

The early warning was unfortunate for the two captive women. Susanna Alderdice and Maria Weichel were both shot by their captors. When the fight was over Susanna was found dead. Maria was shot through the breast but was saved by the company surgeon. The battle at Summit Springs broke the resistance of the Dog Soldier Society in Kansas. Their great leader Tall Bull was dead and his people scattered to the wind. Susanna Alderdice was buried at the site. (20)

Ellsworth had little time to think about Indian attack. The Indians being pushed out of Kansas. Ellsworth's more pressing concern was the suppression of iniquity within its own boundaries. Vigilante justice had been the deterrent of necessity since the town's founding two years before. However, town leaders were bent on living in a civil society and if that meant reinforcing the laws with the force of the majority, then so be it. Ellsworth citizens put their signatures to a vigilante manifesto.

We, the Citizens of Ellsworth, in view of the Acts of Violence against the peace and good name of the Town, do hereby solemnly pledge to each other that we will support the officers in the discharge of their duties, at any and all times when called upon, unless prevented by sickness, that we will drive from our midst all rowdys, roughs, loafers and violent characters, by compelling them to leave and stay away – that the Committee of Bushey, Larkin, Erlech, Newbanks, and Phelps act for the Citizens in saying who shall leave Town – any one threatening or using any violent language to any citizen, to leave Town in 2 hours, or take the consequences. The Sheriff and policeman to notify all rough characters to leave and stay away – any citizen refusing to come to the aid of the officers, to be classed among the rowdies and be subject to the same penalties.

That the law abiding Citizens shall rule the Town, the Vagrants and roughs must leave, the innocent be protected – the guilty to have justice meted out to them, at all hazards the law first – when that fails Judge Lynch to finish up the work. Ellsworth, July 5, 1869.

The document was signed by 42 citizens of Ellsworth. Most of them were the saloon keepers and various businessmen of the town. (21)

While the citizens of Ellsworth were attempting to get their house in order, settlers in north central Kansas were understandably nervous over renewed activity by the Cheyenne. They were not about to let their guard down again and neither were state authorities. The state of Kansas organized four companies of the 2nd Battalion, Kansas State Militia, sometimes known as the Second Frontier Battalion. Each company was located in a blockhouse protecting the Solomon Valley just north of Fort Harker. Ellsworth's Constable Chauncey Whitney joined Company A as its 1st Lieutenant. (22)

With Whitney out of town Ellsworth needed a constable that could handle himself in uncertain situations. Wild Bill Hickok had been interested in an Ellsworth law job in 1867, but as deputy U. S. marshal he spent most of his time in Hays City and further west. Apache Bill Seamans was acquitted on May 20th for the December, 1868, theft of U. S. Army mules. His partner in crime, Alexander Boyd was held over for additional charges.

Some say that it was Wild Bill who sought out Apache Bill Seamans following his release from jail in Topeka. Seamans went from the Topeka jail to Ellsworth Constable in a few short days. Ellsworth was not going to be without a lawman as spring turned to summer and with the support of the vigilante citizenry good order could be expected. (23)

Ellsworth's businessmen were planning on a big summer as the town continued to be promoted as one of the new "end of trail" cattletowns. They were not shy in their efforts to win the cattle trade away from Abilene. Representatives of Ellsworth traveled to Abilene in 1868 to convince drovers of the superior grazing and marketing advantages of Ellsworth. Joseph McCoy found their efforts "utterly unscrupulous … full of low cunning and despicable motives". (24)

Naturally Ellsworth's crafty promoters worked closely with political leaders in

Topeka. The town needed to successfully secure the support of the 1869 Kansas state legislature if they were going to lure the cattle trade away from Abilene. Consequently Governor James Harvey signed an act to establish a new state cattle "highway", not to Abilene as Joseph McCoy proposed, but on a route of approximately 280 miles from Fort Cobb, Indian Territory due north to Ellsworth. (25)

Times were changing quickly on the Kansas frontier. The Western Union Telegraph lines were quickly going up across the state following and serving the Kansas Pacific. By July, 1869, Ellsworth was connected to Hays City. Civilization was carving its way into the prairie providing near instant communication. (26)

They say you can't change a leopard's spots. Unfortunately, Ellsworth city fathers were finding that taming the town's lawless element was going to be about as easy as turning a spotted wildcat into a harmless kitten. In July the Junction City *Union* reported, "...a man was found drugged and robbed in Ellsworth by fellows known as Jim Bush and Rowdy Joe, the people got after them and in a few days secured the robbers and about seven hundred and fifty dollars of the money. They turned the money over to a pal named Howe who was also secured. The parties were permitted to leave the country." In a report on the incident Major George Armes seemed to indicate that Apache Bill's old horse thieving partner, Alexander Boyd, was also serving as an Ellsworth constable. The men were housed in the guardhouse at Fort Harker for safe keeping. Eventually Rowdy Joe, Bush, and Howe were allowed to return to Ellsworth, probably with a stiff warning from the vigilance committee.

The combination of whiskey, women and dancing often resulted in arguments and gunplay. The evening of August 3, 1869, a Texas cowboy enjoyed a little too much Ellsworth hospitality and began brandishing a six-gun, threatening dance hall customers. A wild shot brought Constable Apache Bill Seamans to the scene. The Texan was ready for a fight. Another shot echoed from the dance hall. Seamans fell to the floor shot through the chest with blood erupting from his lungs, the Texan mounted his horse. A posse was organized to follow the hard riding Texan onto the open prairie but nothing could be done for the lawman. Apache Bill died a short time later. The Texan was tracked to Wichita but there the trail went cold. (27)

Within weeks an all too common event on the Kansas plains found notice in the Leavenworth *Times & Conservative*.

Another Indian Attack!

Dateline: Ellsworth, Wednesday, August 24, 1869, 9:40 p.m. under 'Special Dispatch' to the *Times & Conservative*.

This morning at an early hour 18 or 20 Indians appeared near a tie camp on Paradise Creek, north of Bunker Hill Station. Evander Light, the contractor (an Ellsworth businessman), had gone a few hundred yards from camp when he first discovered them. Almost simultaneously an Indian jumped out of the grass near him, and Light knocked him down. The Indian immediately raised his gun and Light attempted to draw his revolver, but ineffectually. As the Indian raised his gun Light struck it downward and the bullet went through his thigh. As the Indian retreated

Light fired at him and he fell into the ravine. Light's party came to his assistance and carried him into camp. The Indians fled on their approach. The tie party immediately came in to the station and Light came down on to-day's train for medical treatment …

But something about the story smelled sour. At the time of the attack Evander Light had a general supply store at Ellsworth, managed by Nathan Dreyfoos. Perry Hodgden who was also a business associate of Light hadn't seen him to verify that he had been wounded and had not personally heard of any loss of property. Dreyfoos, who should have been in a position to know, knew nothing of the incident, except through rumor. He verified that Light supplied his contracting crew with goods from the Ellsworth store and that Light had no other store from which to supply his crew.

Another Ellsworth businessman, Zaremba Jackson, was "… deputy marshal for the purpose of taking the census in Evander Light's wood camp on Paradise Creek". Jackson did not see Van suffering from a wound and "… knew no person who did." Investigations nineteen years later verified that Light concocted the elaborate scheme to swindle the government with a false claim of Indian depredation. (28)

Eighteen-sixty-nine was a year for County Sheriffs to skip the country. Out west at Hays City, Ellis County Sheriff Isaac Thayer disappeared from his job, presumably because he wasn't being paid. He wasn't alone. County officers and justices of the peace abandoned their positions in the face of a bankrupt county.

With only one city officer in place the citizens of Hays followed Ellsworth's lead and formed a vigilance committee. The town was filled with "… thieves, robbers and pickpockets."

For reasons not fully understood today, the Governor refused to appoint a successor to the position of Ellis County Sheriff, saying that the county would have to wait until November to elect a new sheriff. The unbearable lawless condition led the citizens to propose their own election in August. Wild Bill Hickock had moved his "camp" from Ellsworth to Hays City. Presumably Indian Annie was with him. She is found the following year in the Hays City census. They both would eventually return to Ellsworth.

For the time being, there was only one known candidate for sheriff on the bogus ballot for Ellis County Sheriff. Wild Bill was hand-picked by the Hays City vigilantes to represent the law in Ellis County. The election was followed by an announcement that Wild Bill Hickok had gained the position of county sheriff. Hickok would soon make good on his reputation as a killer. (29)

An incident that had occurred in Ellsworth in 1867 brought emotions to the surface in Hays City, September 27, 1869. Sam Strawhun had been one of the toughs in the drunken crowd that had been arrested and tied to fence posts by Hickok and other officers two years before in Ellsworth. Some say Strawhun was setting the stage to gun down Hickok when he created a disturbance in the Leavenworth Beer Saloon. Hickok stepped in to calm the atmosphere, but found an angry Strawhun who made the mistake of moving in a threatening manner. In the blink of an eye Hickok drew and fired. Strawhun dropped dead. (30)

Strawhun was just one of a host of men and women who lived on the edge. Quick

48

money was their maxim and horses often were the means by which that money was acquired. Horse thieves were operating heavily near all the military posts in Kansas. Several men were noted to be the ringleaders of a number of bands of horse thieves. In one way or another they all worked together, including the Sanderson brothers, who operated out of Junction City, Hays City, and Ellsworth. George Sanderson partnered with James White in a livery business along the river at the south end of Walnut Street (Douglas Avenue) in Ellsworth. The livery business was a perfect cover for a horse thief. Horses and mules were constantly coming and going from the Sanderson & White Livery. There was so much activity that Deputy U. S. Marshals were constantly on the trail of one outlaw or another. (31)

The constant vigil required by law enforcement was grueling. Ed Kesler did not run for election to the Ellsworth County Sheriff's position in the November general election. Chauncey Whitney was still with the Kansas State Militia. He would be discharged late in the month. J. Charles Seiber defeated William Anderson to gain the Sheriff's badge. (32)

A fire broke out in the Larkin House in the fall of 1869. The hotel was entirely consumed and most of the buildings on the block were burned. Fires are always tragic but as it turned out Ellsworth was in need of some excitement. The cattle drive for 1869 was estimated at one hundred fifty thousand head of cattle, but Ellsworth's hoped for slice of the cattle trade didn't materialize. If the new state cattle highway from Fort Cobb was used at all, it was not reported. Few if any cattle were shipped from Ellsworth. A correspondent from the Junction City *Weekly Union* was unimpressed with the town and its future. "It does not present a favorable appearance, but on the contrary it affords evidence of being in advance of the settlements of the country. Two or three years ago it had some importance as the temporary terminus of the railroad. When the road was built beyond it, it ceased to be of any consequence. Its old consequence will not be regained until the settlements have reached and passed it …" (33)

Ellsworth had the misfortune of being ahead of its time. The town had reaped the advantage of being on the edge of the frontier when the status of border town gave it a superior position with freighters and military operations. As the extreme frontier moved west, Ellsworth citizens lived in limbo between chaos and order. Civil society and commercial security could be recognized just beyond the horizon, but had not materialized to any degree of certainty. The coming year marked a new decade. It was one that the citizens of Ellsworth intended to make the best of.

Chapter Four

AN UNCERTAIN FUTURE

In early January, 1870, The Junction City *Union* reported a disturbance in Ellsworth. The trouble began when one man tried to rob another. "Two men named Reed and Gardner and a female named Fannie Collins were killed, and another named Nettie Baldwin, was shot through the stomach and breast ..." The shooter wasn't named but legend has it that former Forsyth Scout and Hays City saloonkeeper Jim Curry was Reed and Gardner's intended victim. Curry was the wrong man to tangle with. He was a known killer who had even got the drop on Wild Bill Hickok once in Hays City. Curry, who was also a railroad engineer, hid in the water tank of a locomotive while the vigilance committee scoured the train for him. He was never captured. The only living witness, Nettie Baldwin, was expected to die, but she recovered, going on to even more notorious affairs. (1)

Nettie was a well known denizen of the sporting crowd. Ellsworth police records document that Nettie and friends were frequent participants in city court proceedings. Besides Nettie Baldwin, some of the "working girls" of Ellsworth who were identified as "Fancy Women" were Mag Curry, Lizzie Adams, Cate Low, Ed Hull, Lena Rivers, Hattie Goodall, Samantha Sexton, Belle Thomas and a young woman identified only as "Curlie".

At a saloon known as the Palmera the revelry kindled to new heights as thirty-seven-year-old Lizzy Adams was wed to thirty-six-year-old George Palmer, March 25, 1870. Probate Judge James Miller performed the ceremony. George fancied himself a farmer in addition to being a saloonkeeper. The 1870 census counted George as a farmer while Lizzie was recorded as "keeping house". But Lizzie's form of housekeeping was not of the kind written of in ladies journals.

Four additional occupants could be found living at the Palmera. The census report left little doubt as to their occupation. Eighteen year-old Libby Thompson, formerly of Missouri, described her occupation by inscribing, "Diddles" on the form. Thirty-two year-old Harriet Parmenter seemed most comfortable with, "does horizontal work". Nettie Baldwin, who had miraculously survived the January shooting blatantly teased, "squirms in the dark", while twenty-four year-old Lizzie Harris went right to the heart of the matter with her admission that she, "Ogles Fools". Lizzie was not alone. The census taker documented one son, four year-old John Edward Harris. His birthplace was listed as St. Louis.

Next door three more women were recorded. Josephine DeMerritt was from Virginia, Nellie Burnham was from England and Millie Grofton was from Washington, D.C. Millie was listed as "Cook".

The Cate Low found in court records was actually Rowdy Kate, wife of Rowdy Joe Lowe. Nineteen year-old Kate was often arrested for disorderly behavior, acquiring not only her husband's last name but his soubriquet as well. The 1870 census listed twenty-four year-old Joseph Lowe as keeping a saloon. Twenty-year-old Mattie Dayton was also dwelling at that location, in addition to Joe and Kate. Z. Jackson, the enumerator, felt compelled to note in red ink, "house of ill-fame."

At a campsite near Ellsworth, identified as "Leutz", Ellsworth County census enumerator, Z. Jackson recorded an ox train in the charge of twenty-seven year-old George Hoffman. The train was made up of seven freight wagons, one of which was driven by twenty-one year-old Henry Born. The young man from Michigan was experiencing the plains of Kansas for the first time. Within a few years he would become a legend known far and wide as the renowned horse thief Dutch Henry Born. (2)

Civilization was coming to Ellsworth, even if it was by "slow freight". Ellsworth discouraged the carrying of weapons with an ordinance against, "any gun, pistol, dirk, slingshot or other weapon, within the limits of the Corporation."

Additional evidence of encroaching civilization could be found in far-flung environs scattered over the state of Kansas. Short lived Camp Beecher, at the mouth of the Little Arkansas River in southern Kansas, had been abandoned by the military after a few short months of service in 1868. Now settlers were streaming into the valley as Texas trail herds passed through on their way to Abilene. Traders discovered the advantage of the location, which was officially recognized as the town of Wichita on March 25, 1870. (3)

Further west the U.S. Army patrolled the vacant plains. Following the defeat of the Dog Soldier Society at Summit Springs, Colorado, the plains tribes were confined to reservation land. Encounters with hostile bands were generally west of Kansas, along the old B. O. D. stage route in Colorado.

According to all the rhetoric that precipitated the war against the tribes, once the Indians were forced onto their reservations outside Kansas borders, civilized men would build an agricultural utopia across Kansas, filled with peace and prosperity. But greedy eyes fell also upon those lands ceded to the tribes. In a letter dated March 28, 1870, and referenced in the May, 1870, edition of the *Harper's New Monthly Magazine,* General Sheridan apprised General Sherman of encroachment against the Indians by settlers.

Even after the Indian has been forced to the reservation, he can only be protected in his rights while there by troops keeping off the emigrants who encroach upon his land ... During the last year just as I withdrew the troops from the Sac and Fox reservation the emigrants took possession. A flood of emigration ten thousand strong moved in solid mass and occupied the Osage Reservation, because there were no troops there to keep them off. All the other reservations on which the Indians may yet be placed may be lost in the same manner unless guarded by the military.

The military, it seemed, had its hands full of trouble even without an Indian war. Settlers were taking what they could from the Indian, and thieves of another sort were making off with government property. U.S. horses and mules were prime targets of organized horse thieves operating close to military installations scattered across the plains of Kansas. (4)

Deputy U.S. Marshal Jack Bridges worked tirelessly to bring the horse thieves to justice. Working in and around Hays City, Fort Hays, Ellsworth and Fort Harker, Bridges came into contact with more than his fair share of outlaws. Bridges had once been an Army scout himself. Several of his fellow scouts were presently discovering that army mules and horses provided a first class income if a fellow was willing to take the chance.

Four of those scouts were Jack Ledford, Jack Corbin, James Stitt and Manley Gilman. Horse thieves had been operating in the area even before Fort Hays had been established, which only helped the former scouts in their change of employment. They were soon in contact with two of the most notorious of bad men, Pony Donovan and John Sanderson.

Sanderson partnered with his brothers, establishing bases at Ellsworth and Junction City. From either place stolen stock could be transferred into southern Kansas, near Douglass through Lewis Booth, a former scout and good friend of another scout by the name of Jack Corbin. Jim Smith was a common link between these men. J.R. Mead, one of Wichita's town founders, said that Smith, "… never did anything but steal, gamble and murder since he was a boy. I have known him as a thief for eight years."

Still another of the scouts, Jack Ledford, chose to locate a ranch of his own in Sedgwick County. All along the fringes of civilization the well organized ring of horse thieves could move horses and mules over great distances from ranch to ranch without notice, making a lucrative return for each man's efforts.

In April of 1870, Pony Donovan and a band of desperadoes raided an Army camp at Bluff Creek. The supply train was returning from Indian Territory. The thieves stampeded and got away with one hundred thirty-nine mules, which wrangled Army officials to the bone. A full scale effort was made to bring the outlaws to justice.

Marshal Bridges tracked three of the desperadoes, including Jack Ledford and Jake Black, to Ellsworth. Nine years later in an interview with the National Police *Gazette*, a reporter for that paper related the Bridges' account of the incident.

Happening along the main street of Ellsworth one night, Jack stopped at one of the saloons, and, walking in, came face to face with Ledford, and three of his confederates. Supposing their time had come, they all sprang on Jack at once and he, retaining his presence of mind, but not having time to draw his shoooter, sprang at the neck of Ledford and fastening his teeth as fast as he could to the jugular vein, held on as a vicious dog would to the neck of a bull. In the mean time, the three confederates of Ledford pounded and beat Jack over the head with their revolvers until his cranium resembled a raw steak. He hung to the neck of Ledford with the blood streaming in torrents from his head, and with both eyes the size of saucers. Finding they could not make him let go his hold they ran for the stove-poker and running it into his mouth actually pried open his jaws and released the horrified Ledford. They then jumped on him and tramping him inhumanly with their feet, hurried out and LEFT HIM FOR DEAD.

Deputy U.S. Marshal Jack Bridges was so severely beaten in an Ellsworth saloon that he was left for dead. He survived and swore revenge on notorious horse thief Jack Ledford. Courtesy Ellsworth County Historical Society.

Bridges was carried to the nearby drug store where a doctor dressed his wounds. His skull was fractured and several ribs were broken. As he lay recuperating from the thrashing Deputy Marshal Bridges swore he would kill Jack Ledford. (5)

Ellsworth had operated without a formal government from its founding on May 4, 1867. Prior to incorporation, frontier towns operated under county and township government. Law enforcement was perhaps the most visible example of the government that served the community. Instead of a city police force, Ellsworth relied upon township constables and the Ellsworth County Sheriff to preserve the peace.

The often loose arrangements that formed frontier government could easily pose problems for the fledgling municipalities when interacting with official state formality. Such was the case with the legality of Ellsworth's first Justice of the Peace, H. D. Woodsworth. There seemed to be some question as to his citizenship during the years 1867 and 1868. Therefore the State of Kansas found it necessary to legalize the acts of Mr. Woodsworth during his tenure as Justice of the Peace. A special enrolled bill stated that, "all acts done by him (Woodsworth) appertaining to said office during said time, shall be as valid, and shall have the same force and effect, as if said H. D. Woodsworth had been a qualified elector and a bonafide citizen and resident of said county of Ellsworth."

To alleviate any future problems Ellsworth was incorporated under the laws of the State of Kansas as a Village in the spring of 1870. The Board of Trustees met April 6, 1870, to elect E. W. Edwards as Chairman. Trustee members included Mayer Goldsoll, Nathan Dreyfoos, J. C. Veatch, and Titus Buckbee. Mondays were established for regular Ellsworth Trustee meetings to be held in the office of the appointed Clerk, Michael Newton.

One of the first orders of business for the new Ellsworth Board of Trustees was to establish an authorized police force for the village. Chauncey Whitney was appointed chief of police. A committee was formed to draw up ordinances. The clerk was instructed to give pubic notice to all saloonkeepers to obtain licenses from the board of trustees.

The trustees met the following day, April 7, 1870, with nominations for two policemen from the Chief of Police Chauncey Whitney. George Davidson and Jake Kelly were nominated and appointed. The officers were to be paid fifty dollars per month plus two dollars and fifty cents commission, "in each case where costs are collected against parties violating the ordinances."

Three ordinances were adopted. Ordinance No. 1 made it unlawful to discharge "any Gun or Pistol" within the city limits. "In the North Bank of the Smoky Hill River East of the Round House or West of a point 600 Yards of the East of the R(ail) R(oad) switch in the Eastern portion of the town, and south of the North Line of the town which is about 100 Yards from the foot of the Hills."

The second ordinance addressed drunkenness and disturbing the peace. Public intoxication was subject to arrest and a fine of "not less than $5.00 and not more than 10.00." Any person disturbing the peace "by riotous and unseemly conduct or by shooting or firing of off Guns or Pistols shall be arrested by the Police and subject to a fine of not more than $20 and not less than 10 dollars."

Finally an ordinance was adopted relating to the actions of policemen. "... Any Policeman found in any drinking saloon, Gambling House, or House of Bad reputation while on duty ... shall forfeit to the town of Ellsworth all monies due him for services and be discharged from the service of said town."

Additional ordinances were adopted April 13, 1870. An ordinance for the, "suppression of Houses of Prostitution and assignation within the corporate limits of The Town of Ellsworth..." did not make prostitution illegal within the limits of the village, but allowed for fines of up to fifty dollars for "Keeping a House of Prostitution or Assignation". All inmates of such a "House" were subject to a ten dollar fine.

Another ordinance declared the carrying of deadly weapons (any Gun, Pistol, Dirk, sling shot, or other weapon) unlawful. A fine "Not Exceeding $20.00, and not less than $5.00." was to be exacted.

Filth in the streets was becoming a problem and that too was addressed by ordinance. "... It shall be unlawful for any Person or Persons to throw, or deposit upon any street or alley of said Town any, Dirt, Filth, Garbage, Manure or Matter detrimental to public cleanliness and health."

It was also declared unlawful to, "empty or throw upon any Vacant Lot, or conceal about their Own Premises any decayed or Perishable matter, or any Decayed Meats, Fruits or Swill, but shall cause all Offal to be removed from within the Limits of the Corporation."

All litter was to be "raked, or scraped together" each Wednesday. No additional guidelines were offered as to final treatment for disposal.

Finally, the board of trustees addressed the potential for disorder in saloons during nighttime hours. Police were given authority to close any saloon or drinking house in order to maintain the peace and quiet of the town.

Eighth Judicial District Judge William C. Canfield presided over regular terms of court at Ellsworth commencing on Monday, April 11, and Monday October 3, 1870. The counties of Barton, Rice, Russell, Pratt and Stafford were attached to Ellsworth County for judicial purposes.

Ellsworth was moving ahead to establish a sound, reliable government, even as its population was withering. Railroad activity had moved west. The great wagon trains bound for Santa Fe had long ago made Kit Carson, Colorado, the desired terminal for transfer of freight. Solving the Indian problem only served to reduce the number of active troops on duty at near-by Fort Harker. The expected cattle trade had eluded enthusiastic businessmen who gradually drifted away to other fast moving communities. The population which had hovered around eighteen hundred persons in 1868 was in the neighborhood of four hundred fifty citizens.

The decline had been so dramatic that Ellsworth County was caught unawares as it transferred tax monies for assessed taxable property in January of 1870. So many people had left the county that the properties accounted for no longer existed and in many cases had been abandoned without remuneration.

The State of Kansas rectified the predicament on March 1, 1870, by authorizing the Kansas State Treasurer to return $1,465.26 to the Ellsworth County Treasurer. The action was certified by Secretary of State Thomas Moonlight on March 17, 1870. (6)

Again Ellsworth businessmen turned their attentions to the Texas cattle market as the most immediate way to rescue the failing economy. Ellsworth County was still relatively unsettled giving drovers the benefit of driving through open country away from farms and small ranches.

Texas cattle fever was a major concern to stockmen whose cattle were not immune to the devastating disease carried by the wild Texas Longhorn from the gulf regions of Texas. In addition the Kansas Pacific Railway was enjoying a monopoly as the only railroad far enough west to take advantage of being outside the quarantine line. Although Abilene was technically supposed to abide by the quarantine, Joseph McCoy had initially gained political support in Topeka that allowed the state of Kansas to "look the other way" as far as Abilene was concerned. A few cattle were shipped on the Central Pacific out of Waterville but that trade was really no threat to the tremendous market that the Kansas Pacific enjoyed along its route through the center of the state.

Settlement around Abilene was beginning to threaten that market while rumblings of competition were rising out of the east as new railroads offered potential alternatives to the Kansas Pacific.

On May 1, 1870, the Missouri River, Fort Scott, and Gulf Railroad arrived in Baxter

Springs. New shipping pens were built at the southwest edge of town as Baxter Springs stepped up their competition with Abilene. The town's static population was five thousand people and was known to swell to near ten thousand at the height of the cattle season.

The Atchison, Topeka and Santa Fe built tracks south and west out of Topeka. By August of 1870 the tracks reached Emporia and the railroad was progressing steadily west. The Santa Fe was not a rival to the Kansas Pacific yet, but they were only months away from reaching the western range. (7)

In spite of the competition Abilene was enjoying the benefit of a loyal Texas cattle market, but with that market came the wild Texas cowboys. Abilene had finally found the man who could tame them. Bear River Tom Smith enforced the No Gun law with professional efficiency. By mid-season the random shootings and wild revelry had dwindled to manageable levels. Abilene set its sights on shedding its immoral image. City fathers were making every attempt to rid the city of the horde of soiled doves and sporting men that had descended upon them. When the "ladies" and gamblers tired of the harassment, they packed up and headed for Ellsworth, Hays City, or Baxter Springs where they were more openly accepted. (8)

Wild Bill Hickok kept the peace in Hays City with the approval of the local vigilance committee. Hays City was nearly a mirror image of Ellsworth. Men and women were reckless and carefree. Everyone kept his hand on his pistol. During the evening of July 17, 1870, a typical celebration of carousing lit up the night at Paddy Walsh's Saloon. Walsh was a former Ellsworth man who was said to have killed his man in 1867. As the party boiled over at Walsh's saloon Wild Bill was caught up in a barroom fight with soldiers from the Seventh Cavalry.

Pistols blazed and two men went down. One was dead. The other was seriously wounded. Hickok may have been wounded himself. Evidently he sized up the situation and came to the conclusion that the cards were stacked against him. As troopers from the Seventh Cavalry scoured the saloons for revenge Hickok made his way out of town.

There were a variety of versions pertaining to Hickok's departure from Hays City. Ellsworth attorney Harry L. Pestana often took cases from, and traveled to, Hays City. With a slight leg wound Hickok and his companion, Indian Annie stayed out of sight for a while at Pestana's home in Ellsworth. Once recovered, Ellsworth became Wild Bill's headquarters for the remainder of 1870. (9)

Texas cattle were pouring into Kansas. One hundred and fifty thousand were shipped in 1869. Two hundred thousand were shipped in 1870. No record is known to exist documenting the number of cattle shipped out of Ellsworth prior to 1871. Undoubtedly some herds made their way to Ellsworth, but the expected flood of cattle had not materialized.

One of the big operations that discovered the exceptional grazing of Ellsworth County was the Powers Ranch. The ranch was established along the Smoky Hill River in the southeastern part of the county. The Powers' literally moved in on scattered settlers who had little strength to fight a tremendously powerful ranching operation. David W. Powers stocked mostly cattle used for oxen in the freighting business, but he and his nephews, James W. and David B. Powers were also

56

dabbling in Texas Longhorn cattle. A Powers Bank established in Salina, Kansas, specialized in livestock loans and did a stiff trade with the Texas drovers.

Years of freighting profits allowed David W. Powers to speculate in a new industry that most settlers found unfamiliar. William Kindt related one experience with the Powers Ranch.

BLUFF CREEK RANCH—PROPERTY D. W. POWERS & CO.

The Powers Ranch is today a part of Kanopolis Lake. The hills in the distance and on the left are the South Shore area. The bluff on the right can readily be seen looking west from the dam. Ranch headquarters were at the base of the bluff. Illustrated by Professor Henry Worrall. - Historic Sketches of the Cattle Trade by Joseph McCoy. Author's Collection.

"In the spring of 1870 I worked for Tom Norman and Captain Wiley. That summer the Powers Ranch was started and the cattle ate about everything the settlers raised. The cow punchers wanted to run the settlers out ..." Early in the fall Tom Norman came looking for Kindt. He wanted Kindt to go with him to the Powers Ranch because Powers cattle had been in his corn field. As the Powers brothers had refused to pay for damage to the crop Norman was going over to the ranch and kill them if they did not pay. At the ranch the foreman, Belfort and two of the Powers men were confronted as they were just sending some cowboys out to the cattle. "Norman pulled his gun and told them to settle for the corn."

Norman had the drop on the ranch men and seeing the seriousness of the situation they paid the damages. But that wasn't the end of it. The Powers men were money men with influence and soon the Ellsworth County Sheriff and "four big deputies" traveled to Tom Norman's place and placed him under arrest. Norman was loaded up in a wagon as William Kindt looked on. Kindt was told to appear at court in Ellsworth as a witness but he would have to find his own way to town. By the time he borrowed a pony and rode into Ellsworth Norman's trial was over. He had been fined twenty-five dollars and costs. He was allowed to chop wood for the sheriff for two days to settle up his debt. (10)

Deputy U. S. Marshal Jack Bridges was not the only official on the trail of horse thieves in 1870. Joel Music and Augustus Coring, two government detectives, gained the confidence of the Sanderson gang. One of the headquarters for their illegal activities was the Sanderson and White Livery at Ellsworth. Music and Coring alerted officials when Lewis Booth of Douglass, Kansas and two other gang members tried to sell stolen government horses in Topeka. The arrest led to information concerning activities in and around Junction City.

Deputy U. S. Marshal William White arrested John Sanderson and John Tucker at Junction City. Sanderson made the four thousand dollars bail at Topeka and returned to Junction City.

Tucker remained in Topeka and began to talk implicating Sanderson not only for theft and robbery but murder. A warrant was issued for the arrest of John Sanderson for the murder of Thomas Reynolds of Junction City in 1868. Sheriff Richard C. Whitney, Deputy James Reynolds, and Marshal White arrested Sanderson on August 1, 1870. He quietly submitted.

But as the officers holstered their pistols, Sanderson suddenly brought up a double-barrel shotgun and fired at Reynolds' head. A second shot hit Marshal White. Dropping the shotgun Sanderson blazed away with a pistol as he fled the scene.

Sanderson was discovered hiding in a small stone house near Solomon City on August 4th. He was captured and placed under a guard of some thirty men.

The prisoner was later taken to Humboldt Creek for a preliminary examination before the justice of the peace on August 6th. John Sanderson's brothers, Jonathan and George, escorted the bodyguard. George Sanderson operated a livery in Ellsworth with partner, James White.

At Humboldt Creek an estimated one hundred men confronted the lawmen. John and his brothers were seized but when John refused to make a confession he was shot to death. Jonathan and George were threatened, but upon signing a written statement that they would not return to Junction City the two brothers were released. That very day, Lewis Booth was released at Topeka on bond.

Booth turned out to be the link between the Sanderson gang and the thieves in the Douglass-Wichita area. The horse thieves were playing a fast and dangerous hand. For years they had preyed upon honest settlers. No one was safe from their escapades.

Honest citizens were tiring of looking over their shoulders as they passed over wagon roads while tending to daily responsibilities. The men were mostly Civil War veterans. Cowering in dark corners was not their way. A vigilante organization was formed in the Douglas-Butler County area during the summer of 1870, patterned in a military fashion of order and discipline. Several hundred men formed a citizen's army known as "The Regulators".

The Walnut River was a natural thoroughfare and began to be closely watched by the Regulators. Several hiding places were soon discovered in the thick timber along the river. A cave was also discovered. A stakeout soon revealed the coming and going of the thieves. Men were recognized without being alerted to the hunt. Information was gathered, while observing the outlaw's closest friends.

In early November two groups of silent riders made tracks to the cabin of Jim

Smith, one of the thieves. The Lewis Booth place, north of Douglass, was the second destination.

The riders found that Smith had not reached home from his day in town. Riding to Slayton's Crossing on the Little Walnut River the vigilantes secreted themselves away. Smith would have to pass that way on his way home.

Meanwhile, the other band of Regulators closed in on the Booth place. Lewis's brother, George, and former government scout Jack Corbin were both staying overnight. All had gone to bed when a knock brought Lewis' wife, Jennie, to the door. Masked vigilantes suddenly sprung into the room. The outlaws were dragged from their beds and marched to a grove of nearby timber.

A rope was placed around Jack Corbin's neck and with a jerk he was lifted off the ground. Just before the life was strangled out of him the hangmen lowered him to allow him to regain his stance. The Regulators wanted names. Corbin was again strung up and again brought to the ground. Men were named as Corbin begged for his life. The rope once again drew taunt. Once more, Corbin was swinging from the tree but this time the rope was tied off while the outlaw choked and struggled for the last time.

All the while the Booth brothers watched, alarmed at their own fate. They begged to be shot. The Regulators decided to allow them to run. No man could outrun the hail of bullets that filled the air that night. Both men were dead within moments.

Back at Slayton's Crossing, Jim Smith rode silently toward his destiny. The dark of night could not cover his identity as he crossed the Little Walnut. His white mule was well known and easily recognized. A shot rang out. Smith reeled as hot lead pierced his body. His pistol was out. The dark erupted into a white hot flame as Regulators blazed away. The mule went down and in seconds both Smith and his mule were dead. (11)

The Regulators continued purging unwanted scoundrels, sending waves of alarm across Kansas. Ellsworth's horse thief crowd may have been duly alarmed by the recent turn of events. The loss of horses and mules seemed to subside as men checked their throats for signs of rope burn after waking from a night of sweat drenched sleep.

All the while settlement was inching ever so close. Farmers began taking up land in Ellsworth County. The county produced two thousand one hundred seventy-five bushels of wheat, twelve thousand one hundred sixty seven bushels of Indian Corn, four thousand three hundred ninety-three bushels of potatoes and one thousand six hundred and four tons of hay. The town of Ellsworth may have dramatically diminished in population but the county could boast a populace of one thousand one hundred and eighty-five people. (12)

The Reverend Dr. Levi Sternberg was a great proponent of central Kansas for settlement. He wrote a letter dated December 10, 1870, to Clinton C. Hutchinson, Topeka. Mr. Hutchinson was collecting information for a book extolling the virtues of Kansas.

DEAR SIR: You desire to know if the Plains are well adapted to butter and cheese making, and also my method. In replying to the first inquiry, it may be proper to say that I am not prepared to speak of the Plains generally.

Portions of them may be barren and destitute of water and of natural shelter for stock. My remarks are intended to apply more especially to Ellsworth county, the eastern limit in this part of the State of the buffalo grass region. Whether a country is well adapted for stock and dairy purposes, depends upon its grasses, water and climate.

We have both winter and summer grasses. Our winter grasses are such as keep green, and grow somewhat during the winter, especially in sheltered places in ravines and near the banks of streams. They come forward very early in the spring so as to afford good pasturage, in this region generally about the middle of March. The principal variety ripens about the first of June, and resembles what we used to call the early June grass in New York. When green, it is sweet and tender, and cattle eat it with avidity." Our summer grasses may be divided into two classes, consisting of such as are only fit for grazing, and such as arc also suitable to be cut for hay. The term buffalo grass, includes the gramma grass, or the curled mesquite, both of them remarkably nutritious, even when ripened and dry, and affording almost as good pasturage in winter as in summer, but too short to be cut for hay. The blue joint is our principal grass for hay. It is the latest of our grasses in coming forward in the spring, only appearing about the time when our winter grasses are beginning to ripen. We have at present little more of this grass than is required for hay; but I am sorry to say that it is slowly but surely supplanting the buffalo grass. The milk produced from these grasses is remarkably rich, and our cows have access to no plants giving their milk an Unpleasant flavor, except that late in the fall they sometimes eat a species of wild sage, giving it a bitter taste.

Good water is a prime necessity for a stock and dairy country. It should be running water. Stagnant water affects the quality of the milk injuriously. Water drawn by hand involves too much labor, and is too uncertain a reliance. Our river water, and that flowing from our numerous springs, is most excellent for stock.

Our climate is of a medium character. We are subject to occasional storms, when cattle need some natural or artificial shelter, and it may be some hay. Usually, however, they graze upon the open prairie, in winter as in summer. Thus far I have not been required to feed my cattle more than about a dozen times during the winter, and they reach the spring in fine order, unless they should be pulled down somewhat by some special cause, such as coming in too early. In summer our climate is not warmer than in more northern latitudes. However warm it may be during the day, our nights are invariably cool and refreshing. The heats of summer, therefore, interfere but little with butter and cheese making, to those who have a suitable place for the purpose, and I know of no reason why we may not compete successfully both as to quality and quantity with the dairymen of any part of our country.

In the manufacture of butter, I am careful as to the condition of my cream, not leaving it to stand too long. I use the dash churn. I am careful to work out all the buttermilk, and yet not destroy the grain of the butter. This requires both experience and skill. The salt which should be of the purest kind, and about an ounce to the pound of butter, should be thoroughly incorporated with the butter, and dissolve in it. If the cream be too warm in churning, the butter will be of an inferior quality, and will readily soften in warm weather. The proper temperature is from fifty-six to sixty degrees. The cooler the cream, the longer the butter is in coming, but the better the butter. Yours truly, L. STERNBERG. (13)

As Reverend Sternberg penned his observations, farmers were a very small part of local commerce. Ellsworth County's potentially vibrant agricultural economy would not materialize for several years.

The failing economy unnerved desperate Ellsworth businesses who were confronted with tough times. Ellsworth had always coveted the lucrative cattle trade but that trade continued to elude them. City fathers faced a bleak winter while Abilene basked in prosperity. Joseph McCoy's Great Western Stockyards had become a financial bonanza.

From all points North the buyers came flocking to Abilene … No drover whose stock was good for anything, had any trouble to find a buyer at good prices, and the season closed with the most satisfactory results to all interested. Many 'through' or fresh driven herds sold at thirty to forty dollars per head, and from fifty to sixty dollars were realized for wintered herds, of which there were quite a large number. The season was dry, the grass was rich, and the cattle became very fat." (14)

If Ellsworth was going to succeed in the coming year the town would have to gain a share of the Texas cattle market. Just as winter would eventually turn to spring Ellsworth businessmen looked forward to green grass and renewed prosperity.

Chapter Five

WINDS OF CONFLICT

The days of Abilene's domination of the Texas cattle trade were numbered. Grazing lands were being quickly taken up by settlers. Abilene still expected great numbers of cattle for the coming 1871 season but as they say, "All good things must come to an end".

However Ellsworth promoters also viewed the Texas cattle trade as critical to the economy of their own struggling town. Tens of thousands of cattle guided by hundreds of cowboys virtually guaranteed prosperity. Ellsworth's greatest dream was about to unfold. One can only imagine the excitement on the streets of Ellsworth when they learned of the Kansas Pacific's plans to make Ellsworth the principal cattle shipping point for 1871.

Thousands of Texas Longhorns were already grazing the rolling Smoky Hills of Ellsworth County. Taking advantage of very productive free winter grazing, not to mention the hospitality of nearby Ellsworth, many herds had moved onto the lush open range following the 1870 season.

Even so, Mayor Goldsoll hedged his bets by opening a branch of his general supply house in Abilene. Goldsoll was on the Ellsworth Board of Trustees and had operated the Old Reliable House at Ellsworth since 1867. Perhaps tiring of each year's expected cattle boom Goldsoll opened an Abilene store doubling his chances to gain from the lucrative cattle trade. (1)

Ellsworth's principle leaders intended to be ready for the new season. Saloons were ordered to immediately present bonds. The action served to lend credibility to both the town and its drinking establishments. Constable Chauncey Whitney was authorized to close any saloons not complying with the bond request.

Rowdy Joe Lowe was one saloonkeeper who refused the order. Joe was given an ultimatum by the clerk, "... produce acceptable bonds immediately ..." To Joe's dismay Ellsworth was moving beyond the "wide open" atmosphere that had been its hallmark from the beginning. He had little choice but to give in. For the time being Rowdy Joe Lowe's U. S. House would continue to be a part of the sporting scene in Ellsworth.

Not only was the frontier moving beyond Ellsworth, the civilizing qualities of an agricultural society were beginning to carve a new agrarian order from the ancient sod of the Smoky Hill country.

Ellsworth County's Rev. Dr. Levi Sternberg and his neighbor, Mr. David B. Long were both present at the annual meeting of the Farmers' Institute at Manhattan's

State Agricultural College in February of 1870.

Both men were engaged in the cheese business. Mr. Long told the convention,

> Kansas is looked upon as a great beef-producing State, and we can certainly make as good cheese here as in Ohio, and can do it with less expense. Our cows cost less, and they net more. In Ohio it costs twenty-five dollars a year to keep a cow, in Kansas less than one-half that. Cheese in Ohio brings twelve and a half cents per pound; mine brings eighteen and a half. Good cheese can be made in Kansas. Dairy farming is destined to become one of the most interesting and profitable branches of industry in Kansas.
>
> Some one then asked, 'How much cheese can you make from one gallon of milk?' Mr. Long answered, 'In Ohio, one pound from one gallon, or ten pounds of milk; here, one pound from eight and two-thirds' pounds of milk. This is the quantity from the common cow; from the Alderney, we can make more.'
>
> Dr. Reynolds asked, 'Do cows give as much milk here as there?' Mr. Long thought they did, full as much. 'The buffalo grass produced as much, and richer milk, than the tame grass.' Dr. Sternberg said, 'our season being longer (than that of Ohio) we can have two months more for butter and cheese making.' Mr. Long was asked about exporting his cheese, but he has no need; he finds a ready market for all his in the State ... (2)

For all the benefits of producing cheese on the frontier of Ellsworth County wild men still reigned supreme in 1871. Change had come to Abilene, but change was slow in coming for the relatively uncultivated plains of Ellsworth County. Outlaw activity continued as federal officials and local lawmen concentrated their efforts to bring the outlaws to justice. Despite the breakup of the Sanderson horse thief ring in November of 1870, Pony Donovan and a significant band of thieves were still on the dodge in February of 1871. The outlaws were known to be traveling toward the setting sun, southwest of Hays City along the old stage and freight route famously established by David Butterfield. Troops were dispatched and the gang was captured, minus a very lucky Pony Donovan.

Back in Wichita Jack Ledford had married and declared that he had gone straight. He and Alice Harris began wedded bliss as proprietors of the Harris House. One of Alice's old beaus, discovered that a two thousand dollar reward was still being offered for the capture of Ledford He wasted little time notifying authorities at Fort Harker. Jack Bridges, who often worked out of Ellsworth, was just back from the Pony Donovan chase. Bridges' pride was still stinging from the pistol whipping he had received at the hands of Ledford and three other men a year earlier in Ellsworth. Bridges' skull was fractured and several ribs were broken. As he lay recuperating from the thrashing, the Deputy U. S. Marshal swore he would track down and kill Jack Ledford.

With new information on Ledford, Bridges and another Federal Marshal, Lee Stewart, set out on the Fort Harker military trail to Wichita. The two lawmen were supported by twenty soldiers under the command of Captain Randall of the 5th U.S. Infantry.

The posse rode into Wichita at one o'clock p.m. February 28, 1871. They immediately surrounded the Harris House. An extensive search failed to turn up any sign of Ledford. The soldiers left town, setting up camp beyond the city limits. Bridges, Stewart, and Lt. Hargous carried on the search. One of them finally noticed a privy across the street behind a saloon.

The three stepped across the street and cautiously approached the outhouse while Ledford was watching through a crack in the door. Knowing that the law was on to him, Ledford charged from the outhouse with guns blazing. Marshal Bridges was shot twice in the arm. Another shot just missed Lt. Hargous. Stewert and Hargous returned fire, emptying their guns while they retreated with Marshal Bridges who was bleeding profusely. Their attention was then only on Bridges as he collapsed to the ground.

Ledford made his escape as Bridges fell to the ground. But Ledford had not escaped unscathed. Several wounds to the body and right wrist rocked him but did not bring him down. Ledford staggered into a wholesale liquor store and fell to the floor. He was carried to the Harris House where he died in less than thirty minutes.

Because Ledford was a popular man in Wichita, shock soon turned to anger among the citizens as tensions mounted. Stewart and the military escort hastily loaded Bridges onto a wagon and left town. Bridges was returned to the post hospital at Fort Harker where he took nearly three months to recuperate. (3)

The dust had hardly settled when another Ellsworth man, Rowdy Joe Lowe angered the sensibilities of Wichita citizens. Rowdy Joe was accused of stealing a "Slate Colored Mule" from Thomas J. McAdams of that city. Ellsworth County Sheriff J. Charles Seiber arrested Rowdy Joe Lowe at Ellsworth for the theft. Seiber escorted Rowdy Joe to Wichita where he appeared before Justice Van Treeson March 17, 1871, but Joe's victim, Tom McAdams unexpectedly failed to appear in court. The case was dismissed and McAdams was ordered to pay court costs of forth-nine dollars and forty cents. (4)

Sixty miles east of Ellsworth the city of Abilene, Kansas, was dealing with its own problems. Abilene City Marshal Tom Smith was killed November 2, 1870. The coming cattle season was fast approaching. Mayor Joseph G. McCoy turned his full attention to law enforcement. Not just any man would do. Replacing a man who had tamed the wild Texas Cowboy would not be easy. Few men could fill Tom Smith's boots.

McCoy's bookkeeper, Charles Gross suggested Wild Bill Hickok, whom he had known in Missouri. Gross traveled to Fort Harker and eventually found Hickok north of Ellsworth at Schermerhorn's Ranch in Lincoln County. Wild Bill told Gross he'd come have a look. By mid-April Wild Bill Hickok was Abilene City Marshal. His long time companion, Anna Wilson, who was expecting a child stayed behind in Ellsworth. (5)

Settlement of Kansas continued to steadily extend west to Ellsworth and beyond. Edward Judson Dodge was drawn to Ellsworth in search of property. He arrived by train on the fifteenth of May, 1871. After leaving the train Dodge entered a hotel and sat down to have breakfast. A rough looking man entered the dining hall looked around, and took a seat across the table from Dodge. The desperado pulled his pistol and laid it on the table, a typical frontier custom. The waiter stepped up and informed the desperado that beef and pork were on the menu. The man swore and replied, "That will not do for me; I will have me a piece of a man." With a demoniac look he stared directly at Mr. Dodge. Standing up, he grabbed his pistol, walked to the door and fired. An unsuspecting milk delivery man fell dead in the street. An angry crowd gathered and soon the gunman had a rope around his neck as he tiptoed precariously on the head of a barrel.

Rowdy Joe intervened merely to declare that the doomed man owed him two dollars for whiskey. When informed of the milkman's death, Joe offered to help hang the man, but Rowdy Joe insisted that "words" should be said before the condemned man was hung. Joe was a young German who spoke in broken English. He reentered his saloon and returned with an English Bible. As he read from the Bible he stumbled and struggled with the words. In frustration he threw the bible into the dirt, declaring, "No use making so much fuss and trouble over such a little thing as that." With a lunge he kicked the barrel from under the former "tough" and "… sent him swinging into eternity." The vigilantes adjourned to the nearest saloon which, of course, was Rowdy Joe's. While the whiskey flowed they proceeded to "congratulate each other on their prompt, willing and ready way to punish crime." Few places on earth were more exuberant about crime fighting than Ellsworth, Kansas. It was spring and spirits were high. (6)

The exuberance of spring always brings new life to the prairie. The spring of 1871 was no exception. The return of the buffalo on the open plain signaled the promise of a new year. First sightings found them scattered on the southern horizon. Soon the herd was moving north in a vast column ranging from twenty to fifty miles in width.

Southwest of Ellsworth Colonel Dodge set out from Fort Zarah in route to Fort Larned. Col. Dodge pressed forward toward what appeared to be one solid mass of animals. Driving a buggy into the quietly grazing herd Dodge recognized that the great column of migrating animals was made up of smaller groups of fifty to two hundred buffalo per herd, all slowly grazing northward.

Near Pawnee Rock the buggy startled some of the leaders of one of the smaller herds, causing a great stampede. Fortunately Dodge was an experienced hunter. Reining his horse to a stop, he took aim at the oncoming rush of buffalo. With several sure shots Dodge killed the leaders, dropping them far enough in front of his buggy to cause the rest of the stampede to swing around their prostrate dead comrades. Dodge remained quiet as the thundering herd passed safely on either side of his buggy.

While the buffalo appeared to inhabit the plains in limitless numbers, the eventual extermination of the species was recognized by some. United States Representative R. C. McCormick of Arizona introduced a bill to the U.S. House of Representatives on March 13, 1871, to limit the killing of "bison or buffalo" for only "meat for food or preserving the skin". Wanton hunting was declared unlawful. In April, McCormick again spoke to the House, describing the buffalo as "the finest wild animal in our hemisphere". General William B. Hazen supported McCormick's efforts, declaring that killing the buffalo would have no effect upon the plains Indians as they were already "becoming harmless under a rule of justice". Nevertheless, with fewer Indians to harass hunters, buffalo hunting quickly became an economic staple on the Kansas prairies. The slaughter was just beginning. (7)

The range of the buffalo may have been pressed west of Ellsworth, but to town promoters the loss of the buffalo meant new grazing lands for Texas cattle. The one hitch to their plans was the new thrust by the Santa Fe Railroad onto the plains.

A number of buildings began to appear on the prairie along the intersection of the Chisholm Trail and the Santa Fe Railroad grade sixty miles south of Abilene. The location was the Santa Fe's first real attempt to wrestle the cattle trade away from the Kansas Pacific. Stockyards were being built at the new town site of Newton, Kansas. The new railhead threatened to once again derail Ellsworth's endeavor to become the next great cattle town.

By late spring Newton had swelled to a rambling collection of saloons, hotels, gambling halls, restaurants, grocery stores, and assorted other essential frontier businesses. The town also boasted a separate brothel district cleverly dubbed, "Hide Park". Most Texas trail drivers would only learn of the new town as they approached from the south. (8)

Eighteen seventy had been a very successful year for Texas drovers and with that success word of record profits spread across Texas. Excitement was high in the early months of 1871 as cattlemen prepared for one of the largest drives on record.

In Texas, sixteen year-old Ben Drake hired on to Pete Murchison. "I accompanied Pete to a shoe shop where he ordered a pair of boots made for me. Those boots cost $14.00. He also gave me a pair of bell spurs, a Colt's cap and ball six-shooter, and a rim-fire Winchester as well as a pair of leather leggings which cost $12.00. This was the first time I was rigged out, and you bet I was proud." (9)

George Saunders was seventeen years old and rearin' to go up the trail. He signed on with Monroe Choate, a partner in the trailing firm of Choate & Bennett. The outfit was sending a total of fourteen separate herds north that season. Saunders was with the first outfit to leave Helena, Texas, "… with a full chuck wagon, the necessary number of horses and men," On the Cibolo River near Stockdale the drovers received one thousand steers and pointed the herd north. (10)

Nute Rachal was also on his first drive to Kansas. The outfit was driving big wild steers six to sixteen years of age. "When we reached Bluff Creek at the Kansas line the first house of Caldwell was being put up. It was a log house. Here we found an old friend, Milam Fitzgerald, with a tent full of supplies, so we stocked up. The trail herd stopped at Cottonwood Creek south of Abilene, but perhaps due to the crowded conditions on the prairie at that location they pulled up stakes. "We went from the mouth of the Nueces River to Ellsworth, Kansas, without going through a gate." The trail men moved the herd to Wilson Station just west of Ellsworth. "… Dick Bean, myself and two other Texas boys stayed all summer." (11)

South of Ellsworth on the old Chisholm Trail, Wichita had been a rival of Park City since 1869. Both had fought bitterly to gain the Sedgwick County Seat. Wichita won the election in October of 1870, but some ballots favoring Park City were surprisingly found in the Arkansas River. Park City understandably opposed virtually anything that would benefit Wichita.

Recognizing the conflict between Park City and Wichita, the Kansas Pacific supported Park City in an effort to divert the trail herds onto a new route leading to Ellsworth.

Major Henry Shanklin was the trail representative for the new Ellsworth Trail. The Major knew the country and the people well. Shanklin had been Indian agent for the Wichita tribe.

Beginning at Park City Shanklin quietly staked a new Chisholm Trail Cutoff intersecting the Chisholm Trail as it crossed the Ninnescah River southwest of Wichita. From there he continued south across Indian Territory to the Red River.

The first herds of early spring were met by Major Shanklin as they crossed into Indian Territory. There he informed the drovers that the old trail to Abilene had been closed by settlers, "who would shoot and stampede their cattle." He offered to guide the first herds through to the new stockyards that had been provided by the Kansas Pacific in Ellsworth. Most drovers had become accustomed to doing business with the Kansas Pacific. The drovers that Shanklin spoke to readily agreed to follow his advice taking the new trail to Ellsworth.

Major Shanklin may have thought he had done his work discreetly but the fine folks in Wichita were soon alerted to his activities. Four prominent men quickly rode down the trail to intercept the leading herds. At McLain's Ranch (Clearwater, Kansas) on the Ninnescah River the riders were told that Shanklin had already turned four herds north toward Park City. The night was dark and cloudy, leaving little opportunity to trail the herds over the prairie. The men held up at the ranch till early morning.

Before first light the Wichita riders, described as the "Four Horsemen" pointed their ponies north, riding with a vengeance. The trail herds were strung out following the newly staked trail. The leading herd was soon within sight. The Wichita men boldly rode to the front and called a halt to the drive. Drovers gathered around as the horsemen argued their point, but the cattlemen trusted Major Shanklin. They were determined to continue to Park City until one of the "Horsemen" brought the trail boss to his senses with a bribe. The herds were soon turned about and driven right down Wichita's Douglas Avenue. Wichita regained the cattle traffic through its thoroughfares. Ellsworth had lost an important battle. Most Texas cattle continued to trail through Wichita and its businessmen reaped the benefits. (12)

The Kansas Pacific representatives persisted in their efforts to divert traffic to Ellsworth, even if they were only nominally successful. Gunman John Wesley Hardin was an eighteen-year-old drover for Columbus Carroll. Hardin described meeting a party of men at a place called Cow House (McClain's Ranch), which was the same place Major Shanklin had chosen to turn the cattle north from the Chisholm Trail. "We followed a plough furrow on this trail and these men furnished a guide." Upon crossing the Arkansas River, a Park City delegation met the drovers, inviting them to take in the town. "About sixty cowboys went to that town and it is needless to say filled up on wine, whiskey, etc., some getting rather full." But, instead of driving to Ellsworth the cattlemen turned their cattle northeast toward Abilene, making their own way. They were soon on the Newton Flats. (13)

Nevertheless herds did arrive on the prairie surrounding Ellsworth. Texas cattle drover James F. Ellison delivered two thousand head of cattle to D. W. Powers of Ellsworth during the summer season. The beef steers sold for two and one half cents per pound.

On the trail cattle could sometimes be seen strung out for miles.
Illustrated by Professor Henry Worrall - Historic Sketches of the Cattle Trade by Joseph McCoy.

Jacob Ellison was with one of the herds of "big steers" that were delivered to the Powers Ranch. The cattle had been driven north to Newton, eventually striking the Santa Fe Trail. The herd was driven west to the Little Arkansas River, which Jake described as, "… a big fine creek." A few miles north Ellison's herd joined another herd bossed by John McGill.

Augustine Bellmont was in charge of the cattle on the Powers Ranch. "He classified the stock, grazed and fattened them on pastures, and then sold those ready for market to buyers who came out from Kansas City and Chicago."

According to Joseph McCoy, the ranch was one of four Kansas ranches where the Powers would "… annually winter about three thousand head of cattle and sufficient cow ponies to handle the stock." (14)

Cattle ranches and farms were beginning to take up the open prairies. Settlement would eventually force Texas trail drivers to shift operations west causing Ellsworth to eye Abilene with jealous desire. The trail business would soon leave Abilene but as the shipping season opened in 1871 Abilene was still king and Wild Bill Hickok was the law.

Anna Wilson eventually followed Wild Bill to Abilene. She lived with him for about a month in a two story wooden cabin on the south end of town. Charles Gross did not remember her name but said that Hickok grew tired of her and after paying her some money, sent her away. Perhaps he was unhappy with her pregnancy. In any event, Anna returned to Ellsworth where she raised her son, supporting him by washing clothes, scrubbing floors and reading fortunes with cards. (15)

Trouble continued to erupt in Ellsworth. On June 18, 1871, Richard Cavanaugh and Constable John T. Snyder argued in Little Jake's Saloon. Snyder was a sometime fiddler in Rowdy Joe's saloon. As the argument peaked, Cavanaugh and

68

Snyder were told to take it somewhere else. Cavanaugh stepped from the door to boardwalk. Snyder followed closely behind. The two barely cleared the doorway when pistols were drawn. Shots were fired nearly simultaneously. Then each man grabbed the other in a death grip. Rowdy Joe and Chauncey Whitney pulled the men apart. Joe had wrestled the pistols away from both men. According to Whitney both weapons had fired one shot. Whitney took Snyder across the tracks where he collapsed from a gunshot wound. Cavanaugh was unhurt.

During a period of nine bedridden days Snyder was nursed back to health by his wife. He then brought suit against Cavanaugh over the shooting. The trouble arose over the simultaneous shooting. Snyder claimed that Cavanaugh had fired both shots. It was implied that while the pistols were in Rowdy Joe's possession he might have loaded one round into Cavanaugh's pistol to make it look as though only Snyder had fired. Constable Chauncey Whitney believed Snyder but the jury evidently did not believe that Joe had anything to do with loading of Cavanaugh's pistol. The case was rendered "Not Guilty". (16)

Stolen horses still held a strong attraction for many of Ellsworth's residents. The death of John Sanderson at the hands of Junction City vigilantes in August of 1870 only temporarily slowed his brother, George Sanderson. In May, Ellsworth County Sheriff J. Charles Seiber discovered that Sanderson was wanted for theft of government property, namely horses. Another brother, Jonathan Sanderson returned to Junction City. Seiber and two deputies approached George Sanderson's place in Ellsworth with a warrant for his arrest. They were met at the door by Mrs. Sanderson who informed the officers that George indeed was there. She then informed the Sheriff that if he attempted to enter the place George would blow his head off. Amazingly, none of the officers were carrying weapons.

Sheriff Seiber left the unarmed deputies to guard the door while he set off to get a pistol. In the Sheriff's absence, George Sanderson charged out the door, pistol at the ready. The officers had no recourse but to watch as Sanderson mounted a pony and made his escape.

A series of seesaw events ensued. A posse caught up with Sanderson. He was sent to Topeka, released on bail, rearrested and re-released on bail. Sanderson and his partner, James R. White, attacked Sheriff Seiber, beating him over the head with a revolver.

The Sheriff, who also served as a Deputy United States Marshal, went to Fort Harker and enlisted the aid of the Fifth Infantry to once again arrest George Sanderson as well as James White and one of their employees named Jackson. The men were rounded up at three a.m. and delivered to the guardhouse at Fort Harker.

Rowdy Joe was at the head of a group of irate Ellsworth citizens who pressed the local court to gain a release of the prisoners, but Sheriff Seiber was ahead of them. He removed the prisoners under military escort and transferred them to Brookville. At Brookville he learned that Rowdy Joe and his friends were still determined to gain the release of their friends. The soldiers were alerted that fifteen to twenty "roughs" from Ellsworth were planning an attack.

But the Ellsworth crowd was slow in reacting. Upon their arrival at Brookville, the Ellsworth crowd proceeded to develop a strategy at one of the local saloons.

Fort Harker was telegraphed. Troops were sent by train to Brookville while the strategy session continued. The additional troops forced Rowdy Joe and the boys to back down. Sheriff Seiber was allowed to leave Brookville with his prisoners. At Topeka bail was set and the prisoners were set free.

Certain Ellsworth elements were doing their best to live up to the wicked reputation that had made Ellsworth a living legend. Vice and corruption had prospered in frontier Ellsworth. Rowdy Joe, George Sanderson and their cohorts thrived on chaos.

Back in 1869, Bvt. Lt. Col. Leib, Commanding, Fort Harker, described the Ellsworth that Rowdy Joe loved in a letter to his superior, "I am forcibly impressed with the idea that there is a class of officials at Ellsworth who live by 'Black Mail' entirely as they seem to have no other visible means of support." (17)

The heat was unquestionably on anyone who stood in the way of the powerful gang of horse thieves led by George Sanderson. Sheriff Seiber left the county in July. His bonds for sheriff of Ellsworth County were declared insufficient and his resignation accepted. The governor was requested to appoint a new sheriff. (18)

Meanwhile cattle began to stream toward Ellsworth, filling the surrounding prairies. Good grazing and fast markets combined to produce a cattle Mecca in the land of Kansas. New towns were beginning to see the fortune to be made in the cattle business. Railroad service was the key to the future.

The Kansas Pacific bought the stockyards at Ellsworth and expanded them. By July 14, 1871, thirty thousand head of rangy Texas Longhorns were grazing over the Smoky Hills that surrounded Ellsworth. More cattle arrived every day. (19)

Ellsworth's most persistent lawman, Chauncey Whitney had served the town as a loyal lawman from its earliest days. He was evidently appointed Ellsworth County Sheriff by the governor as his bond as sheriff was approved by the Ellsworth County Commissioners July 21, 1871.

Whitney was always there in time of need. He fought at the Battle of Beecher Island in defense of his community. Living on the edge of civilization had nearly driven him to desperation, but one person had brought peace of mind to a mad world. He had watched her grow from a sickly young girl to a budding and beautiful woman. On July 23, 1871, Chauncey Beldon Whitney was married to Nellie Viola Henry. He was thirty-nine years old. Nellie's wedding day was also her sixteenth birthday.

Besides serving as Ellsworth County Sheriff and Constable of Ellsworth Township, Chauncey Whitney worked as a carpenter. Making a living strictly from law enforcement was next to impossible. There was never enough money. Nellie later recalled, "We bought a lot – but did not pay for it. We also put up a one room house but the lumber was not paid for." (20)

The Cavanaugh-Snyder fight and the Rowdy Joe-George Sanderson fiasco prompted city fathers to look for new ways to tame the town. Their solution was to form Ellsworth into a 3rd class city on July 27, 1871. Mayor Captain H. F. Hoesman led the city council through a series of ordinances. The first order of business was to set the time and procedure of City Council meetings. But foremost on the minds of City Council members was law enforcement. Ordinance No. 2 set the City Marshal salary at fifty dollars per month and two dollars and fifty cents for every conviction. The Assistant Marshal's salary was forty dollars per month plus the two dollars and fifty cents per conviction. The City Clerk received thirty dollars per month and the City Treasurer fifteen dollars.

Ordinance No. 3 prohibited the carrying of weapons within the City of Ellsworth. Individuals were subject to arrest if found in possession of a "pistol, bowie knife, dirk, or any other weapon". The fine for such an infringement could be up to fifty dollars and-or imprisonment of no longer than one month. Ordinance No. 4 pertained to "drunk and disorderly' behavior and carried the same penalty as Ordinance No. 2. The City Council passed a total of twelve ordinances. Chauncey Whitney was appointed City Marshal; Tom Clark, Assistant Marshal. (21)

For Rowdy Joe, Ellsworth was becoming much too "civilized." Joe and his paramour, Rowdy Kate moved to Newton where they established a dance hall with a "fast" reputation. (22)

With Newton and Ellsworth vying for the Texas cattle trade Abilene was only too happy to turn its interests toward its law-abiding farm community. A Farmers Protective Association met to drive the Texans from Dickinson County.

Abilene's city fathers agreed. On September 2, 1871, Marshal Wild Bill Hickok was ordered to, "... suppress all Dance Houses and to arrest the proprietors if they persist after the notification." Many proprietors in the district closed up shop, shifting operations to Newton and Ellsworth. (23)

Drovers were also looking for quieter headquarters than either Abilene or Newton. In spite of Ellsworth's earlier reputation, bloodletting seemed to have been brought in check under the leadership of former Forsyth Scout, Marshal Chauncey B. Whitney. Shanghai Pierce, an influential Texan, moved his headquarters to Ellsworth, but cautioned the city that new and larger stockyards would have to be built if Ellsworth intended to take in numbers equal to Abilene.

While a great amount of cattle activity continued to occur at Abilene during the summer of 1871, the market was beginning to shift to Ellsworth. Major Seth Mabry and Shanghai Pierce had already turned to Ellsworth as headquarters for their cattle operations. Capt. James D. Reed also traveled to Ellsworth to inspect conditions at that location. Reed had lost an arm in the war, but the lack of an arm hadn't stalled his cattle instincts. Mabry and Pierce were known to be very sociable at the end of the trail. They soon invited One-Armed Jim Reed to help them round up the town. The sight of the six foot Pierce, five foot four inch Mabry and one-armed Reed carousing the dance halls and streets of Ellsworth must have been a memorable one indeed.

The *State News* at Topeka took notice of the activities in Ellsworth and announced, "As we go to press, Hell is still in session at Ellsworth.

Being one to easily fall for a lady's affections, Shanghai stepped into a trap laid by his friends at Ellsworth. "There was a certain fair lady sojourning at an Ellsworth hotel who had commented favorably upon the appearance of the tall man ... it was (also) common knowledge that an interested bad man had served notice that his fair one was not to be molested by any cattleman." As Shanghai prepared to board a train loaded with cattle he was lured by the conductor to pass by the window of the fair lady.

Major Seth Mabry of Austin, Texas, drove cattle
to virtually every major cattle town in the West.
Illustrated by Professor Henry Worrall - Historic
Sketches of the Cattle Trade by Joseph McCoy.

Abel Head "Shanghai" Pierce "cut a wide
swath" wherever he went. His ranch on the
south coast of Texas produced big Texas
longhorn cattle known as Shanghai's Sea
Lions. Illustrated by Professor Henry Worrall
Historic Sketches of the Cattle Trade by
Joseph McCoy.

One-Armed Jim Reed of Goliad, Texas, bought
and sold cattle at the end of the trail with enthusiasm. The loss of an arm in the Civil War never
slowed him down. Illustrated by Professor Henry
Worrall - Historic Sketches fo the Cattle Trade
by Joseph McCoy.

He saw her within the dimly lighted room. Reaching over, he tapped upon the open window. She gave no heed to his signal. He repeated it. Then a man, resembling her six-shooter friend, appeared at the window with a cocked pistol in each hand. The picket fence which separated him from the rail road tracks crashed flat with Shanghai's first charge. He ran rapidly to the accustomed place to board the train and hid in the weeds. He could hear men searching for him. The train approached with the engineer holding the throttle wide open. Shanghai could stand the pressure no longer, and making a run for it, he tried to flag the engineer. When the caboose passed, laughing men fired their pistols in the air. Again he took cover and lay in the grass throughout the night, only to learn when the next morning came that he was the little goat his drover friends had left behind. (24)

According to Joseph McCoy, fully six hundred thousand head of Texas cattle arrived in Kansas in 1871. The season had been a rainy one. Early good grazing turned to washed-out grass with little nutrition. Unlike previous years on the plains the cattle lost weight. Buyers weren't interested in the poorly conditioned cattle. To make matters worse, severe storms had resulted in numerous stampedes, wearing out both man and beast. Three hundred thousand head of cattle were unsold at the end of the season. Drovers chose to hold their cattle on the dryer buffalo-grass range of western Kansas and Eastern Colorado. Some drove north to the river bottoms of the Platte River. Ellsworth reported that eighty thousand head of cattle were being prepared to winter over in Ellsworth County. (25)

The nearly inseparable Mabry, Pierce & Reed developed a business relationship with each of them having more cattle than they could market. The men decided to throw their cattle together and "winter them over".

Capt. Reed ponied up approximately sixteen hundred head of steers while the others brought the total to three thousand head of Texas cattle grazing the Kansas range over the coming winter of 1871-72. Many drovers besides our trio were beginning to "winter over" manageable numbers of cattle in order to sell on an early market the following spring. The practice allowed them to gain handsome profits before larger and more traditional trail herds reached Kansas. A Kentucky man, Tom Hamilton, was hired to handle the winter herd. (26)

Nute Rachal and three other cowboys stayed on the prairie west of Ellsworth herding a set of big wild steers. "All went well until October when the buffaloes began to come in vast herds, stampeding our horses and causing much annoyance." The market was glutted with no buyers for the cattle. The owner of the steers, Captain Pulliam, shipped the cattle to Chicago himself taking bankrupting slaughter prices at that location. (27)

The continuing Wild West soap opera between George Sanderson and former Ellsworth County Sheriff J. Charles Seiber fell to a new low when Seiber was arrested on a charge of assault with intent to kill. The charge amounted to harassment from the Sanderson gang who appeared to be intent on dismantling Seiber's reputation after his persistent pursuit of their horse thief activities in and around Ellsworth.

Melvin Clay (M. C.) Davis was elected Mayor. Davis believed that Ellsworth could support a newspaper.

He confided this view to his brother-in-law, J. B. King of Moulton, Iowa, who was visiting in Ellsworth at the time. Mr. King replied that he knew a printer in Moulton who would be just the man to undertake the new venture, and was given the authority to make the deal.

Mr. King returned to Moulton, laid the proposition before Mr. (John) Montgomery, who was foreman of Mr. King's newspaper there, and after some preliminaries the prospectus for the Ellsworth *Reporter*, so named by Mr. Montgomery, was printed at Moulton and sent to Ellsworth for distribution among prospective subscribers.

Leaving Moulton for Ellsworth, Mr. Montgomery took with him a half dozen fonts of type from King's shop. He stopped off at St. Louis and purchased a Washington hand press and additional type. At Leavenworth, in a monument plant, he acquired a marble slab to serve as an inking stone.

Mr. Montgomery reached Ellsworth November 16, 1871, and three weeks later on December 8, the first issue of the Ellsworth *Reporter*, 500 copies, was run off the press. Mr. Montgomery unaided, had set all of the type for the news and advertisements. He ran off this first edition with the aid of Paul Call, a 13 year old boy, who inked the press.

The *Reporter* office was established in the old Marshall House, near the big bridge. The first issue was a four page paper ... (28)

Declaring, "FOR THE FUTURE IN THE DISTANCE, AND THE GOOD THAT WE CAN DO.", the Ellsworth *Reporter* started with a subscription list of five hundred at the rate of two dollars per year, paid in advance. (29)

Issues of the first edition of the Ellsworth *Reporter* were sent to existing papers across the state and to selected out-of-state papers. Several responded with congratulations. One in particular provided an interesting bio for the editor.

We acknowledge the receipt of a remarkably neat paper from Ellsworth, Kansas. – It is No. 1 Vol. 1 of the Ellsworth *Reporter*, and it flies at its mast-head the familiar name of M.C. Davis, as editor and proprietor. We know that boy – we ought to know him. Mel was a drummer boy in the old 15th, during two or three campaigns, but when we got into the heat of the Atlanta affair, the boy dropped his drum and shouldered a musket. Right in the head of a July day, when a line of rock – hidden rebels raised a veil of blue smoke ahead of our skirmishers, we saw him borne to the rear with a knee full of musket balls. We wish the *Reporter* the greatest success imaginable. If any editor in Kansas knows how to make a good paper, M. Clay Davis is that editor, and if any little paper in Kansas is showy and neat and readable the Ellsworth *Reporter* is its name. Our (hand) goes out in greeting to our old-time comrade and present fellow – inkslinger. – Send us a buffalo hide, old boy. – Montezuma (Iowa.) *Republican*. (30)

In November, a severe rainstorm set in, followed by a cold wind which froze the water. The grass became covered with a sheet of ice two or three inches thick. A furious gale blew for three days and nights. Many men and horses were frozen to death and thousands of cattle perished. Mrs. W. F. Burks was with her husband's drive. "On stormy and rainy nights a candle always burned in my tent to guide the men." The outfit survived the snowstorm but witnessed young cattle that lost their horns from the cold. The early cold weather convinced Mr. Burks to sell his cattle at any price and return to "Sunny Texas". (31)

The storms continued to crawl across Kansas one after the other. M. C. Davis, editor of the Ellsworth *Reporter* lamented. "... it seemed impossible for any living creature to survive one nights siege on open ground." A young man by the name of Reison traveling by wagon lost his way in the storm. No longer able to control his team he turned them loose and set out on foot to find his camp.

For...two days and three nights he wandered around, without a particle of food, and the last day and night barefooted; he finally made his way to camp, crawling the last four miles on his hands and knees, having lost the use of his legs below the knee joints. He was placed in the hospital at Ft. Harker where he lingered for several days.

Thousands of cattle were scattered over the country, seeking shelter in the beds of creeks and ravines; when the storm abated stockmen gathered their cattle into camp, finding a small per cent dead and the balance thin in flesh and hardly in condition to survive another such storm.

Last Friday another storm set in and the ground is now covered with several inches of sleet and snow; cattle are again scattered and the prospect looks blue; men who come in report the ravines full of dead cattle, and if the sleet remains on the grass and the streams stay frozen much longer the losses of stock men will be counted by hundreds of thousands.

Last winter thousands of cattle were wintered in this country without feeding a pound of hay, but men who are trying the experiment this winter will pay for their experience at from sixty to one hundred per cent of the capital ventured.

The storms turned even the best preparations to disaster. One Ellsworth County farmer who signed himself, "D. B." wrote to the Ellsworth *Reporter* calling for the merchants and citizens of Ellsworth to support protection of the farmers from the free-ranging cattle herds that had invaded the county.

There must be some protection in this matter, (and here is where the town can help the farmer.) ... I will endeavor to show that the farmer and producer has been, and is now unjustly dealt with, and unless the town people will unite with the farmers and put a stop to such unjust and damaging practice as has been perpetrated upon settlers of Ash Creek for the past six weeks by a few Texas cattle dealers, the settlers will be compelled to leave and go elsewhere. Fields of corn that were ungathered, stacks of hay fenced and unfenced alike have been destroyed; orchards and forest trees have been browsed. – The range protected by the settlers for their own stock by hard fighting fire night and day has been grazed closely, so that large loss of stock is inevitable to the farmer. On Ash Creek alone not less than 2000 head have been feed(ing) for the last five weeks and not a single field or stack has escaped those half starved 'sand loppers.' When justice is asked from the owners of these cattle you are told, they are not my cattle. Nobody appears to own more than 25 or 30 head. They are badly mixed, and the owners think they are doing well enough, say they can't round up as they call it, but the farmers are getting their property used up and getting nothing for it. (32)

From - Historic Sketches of the Cattle Trade by Joseph McCoy.

Chapter Six

BOOM TOWN

The winter of 1871-1872 was exceptionally challenging to cattlemen who wintered stock on the open range. Not only had they lost cattle to the severe cold, farmers shot the starving beasts as they invaded haystacks intended for their own cattle. The hides were something to salvage but skinning a branded carcass was equal to stealing a live animal. However that hadn't stopped hide hunters from harvesting the only thing of value left to cattlemen.

The Stockmen's Protective Association was organized to curb skinning by unlawful parties and give the cattlemen a chance to at least recover a small portion of their losses. Membership in the association was two dollars. Hide inspectors were authorized by the association to verify ownership of hides sold at Fossil Station (Russell), Bunker Hill, Zarah (east of Great Bend), Ellsworth, Wilson, Larned, Sedgwick City, and Newton. (1)

The presence of stockmen throughout the winter months was an added bonus to the railhead economy. In the past trail men sent their crews home soon after arriving at the end of the trail as grazing herds did not require a full outfit of men. Once the cattle were shipped the rest of the crew was sent home. But as cattlemen turned to winter grazing businessmen reaped a supplementary market. Jake New advertised his Ellsworth Billiard Hall and restaurant as having "Good Fare" with "Reasonable Rates" while proudly announcing, "Cattlemen make 'Jakes' their headquarters."

In addition to Mayer Goldsoll's large stock of goods at the "Old Reliable House" in Ellsworth, plans were announced to open a branch store at Fossil Station, "... for Texas cattlemen wintering at Fossil and Fort Hays." Goldsoll advertised the, "largest stock in Western Kansas, of Fancy and Staple Groceries and Provisions, also Liquors, Cigars and Tobacco."

Having been host to many great generals of the United States Army and other important notables, citizens of Ellsworth had grown somewhat used to excursions of the famous and noteworthy. The Grand Duke Alexei Alexandrovich of Russia made quite an impression with a magnificent tour of the United States, incorporating a flamboyant buffalo hunt with Generals Sheridan and Custer and the noted buffalo hunter and scout Buffalo Bill Cody. At Denver the Grand Duke boarded a Kansas Pacific train bound for St. Louis. The Ellsworth *Reporter* noted, "Duke Alexis did himself honor to pass thru Ellsworth the other night, sleeping in seven palace cars.

77

He did not call at the *Reporter* office and we don't care. It will be a good excuse for us not calling on him when we go to Russia." By the time they reached St. Louis the Grand Duke's supply of caviar and Champaign was reportedly exhausted. (2)

While the Grand Duke was frolicking over the prairies, development of those prairies held men's livelihoods in the balance. As stockmen met in Ellsworth to protect their investment, farmers were strengthening their efforts to banish the Texans from the railhead sixty miles east at Abilene. A notice was placed in the February 8, 1872, Abilene *Chronicle*, "We the undersigned, members of the Farmers' Protective Association, and officers and citizens of Dickinson County, Kansas, most respectfully request all who had contemplated driving Texas cattle to Abilene the coming season to seek some other point for shipment, as the inhabitants of Dickinson County will no longer submit to the evils of the trade." (3)

The Abilene City Council had also had enough of the gunmen they had hired to keep the peace. Deputies Tom Carson and Brocky Jack Norton were fired November 27, 1871. A little over two weeks later, December 13, 1871, the council followed up by discharging Wild Bill Hickok. Abilene was fully ready to become civilized.

Abilene had seen its last year as a major cattle town, but the city was about to witness one more violent act before sending the cattle trade to other railheads. The Abilene *Chronicle* for February 1, 1872, reported a shooting between Wild Bill Hickok's former deputies, Tom Carson and Brocky Jack Norton. It appears the two men "quarreled bitterly". Tom Carson reacted, "… the way he new best, with pistols blazing." Norton was wounded, but survived. "Brocky Jack, the man whom Tom shot, is recovering." Carson was arrested and sent to Junction City to be held for trial.

Within days, February 18th to be exact, Tom Carson and three other inmates escaped from the Junction City jail. The Junction City *Union* proclaimed that, "… it will be an easy thing to capture and fetter them so that they will 'stay'." Carson was never heard from again. Perhaps he met the same fate as John Elsizer who was reportedly taken from the Abilene jail and "… hung … by persons unknown as yet." Brocky Jack Norton headed for Ellsworth. (4)

A copy of the proposed herd law presented to the legislature was posted in the February 22, 1872, edition of the *Reporter*. The law ordered drovers to herd their cattle during the winter months rather than mandating farmers to fence their land. County commissioners were given authority to impose the herd law or reject it. Ellsworth County Commissioners J. C. Howard, a local stockman and Leo Hertzig an Ellsworth saloonkeeper were decidedly anti-protection favoring the cattle trade. Z. Jackson, owner of a general merchandise store, also owned a farm, thereby favoring the farm constituent. But the herd law failed by a two thirds vote. Despite Governor James M. Harvey's support of the law, Ellsworth County would remain a free grazing county for the time being. (5)

Meanwhile, marital difficulty created its own set of problems for a sporting couple in Ellsworth. Lizzie Palmer had been the premiere madam of Ellsworth since its earliest years when she operated as Lizzie Adams. George Palmer had always been her lover and in March of 1870 the two married and moved to a farm outside of town. Unfortunately, Lizzie began to miss the old lifestyle. Perhaps the recent long winter had been too dreary. By early 1872, Lizzie moved back to her old haunt in Ellsworth, popularly known as the "Nauch." The place was evidently a dance house.

The term "nauch,' meaning "dance," originated in Indian. The expression referred to the dancing girls or "Nautch Girls" who performed dances for the pleasure of human beings. Through the broad reach of the British Empire the term spread throughout the world, making its way to Lizzie Palmer's dance house where cowboys paid for the pleasure of a dance with one of the girls and perhaps a visit to her perfumed crib.

At The Nauch, Lizzie took up with a Texas cowboy and sometime horse thief by the name of Taylor DuBoise. Incensed at her treachery, George Palmer took out a notice in the *Reporter* in late February stating that he would not be responsible for debts contracted by second parties, notably Lizzie. In another story of that same issue the *Reporter* admonished two of the fancy ladies, one of which easily could have been Lizzie, not to allow their wantonness to lead them into Ellsworth's halls of justice. "Those two soiled doves of the class demimonde, who got away with the upper story of each other's heads at what is denominated the 'nauch' had better draw it slow or they and their married man will have a chance of loaning the school fund their surplus stamps."

That very night, February 22nd, Lizzie's house burned to the ground. George Palmer was the most likely suspect for the arson. The fire began around ten p.m. but was extinguished, or so they thought. "About two o'clock the next morning a cry of fire was heard and on running out we could see a small blaze on the kitchen roof attached to the main building."

The *Reporter* poked fun at Lizzie's customers. "What did we see? We saw quite a few fair haired boys minus hats, coats, etc. in an awful big hurry to go someplace, We saw Ghosts! Yes, they were gliding around town in their shrouds, winding sheets and other white fixins."

A strong wind carried the fire and within five minutes of the initial alarm completely engulfed the house. A nauch is nothing without a fine piano to dance to and Lizzie had spared no expense in obtaining a fine hardwood piano valued at twelve hundred dollars. After the house was completely burned to the ground the piano stood on its legs, eerily white hot for another ten minutes.

Although not named, the *Reporter* continued with a description of Lizzie Palmer. "We saw a woman who stood watching several thousand dollars worth of her hard earnings while it was enveloped in flames, without a tear in her eyes, and with an eye to business trying to get a bid on the old hardware."

George Palmer and a stockman by the name of Penny were arrested but released two weeks later for want of evidence. Meanwhile, the embers were smoldering white hot in a love triangle that could only end in violence. (6)

Meanwhile, although Rowdy Joe was no longer in town, he was still making the pages of the Ellsworth *Reporter* in February of 1872. A note from a paper titled the *Daily Call* was reprinted with a reference to a tragedy at Newton, Kansas. "It seems that Rowdy Joe, a character well known in Ellsworth and at different points along the line of the K. P. Railroad, got into an altercation with a man named Sweet, who kept a saloon there known as the 'Through Ticket', and shot him through the heart, killing him instantly. Rowdy Joe after doing the job skidaddled and has not been heard of since-" The *Reporter* added that Rowdy Joe was arrested, tried and acquitted on a plea of self defense. (7)

The city of Ellsworth recognized that vice was the source of most violence and worked diligently to control it within the city limits. The city council ordered Marshal Whitney on March 6, 1872, to "… instruct all 'soiled doves' that they will not be permitted to live in or carry on their business within the limits of the city of Ellsworth." Ordinance #8, passed in August of 1871, was recently published for public notification in the *Reporter*. The Vagrant's Law prohibited "loitering around houses of ill fame, gambling or where liquors are sold or drank." Anyone without visible means of support could be fined from ten dollars to fifty dollars or imprisonment of up to thirty days.

Evidently Lizzie made the best of her recent loss by relocating southeast of town, just outside the city limits between the Smoky Hill River and the city. She reopened a month after the fire. Although out of the city limits (and therefore outside the authority of city law) she was actually only a little over one block from South Main Street. On opening day she wrote a poem to her one and only George.

Take Me Back Home Again
Take me back home again, take back home,
Hopeless and helpless, in sorrow I roam;
Gone are the roses that gladdened my life,
I must toil on in the wearisome strife.
Once I was happy and friends were my lot,
Now I'm a wand'rer, despised and forgot!
Lonely and weary, in sorrow I roam,
Take me back home again, Take me back home,
Take me back home again, Take me back home.

George, dear George, so gentle and mild,
Look once again on thy pitiful child!
Since we were parted I never have known
Love and affection so pure as thine own!
Days of my childhood, I dream of you now,
While in my sorrow and anguis I bow!
No one to love me 'neath yon starry dome,
Take me back home again, Take me back home,
Take me back home again, Take me back home.

Oh, could I live but the days that are flown,
Dearest and sweetest that ever were known,
Fondly I weep in my desolate pain, Longing to be with my George again!
Weary, so weary, my heart yearns for rest,
Poor wounded bird that is robbed of its nest!
Child of affliction! Dear George I come,
Take me back home again, Take me back home,
Take me back home again, Take me back home.

George could not resist Lizzie's call. According to the Ellsworth *Reporter*, March 28, 1872, George, "… went, we presume, to take her back home again, stayed for supper; drank whiskey and got mellow, in fact was drunk."

Unfortunately, Lizzie's young Texas cowboy, Taylor DuBoise entered the house and found the blissfully reconciled George and Lizzie sitting on the bed talking, "... both drunk and happy and unsuspecting danger." An argument erupted. George stood up to defend himself and was immediately knocked to the floor by DuBoise. The jealous cowboy then drew his pistol. Three shots were fired, each one passing through George Palmer's forehead. The paper reported that Ellsworth lawman Chauncey Whitney failed to apprehend DuBoise but police records show that he was arrested and ordered held in Salina. Ellsworth's jail was not safe, considering that he had friends who were capable of helping him escape. Taylor Duboise was described as twenty-four years of age, six feet tall with gray eyes and light hair. (8)

March 27, 1872, the City of Ellsworth moved to pay Whitney four hundred fifty dollars for back pay, covering the previous six month period. In those proceedings he was referred to as "Sheriff".

The same issue that reported George Palmer's death addressed a rumor that the Ellsworth County Sheriff had been shot to death while stealing horses at Wichita.

> That's hard on Capt. Whitney but presume he can draw some consolation from the fact that he is getting well, that he was not shot while stealing horses, that he has not been shot since he has been filling the sheriff's office, and that he was not in the wicked burgh mentioned.
>
> We presume the story originated with J. C. Sieber, an ex-sheriff of this county, by a deputy U. S. Marshal.
>
> Sieber was charged with stealing horses, the marshal undertook to arrest him, he resisted, got shot, is badly wounded but will hardly die, such men are hard to kill.

Sieber survived. He was charged with misappropriating government property. He was released from jail on a five hundred dollar bond. For an undefined few weeks of early 1872, Chauncey Whitney was serving simultaneously as Ellsworth Township Constable, Ellsworth City Marshal and Ellsworth County Sheriff. (9)

Even as Ellsworth was being promoted as the next great railhead for Texas cattle, settlers were already filling in the eastern part of Ellsworth County. From a meeting at the Thompson Creek school house, the Ellsworth County Farmers' Protective Society argued their solution for a better society.

> That farmers must leave their vocation which is the life blood of every county or community and the germ of civilization. Give this country into the hands of the herdsman and you will make it half civilized or barbarous country without schools or churches – and controlled by a few large stockmen having many poor illiterate men dependent upon them for support.

As winter passed into early March, the disaster of the previous winter continued to be on the minds of both cattlemen and farmers. Several hundred cow ponies and an estimated quarter of a million head of cattle had been lost. The skinning business was making quite in impact all across western Kansas. Kansas Pacific Agent Shryock reported in mid-March that 5,269 dry hides and 2,353 green hides had been shipped from Ellsworth since December 1ˢᵗ of 1871. The total of 7,621 hides weighed 249,225 pounds. "Larkin & Relphe were the heaviest shippers; shipping 2,870; B. Frank, 1,693; Goldsoll, 1200; Larkin & Jackson, 948; Phelps, 737; Beebe, 63." Even as Agent Shryock was filing his report, hides continued to pile up. Carloads of green hides could be seen stacked behind and in front of Ellsworth businesses. (10)

The loss was widespread in cattle country, extending all the way into south Texas. James T. Johnson described the aftermath in the Lone Star State.

> I helped skin dead cattle on the prairies in Goliad, Victoria and Refugio counties, (Texas) as the cattle were starving to death by the thousands, and very few grown cattle lived through this terrible winter. I have seen as many as a thousand head of dead cattle in one day's ride on the prairie near Lamar. Horses, cattle, deer and sheep suffered awfully ...

Even though the entire cattle industry was shaken, cattlemen persevered. Scores of cattle had survived in the brush country of south Texas. New herds of wild cattle were gathered and sent north on the long trail to Kansas and beyond. (11)

The face of Ellsworth was changing rapidly. Twenty car loads of material arrived, putting some thirty men to work building a new hotel on South Main Street. Abilene's Drovers Cottage was partially dismantled and shipped by rail to Ellsworth. The new hotel would be half again as large as the original Abilene establishment. The Ellsworth *Reporter* could hardly contain itself. "We hear of people coming from every direction to Ellsworth. – Half of Abilene will be here in two months."

The town was looking to the future. Voters were asked to approve the building of an Ellsworth County Courthouse and Jail and a proposal to approve bonds to bridge the Smoky Hill River, "... at the foot of 'F' street ..." was on the ballot.

The same issue quietly acknowledged of "... some talk that Fort Harker will be abandoned and sold." (12)

The election on April 2, 1872 approved the bonds to build the Smoky Hill River bridge. The combination courthouse and jail was declared a certainty. *Reporter* editor, M. C. Davis was elected mayor. Chauncey Whitney and Thomas O'Laughlin were elected as constables.

Whitney resigned as Ellsworth City Marshal April 3, 1872. John L. Councell was named as his replacement. (13)

On a lighter note, Ellsworth pranksters found the trick played on prominent drover Shanghai Pierce a year earlier to be more fun than could be resisted. The trap unfolded once more in early April of '72.

> The young men of Ellsworth are as susceptible to the 'tender passion' as the young men of any other town are. A few evenings since a young man, of high standing in this city, was handed a sweetly perfumed note, in which the writer, whose signature indicated that 'he, she or it,' was a female, stated that she for a long time felt a 'friendly feeling toward him, and that that feeling had now attained the name of love,' – (*Verbatim*.) A meeting

was desired to be held at the corner of Main and F. street. The anxious swain was promptly on the appointed spot. Closely muffled, he waited long and patiently, but no Pythias appeared to clasp in her arms the expectant Damon. 'The clock in the steeple struck one,' and the disconsolate Damon retired to his couch. Next morning he received another note from his 'dear' in which 'he she or it' explained that the appointment for the evening before was not filled for the reason that an over-watchful mamma had prevented it, 'but, dearest, be at trysting spot tomorrow night, at ten o'clock, sharp, and I will be with you.' Promptly was Damon present, expecting a lovely time 'among the roses.' Ten o'clock came and so did Pythias. With a fluttering heart, and no walls to talk through, Damon approached Pythias, poked his 'mug' inside a bonnet, implored a kiss encountered a bushy pair of whiskers, uttered a few 'bad words,' took to his heels, and does not know to this hour whether it was 'he she or it. (14)

People continued to pour into Ellsworth. The *Reporter* declared, "Loafers are multiplying. The town is full of strangers." At least they had rooms to stay in. The Drovers Cottage was completed bringing praises from the paper. "The new hotel adds greatly to the look of Main Street. It is 3 stories high 100 foot front and runs into next week."

By the wording of a report in the paper, Ellsworth apparently had the benefit of a street car, "Ellsworth has another new street car. Sanderson & White are the conductors."

Who had time for disquieting news in Ellsworth, Kansas? Editor and Mayor M. C. Davis noted, "Only one funeral in town this week so far." The world was changing and that change was never more evident than on the plains of Kansas. Settlement of farm land was pushing, always pushing Texas drovers further west in search of open range. But there was plenty of free grazing left. (15)

Under the byline, "STLL THEY COME," *Reporter* editor M. C. Davis welcomed a new paper to Kansas. The Wichita *Eagle*, edited by M. M. Murdock late of the Burlington *Chronicle*, began business in the busy little town situated prominently at the Arkansas River crossing of the great Chisholm Trail. Davis commented, "The *Eagle* is a large eight page, neatly arranged and well printed paper, and is really a thing of beauty. – 'Long may it wave.' " (16)

The *Reporter* picked up a piece printed in the Junction City *Union* recalling Ellsworth's violent beginnings. "Three years ago, a man named Hall shot another man named Erlick, storeroom keeper for Larkin & Relfe. Erlick severely wounded took Hall's revolver away, beat him over the head till dead. Hall's relatives recently removed his body "from the banks of the Smoky."

Editor Davis made his feelings unmistakable on the subject of a recent arson. "At 3:00 A.M. yesterday morning a house owned and occupied by a colored woman called Martha (was) discovered on fire by the night watchman at Drovers Cottage.

The house was consumed along with the fence and an outbuilding of one Mr. Buckminster. The folks who keep a questionable house above town, and who threatened to burn Martha out ought to be taken care of."

Whether the "house above town" was Lizzie's nauch or another of the class known as demimonde is not clear. At about this time others who were told to ply their trade outside of the city limits were at least in the process of moving. (17)

Along the Arkansas River, approximately thirty-seven miles southwest of Ellsworth, a pair of Ellsworth entrepreneurs, Perry Hodgden and Titus Buckbee were promoting the former site of Fort Zarah as the new town they naturally named Zarah. Their mercantile served travelers and drovers in the area.

On April 30th a drover by the name of Perry entered the store, inquiring of crackers to eat. Zack Light, brother-in-law to the owners, was behind the counter managing the store.

Perry received his crackers and then asked for some cheese. Zack took offence at the way the question was asked, pulled a pistol and killed Perry. As Perry's brother entered the door Zack fled out the back, mounted a pony which he rode hell bent for leather in the direction of Ellsworth. The surviving brother rode after Zack, but the killer reached Ellsworth in time to turn himself over to the protection of authorities, evading the brother and his own brand of justice.

Seeing that nothing could be done to avenge his brother's death, the cowboy turned back toward Zarah. The cowboy was never heard from again. Consensus in Barton County was that Zack's own brothers found the cowboy out on the trail and killed him, ending the threat to Zack. Frontier justice was often swift and just as often not so just. The case against Zack Light was eventually dismissed. (18)

Ellsworth's intrepid lawman Chauncey Whitney not only faithfully served to keep the peace, as a carpenter he helped build the town. May 1, 1872, he and George Kendall entered into the furniture and undertaking business. According to the *Reporter*, "Both of the men are mechanics and practical businessmen.

Many different types of stores were opening across town. Jake Karatofsky of Abilene opened a branch of his Great Western Store in Ellsworth. He billed the store as "Cheap Jake's."

The town boasted the medical services of three doctors. Two men who were for a time associated as partners stirred up a comical image as Dr. Duck and Dr. Fox. The third medical rep was Dr. Minnick. Considering the lively twenty-four hour a day standard of living all three men carried on successfully.

Oscar Seitz, a native of Cassel, Germany, was one of the original businessmen in 1867. Seitz Drug Store was a popular establishment. Oscar's brother, George Seitz arrived in 1868 and assumed management of the store. Soon Dr. Seitz, "... as the boys call him ... became known as one of the best businessmen in the city. An educated druggist, neat as a pin, courteous and public spirited ..."

Oscar was occupied with the management of an additional drug store in Salina. George guided the Ellsworth store with capable talent and purchased his brother's interest to become sole owner in February, 1872.

The excitement of the Texas cattle trade brought only a passing recognition of the waning importance of nearby Fort Harker. Three companies of Infantry left the post in late April. The remaining company of Cavalry had received marching orders, leaving twelve men to guard the seemingly forsaken post. (19)

Unbelievable amounts of money changed hands on the streets of Ellsworth. The city was a fortunate recipient of the enormous cattle trade. According to a statement in the *Reporter*, ten saloons were paying license and giving bonds amounting to fifty-five thousand dollars per year and that did not include the dance halls and bordellos that had left the city.

Lizzie Palmer started something when she moved outside the city limits of Ellsworth. A plat titled "Out Lots" was recorded with the Ellsworth County Register of Deeds, May 12, 1872. One street, Bayers Street, lined with thirty-six lots on either side made up the official red light district. August Bayers was a blacksmith and freighter with a shop at the east end of South Main Street, near the entrance to the Out Lots. Little else is known of his connection to the Out Lots. Perry Hodgden held a majority of the lots, evidently renting to the various dance halls and brothels. This "town" was initially referred to as the "addition" and sometimes called the "bottoms", but Lizzie Palmer's "Nauch" had put its stamp upon the district which most commonly was referred to as Nauchville.

Brocky Jack healed up from his gunfight in Abilene and was now Assistant Ellsworth City Marshal under Marshal John Councell. The adventurous life of being an Ellsworth lawman was noted in the May 16, 1872, Ellsworth *Reporter*:

Female Politician – The other morning we witnessed the Marshall and assistant arguing a point with a woman. The point in dispute seemed to be the proper way to go to the cooler. The Marshall insisted on her walking and she insisted on being carried. As is always the way the woman came out victorious. Drunk was no name for it.

There was no indication as to the whereabouts of Marshal Councell and Deputy Norton when their absence was duly noted by the Ellsworth City Council at the June 8th meeting. The city clerk was instructed to "notify the City Marshal and Policeman that their presence is required within the City limits at all times." Norton's earlier association with the Abilene brothel district and later known activities at Ellsworth seemed to indicate that the lawmen were spending more time at the newest sporting attraction just outside the city limits. Nauchville's collection of dance halls and brothels were evidently a hard thing for the officers to resist. (20)

Meanwhile new inroads into the Texas cattle business were shaping up in Wichita. The Santa Fe Railroad steamed its first engine into Wichita on the dark, stormy night of May 16, 1872. Stockyards would soon be built, providing prosperity and a new rival to Ellsworth and the Kansas Pacific Railway.

To avert traffic away from Wichita, a new route was suggested. The trail turned northwest from the Chisholm Trail at Pond Creek in Indian Territory. It then crossed over open prairie to a point near Raymond on the Arkansas River, then north to Ellsworth. As the trail was unmarked, little is known as to how many herds actually attempted the new route. (21)

A New England native, George Atwood purchased the Ellsworth *Reporter* from M. C. Davis in mid-May. Atwood published his first issue June 6, 1872. His former paper had been the Dallas *Gazette* of Iowa. Atwood introduced himself saying, "We located here because we believe in the grand future of Ellsworth City and County. We are ambitious to publish a live paper and therefore come to a live town."

The Drovers Cottage on South Main Street was destined to be a hit. It was situated an easy distance from the stockyards, boasted eighty-four rooms, a dining hall seating one hundred and a saloon with four billiard tables. A large livery stable completed the convenience of staying with Major and Mrs. Gore.

The Gore's were in fact well known to drovers. They had operated at Abilene and Mrs. Gore was held in the highest esteem by one and all. (22)

The devastation of the previous winter turned out to be only a slight falter to the cattle trailing business as new herds of Texas Longhorns began arriving on the Kansas prairies in ever larger numbers. The cards were stacked for another round of heavy trade on the streets of the Kansas cattle towns.

Heavy rains and Indian troubles in the "Nations" south of the Kansas line slowed the herds on their way north. Buffalo herds also proved to be a nuisance that kept F. M. Polk on the lookout along the cattle trail. "One man was always sent ahead to keep the buffaloes out of the herd and scout for Indians, for they were very savage at this time and we never knew when they would attack us."

Another drover, V. F. Carvajal reached Ellsworth only to find his boss had other plans.

> My boss, Colin Campbell, was there waiting for me, and he ordered me to go to North Platte, Nebraska, and he would meet me there. He bought me a compass and a map of the state of Nebraska. In those days the western part of Nebraska was nothing but wilderness. So we started for … (North Platte) without any roads; just following the North Star by the compass and examining the map to find out where we could get water for the cattle.

North of Ellsworth Carvajal found his way into trouble with an estimated twenty armed homesteaders, which he termed "short horns". With double barrel shotguns leveled at him, "… they stopped me from watering the cattle …."

> All at once there came a 'short horn' on a big horse to where I was. I asked him if he had a section of land on this side of the river where we were watering the cattle. He said yes, about half a mile below here. I told him that I would give him $100 gold or two cows and calves if he would let us water on his land; he told me all right, but you must not cross the river here, that we would have to go about twenty miles west and cross it on the government lands. So I watered the cattle and went west and crossed the Solomon River … We continued our journey toward North Platte, Nebraska … where we found our boss, Colin Campbell, waiting for us, after being on the trail for six months. (23)

The first shipment of cattle through the improved Kansas Pacific stockyards at Ellsworth was reported June 6, 1872. Sixteen cars of, "… poor brutes were started on the road to Brighton." Some of the largest and most respected Texas drovers had just arrived. Capt. A. G. Evans, John Bunton, Jonathan Dewees, N.P. Ellison, and Mark Withers were some of the men mentioned. Forty thousand head of new Texas cattle were grazing in cow camps on the range between the Arkansas River and the Smoky.

The streets of Ellsworth teemed with excitement. The *Reporter* boasted, "Not less than 1,000 people go to bed every night in Ellsworth." J. H. Dixon opened a Bakery and Ice Cream Saloon. Nick Lentz advertised, "Swimmers come forth! All you gentlemen who desire at any time to invoke the god of the sea to wash away

Drovers Cottage was partially dismantled in Abilene and shipped to Ellsworth by rail. Additional construction resulted in a much larger hotel than the original at Abilene. Courtesy Ellsworth County Historical Society.

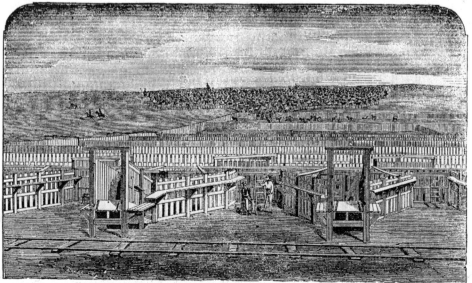

YARDING A HERD FOR SHIPMENT ON THE KANSAS PACIFIC RAILWAY.

The Kansas Pacific Stockyards were at the west edge of town. The hill on the horizon behind the cattle is now the location of the Ellsworth Correctional Facility. Illustrated by Professor Henry Worrall - Historic Sketches of the Cattle Trade by Joseph McCoy.

your sins – Call on Munn in the rear of Nick Lentz's Billiard Hall and you can be gratified to your heart's content. Baths! Baths! Baths! Hot, Cold, Medicated & Vapor Baths. Sic Transit Goria Mundi."

Theodore Sternberg, son of an active opponent of the Texas cattle trade took an opposite approach to his father. The younger Sternberg noted the quality of range and water in Ellsworth County and even boasted that Ellsworth was the best shipping point in Kansas. "In order to reach Ellsworth from the cattle trail it is not necessary or advantageous to drive through the settlement ... By a little care on the part of the drovers, there can be no trouble ... But keep in mind the motto, 'live and let live;' and do not drive your stock over the range of domestic cattle, of which there is no necessity, and your cattle men will not be troubled."

The Reverend Dr. Levi Sternberg's attentions were drawn elsewhere. Upon the abandonment of Fort Harker something had to be done with the reservation. Reverend Sternberg suggested an answer. "I have long thought that when Ft. Harker is finally abandoned it should be donated to the State for educational and kindred purposes such as forest tree and fruit culture ... All the present State institutions are in the Eastern portion: the western three quarters are entirely unprovided with higher institutions of learning ..." Reverend Sternberg suggested that the State of Kansas should be approached on the matter during the coming winter as, "Congress will by that time, probably make some final disposition of the Fort Harker Reservation."

As Reverend Sternberg's words were being printed for publication in the *Reporter*, a neighbor was struggling to take his last breath. Even for an experienced plainsman, death can catch a man unaware. Irwin Faris was one of the earliest settlers in Ellsworth County. He arrived with his brother, Henry, in 1860. They found a virtual oasis on Clear Creek. The Smoky Hill Trail had only recently been promoted as the shortest route to the Colorado gold fields. Travelers needed supplies. The Faris brothers established a road ranch at the trail crossing of Clear Creek and became well known for their knowledge of the country. Irwin scouted a new trail from Fort Ellsworth to Fort Zarah in 1865.

As he set out for a mid-summer buffalo hunt, Irwin probably felt little sense of danger. He and his brother were perhaps the most experienced buffalo hunters in the county. Who would have expected a rabid skunk to attack the camp. Irwin was bitten and soon showed signs of the dreaded hydrophobia. Forty-two year old Irwin Faris died an excruciating death June 6, 1872. (24)

Meanwhile, the Atchison, Topeka and Santa Fe Railroad built to Raymond and on to Great Bend. Raymond immediately took advantage of the cattle trail to Ellsworth. Stockyards, hotels, saloons and buyers were all a town needed to become a cattle town. Great Bend immediately threw its hat into the ring to vie for the cattle trade. Nineteen year-old D. W. "Doc" Barton drove two thousand Texas Longhorns to Great Bend's new railhead. The herd filled forty-six cattle cars, giving Great Bend a legitimate place among the cattle towns. It seemed the competition for the cattle trade was insatiable as survey stakes stretched ever westward toward Fort Dodge and the potential of another new town on the very edge of the frontier.

But that part of Kansas would have to wait its turn. Just as Ellsworth had once been too far out on the border, the Indian frontier of western Kansas offered too great a risk for cattlemen. (25)

Herds arriving on the grazing grounds of Ellsworth County immediately set up a "Cow Camp" to serve as headquarters. The cattle would often be grazed for the entire summer before being sold. Illustrated by Professor Henry Worrall - Historic Sketches of the Cattle Trade by Joseph McCoy

Large herds of cattle were arriving daily on the grazing grounds near Ellsworth. As a man rode through the country it looked as though there was but one vast herd, the cattle were so numerous.

One particular herd, passing through, ten miles east of Great Bend, gave rise to the story of 'The Return of a Western Sheriff,' the recollections of Barton County Sheriff G. N. Moses. Moses recalled that among the men with the herd in question was one man who was said to be a dead shot and "a general bad man."

He had reportedly killed several men on the trail, and as will appear hereafter, his companions even, were afraid of him. This man, thinking he was a privileged character, entered a settler's dugout while they were passing and finding no one but a young woman there, his brute instincts took possession of him, and he ravished her.

Shortly afterwards, her husband returned and learning what had happened, came to Great Bend and swore out a warrant for the man's arrest.

The warrant was placed in my hands for service, I being Sheriff of the county, and I called in James Gainsford to assist in my search for the man. (Gainsford tracked down and arrested the killers of Abilene Marshal Tom Smith in 1871) Gainsford, the husband, and myself went through all the herds of cattle between here and Ellsworth, hearing several times of the herd of which we were in search but lost track of them a few miles this side of Ellsworth. It being too late to continue the search that night, we concluded to ride into Ellsworth for the night and get an early morning start, and also thinking that we might see someone there who could give us some information as to the location of the particular herd, as there were a great many cattlemen in the town.

89

We rode into town, got our supper and then started out to prospect, and after inquiring of a large number of owners of herds, at last found one who told us that the owner of the particular herd in question was at a particular dance house, so we went there and found him, but not a word could we get out of him as to the whereabouts of his herd or the man we were after. After laboring with him for some time, we left him, thinking that we might get the information from someone else.

We kept up our search through the different dance halls and saloons until about half past twelve or one o'clock, when we came on to the owner of the herd again. As we were passing him, he touched my arm and whispered to me to follow him. Meantime we had sent the husband to bed, and Gainsford and myself were then alone. We followed him up the railroad track for about half a mile, and I was beginning to get nervous, thinking there was a trap laid for us, and I whispered to Gainsford, 'It don't look good, be ready for whatever may come.' About this time, the man stopped and faced us and said, 'Now, I will tell you where your man is, but before I tell you I want you to pledge me that when you run on him and he starts the fight that you will finish it by killing him; and if you should fail to kill him, that you will never tell who told you where he is. If he lives, and finds out that I told you, my life wouldn't be worth a cent, for he is a killer and one of the best shots in Texas.' We promised him what he wished and he then told us that the herd was located in the brakes of Turkey Creek and the men were herding the cattle in the Smoky River bottom. He also told us that we would find our man at the camp and not with the cattle. We thanked him for the information and started back for town. His last words were, 'Be sure and kill him.'

We went back to the hotel and slept until half past four; we then routed out the husband, got our horses and started for the brakes of Turkey Creek. On the way, we told the husband what we had learned about the man and where we were going. I then asked him if he had ever been in a shooting fracas or if he was used to handling a gun? He said he had never handled a gun much, but he wanted to get a shot at this fellow anyway. I told him that according to the description given us, we could ride within three or four hundred yards of the camp before they could see us and that when we got there and the shooting commenced, we had better dismount and he hold the horses and I did not know whether they would stand shooting or not and that we could do better execution on foot than on green horses. We had hard work to persuade him, but he finally, but very reluctantly, agreed to hold the horses. We rode on until we came to the bluff which had been described to us and sure enough, as we rode up to where we could look over into the draw, there was the camp. No one was there but the black cook and the man we were after. The cook was working or stirring something in a kettle over the fire and our man was sitting on a stick of wood between the wagons and the fire, his Winchester leaning against the wagon. When we came in sight, he grabbed his gun and commenced shooting. I started to dismount, as we had arranged, and as I looked back to see where our man was in whose care the horses were to be left, and I saw that he had taken the back track, his horse going as fast as he could make him with whip and spur, and that was the last I ever saw of him. I then said to Gainsford: 'Stay with your horse and charge.' We rode down the slope toward the wagon, and meantime the man we were after had gotten up and was resting his gun over the wagon box shooting at us. Some of the bullets nipped very close, but we were not hit. When we got within about a few yards of the wagon, he made a run for the creek bottom, which was dry and full of brush and trees. We did very poor shooting, owing to our horses acting so badly. He got to the brush, he shooting at us and we at him until we had worked down about a quarter of a mile. There was a deep ravine came in close to the creek there, and he undertook to run up over a point to get into this deep cut. I saw if he made it over the point he would sure get away. A short distance of his climb was quite steep and a part of it brought him in full view. He had nearly made it over, was just at the top, when I dropped off my horse, catching the bridle rein on my arm, and using my rifle now for the first time, my other shooting having been done with my holster pistols. I caught as good an aim as I could, considering the horse pulling on my arm, touched the trigger, and as the smoke cleared, saw the man grabbing at the brush and rolling down the bank into the brush and out of sight. I did not know how badly he was hurt and did not want to take any unnecessary chances, so I told Gainsford to ride back to the crossing at the camp and cross over and come down on the other side where he could get a view of him and see what condition he was in, and that I would stay and watch so that he could not get away. We could not go down into the creek bottom with our horses and did not feel like leaving them, for we did not know what we might run up against at any moment. We had had dealings with that kind of men before, and did not know how soon some of his friends would come to his rescue when it might be good judgment for us to take to the hills ourselves.

Gainsford started back to the crossing and got nearly there, when I heard the clatter of horses' hoofs to my left, and looking in that direction, saw six horsemen coming at full speed, with their guns in their hands, ready for action. I yelled to Gainsford to come back, thinking that there being only six, we could run a bluff on them.

When they got within about a hundred yards of me, I dropped on one knee and threw my rifle on them and told them to halt. By that time, Gainsford was at my side with his gun on them. I told the men we were having a little gun play there and asked them if they had come to take a hand in it. They answered by saying that they wasn't hunting any fights, but that was their camp and they had heard the shooting and had come to see what it was about. I told them what we were after and if they wanted to go to camp, they could circle us at a proper distance and go there and that they must stay there.

We had lost so much time parleying with these herders that we concluded that we could lead our horses down to the bank, tie them, and make a run through the brush afoot. We did so and searched for some time but our man was gone. After giving up the search, we started home, very much crestfallen, for I had been Marshal and Sheriff both in Missouri and Kansas for a long time and this was the first time I had ever failed getting a man I had been sent after. We returned home early in the morning of the next day, very much fatigued, mad and hungry, and in this frame of mind I went to the office of the Justice of the Peace, whose name was Martin, and I made the return in question, which read as follows:

'Received this writ _____ day of _____, 1872. Served the same by shooting at the d____d son of a _____ but didn't get him.

G.N. Moses, Sheriff,   Barton County, Kan.'

Afterwards the owner of the herd told Gainsford that our man 'had crawled into camp' and got a herd horse and that they followed him as far as Cow Creek, where they found him dead, and they buried him. (26)

Being a sheriff in Kansas was not an easy job and being a Sheriff in Ellsworth County was even more difficult. One wonders if, in rare quiet moments, Sheriff Chauncey Whitney recalled the days he spent on Beecher's Island in 1868, longing for a "quiet home". Ellsworth was not an ideal setting in which to raise a family.

On July 3, 1872, Whitney's wife, Nellie, gave birth to Mary Elizabeth Whitney. She was affectionately branded Bessie.

The day of Bessie's birth the *Reporter* reminded one and all that Ellsworth was far from the "quiet home" Whitney had longed for. "We shall never forget the display of bravery in the discharge of his duty, which Ed Hogue performed last Saturday in making an arrest surrounded by a thousand men." No details were given about what must have been a very dramatic moment. We are left to our imagination.

The stockyards were of keen interest. They would have to be ready for the great herds of longhorns. "The K. P. Railway is hauling 200 carloads of sand for the stockyards." The yards must have been a spectacular sight as the first herds prepared to ship. (27)

The City of Ellsworth was dealing with the same problems that had plagued Abilene. City Marshal Councell and his assistant Brocky Jack Norton evidently were not performing as expected. On July 24, 1872, the city council gave instructions to the clerk to notify Councell and Norton that, "they had this day been removed from office."

However, the city council could not agree over who to appoint to the City Marshal position. A compromise resulted in Ed Hogue being appointed to a temporary position designated as "Chief of Police" rather than Ellsworth City Marshal. Hogue was a fiery character of French decent, reportedly "born at sea". He had earlier tended bar in a Hays City saloon where he killed a man in a ferocious gunfight. (28)

Ellsworth had been relatively quiet, considering the abundance of men and women actively living as far on the edge of life as they could possibly get. Texas drover Print Olive was no stranger to pandemonium. He had seen more than his share during the Civil War and was known as a man who dealt swiftly with anyone who dared to cross his path. Olive found suitable grazing for his cattle near Ellsworth in early July and set up his headquarters at Drovers Cottage. Many hours were spent negotiating with buyers and playing cards in the various saloons. The "No Gun" law forced Olive to walk the streets without his six-gun. He was uncomfortable but complied with the law in order to do business. During a game at Nick Lentz' Saloon the morning of July 20th, Olive sat in on a game with Jim "Spike" Kenedy. Spike was the son of Miflin Kenedy, one of the largest cattlemen in Texas. The cards fell against young Kenedy and as "Lady Luck" continued to ignore hand after hand, Spike accused Olive of cheating. The elder Olive reprimanded Kenedy in uncomplimentary words, telling him to "cash in his chips," which he did. Kenedy left the game with an angry vow to someday make Olive pay.

By six o'clock p.m. Olive had moved to a new game at the Ellsworth Billiard Saloon owned by Jake New. Kenedy entered the saloon unnoticed; walked to the rear of the bar and picked up a pistol that had been "checked" in accordance with the "No Gun" law. With a spin of the cylinder he knew the weapon was loaded. Kenedy turned, walked directly toward Olive and warned Olive that now he would "pass in his checks!" Four shots rang out.

Jim Kelly had grown up with Print Olive. They were close friends even though Kelly's family had been slaves to the Olives. Olive had relied on Kelly in many close shaves. Kelly and a Mexican drover entertained themselves by watching people pass by in the street. They were standing near a window outside New's saloon when shots won their attention. Quick as thought, Kelly drew a concealed pistol and fired. Olive was lying helplessly on the floor. Kelly's shots through the window brought Kenedy down just as he was about to put a bullet in Olive's brain. Kenedy was arrested while doctors performed surgery on Olive who was spread across a card table. Olive survived, but carried a piece of watch chain in his groin the rest of his life. That night Kenedy escaped with friends. (29)

By mid summer there was no denying that Ellsworth was the new cattle mecca. A traveler wrote his impressions of Ellsworth.

> There were shipped from this place alone last season, over nineteen hundred cars of cattle, and this year they expect to ship four thousand. There are also many herds driven from here to California and the territories. One herd started to-morrow for Montana … Here you see men in the streets from every State, and I might say from almost every nation – The tall long-haired Texas herder with his heavy jingling spurs and pair of six-shooters; the dirty greasy Mexicans with unintelligible jargon; the gambler from all parts of the country, looking for unsuspecting prey; the honest immigrant looking for a homestead in the great free west; the keen stock buyers; the wealthy Texas drovers; dead beats 'cappers'; pick-pockets; horse thieves; a cavalry of Texas ponies, and scores of demi monde. (30)

There was no doubt that by midsummer, boom town Ellsworth was seeing a very eventful season.

Chapter Seven

A TOWN DIVIDED

Ellsworth became the center of attention on many levels during the summer of 1872. Cattlemen finally recognized the town as a viable trading center. Buyers enthusiastically followed the cattle to Ellsworth and so did the sporting crowd. The desperate seed that had struggled for years to find life in a foreboding land reached for the stars with a renewed sense of well-being.

Excitement could be found on every street corner. At Joe Brennan's Billiard Hall a historic occasion demanded more than the usual attention when William Rivers of New Orleans and J. Montgomery of Ellsworth squared off on the billiard tables. Rivers had recently gained national attention for his skill with a cue stick by defeating former U.S. champion John Deary not once, but twice in renowned matches held at Kansas City and Topeka. News of River's presence in Ellsworth drew a large number of spectators to Brennan's. The occasion of a local billiard player contending with someone of William Rivers' reputation was an event to be celebrated. The diversion proved to be all that one could have expected from two heroes of the pocket table as they vied for sovereignty. Rivers defeated Montgomery with the largest average every exhibited in a match game in the state of Kansas. The *Reporter* declared the event, "Good Billiard Playing."

Horse racing was one of the most popular sports of the day and no town could be complete with out a "track." Just outside of town on a grassy flat, speculators and sightseers could be found at the horse races. Ellsworth's track was merely a straight course allowing for races of a quarter-mile, six hundred yards, or half a mile distance.

Bill Tilghman, who would later gain fame as a deputy U. S. Marshal, recalled a summer day in Ellsworth when he was a young buffalo hunter eighteen years of age. Tilghman led an extra horse into Ellsworth to have it shod at one of the blacksmith shops. While the blacksmith was tending to his horse Tilghman heard a voice from behind. "Mister would you let me ride your horse out to the track?" Tilghman turned to find an Indian boy of perhaps fourteen. There were four races that day and everyone wanted to be there.

Tilghman liked the lad and tossed the halter rope his way. After settling up with the blacksmith the two mounted up to take in the races. Tilghman noticed how well the young man handled his horse. "What's your name?"

"Charley," was the reply.

Tilghman had developed an affinity for a particular lady's pies and the thought occurred to him that the young Indian boy just might like them too. "As they passed the pie shop, he bought an apple pie. Breaking it, he handed the larger piece to Charley. The boy's eyes glowed." Charley told Tilghman that he had quit a wagon train that morning and hadn't had anything to eat.

Charley was looking forward to the horse races. "I can ride races." Charley eagerly told his new friend.

At the races one of the jockeys was kicked and would not be able to ride. The owner of the horse inquired for a rider and Tilghman quickly recommended Charley. Tilghman recalled, "Though he rode with only a blanket, he stuck like a burr as his mount made the lightning whirl to start. Charley's services were thenceforth in demand."

What Tilghman didn't know was that he had just participated in an age-old horse racing deception. The owner of the horse was actually Charley's grandfather. Charley was Indian alright, but his father was white. He had grown up spending time both on the Kaw reservation at Council Grove and his grandfather's home in Topeka.

Charley had been racing since he was eight years old. The injured jockey was merely a ploy to get a young, seemingly inexperienced Indian boy into the race. The bets literally soared as gamblers placed their money.

Charley also became well known in later life. His biography does not refer to the scam but simply states that Charley went on a tour.

> ... on a tour of Western Kansas as far west as the notorious cattle town of Ellsworth. Here Charley and Carrie won a very profitable race, and the mixed-blood became an instant hero with the cowboys, saloon keepers, and prostitutes.
>
> I never knew how much money our crowd actually won but I know it was a very large sum and the gamblers and the madam insisted on taking me to her house and then up town and bought me a new suit of clothes, boots, hat and all, and the madam had a new jockey suit made for me. I was proud of my good luck, the suit was a good one. They gave me money and bought me candy and presents and they came to our camp every day ... I had never been so petted in my life and I loved it.

"Charley" Curtis would later become the Vice President of the United States, the only Native American to do so. Curtis served in Herbert Hoover's administration from March 4, 1929, until March 3, 1933.

A good many years after the Ellsworth horse races Bill Tilghman visited Curtis during his term in Washington. In the Senate dining room Charley ordered pie. "But none of it ever tastes so good as that apple pie you bought me at Ellsworth, Bill." (1)

Just as Ellsworth was finally gaining in status as a town with a future, Fort Harker was declining. The primordial sea of grass with its essential network of flora and fauna and the people who depended upon it were being forced out of existence. The

"Lords of the Prairie", the Cheyenne, Arapaho, and Sioux; the Kiowa, Comanche and Pawnee were relegated to the reservations below the Arkansas River and above the Platte. The great battle for the sacred Smoky Hill country was won by an invading culture whose insatiable hunger for land sought to change the face of that land forever. There would be no need to guard the settlement of central Kansas. Fort Harker was slated to be abandoned. The Ellsworth *Reporter* announced that government property at the Fort would be sold Monday August 12, 1872. (2)

The loss of Fort Harker and its monetary benefit made the cattle trade more important than ever to Ellsworth's economy. Providing proper facilities for the cattle market could not be ignored. Abel "Shanghai" Pierce was well aware of the great demand the cattle trade had placed on Joseph McCoy's Great American Stock Yards in Abilene. Ellsworth followed the advice of Pierce who had criticized the small stockyards at the west edge of town. The Kansas Pacific yards were not only enlarged, they were now the largest cattle yards in the state.

One hundred thirty-five thousand head of cattle were grazing the cow camps surrounding Ellsworth, just waiting for a turn to pass through the new stockyards. The yards were opened for business just as the main shipping season was about to commence. Texan Col. Robert D. Hunter, favorably known among the cattlemen, was superintendent of the yards. Shanghai Pierce was known by virtually everyone in the cattle business and he was not shy in saying so. Ellsworth businessmen were convinced that Pierce was just the man to promote Ellsworth as the most important market in cattle country. Town leaders were willing to put all bets on Shanghai Pierce, offering him an undisclosed amount of money to represent Ellsworth to cattlemen as they drove their great herds north to the Kansas railheads.

Pierce's reputation as a prominent "mouthpiece" in the cattle industry was noted by a correspondent for the Manhattan *Nationalist* and reprinted in the *Reporter*.

> When I first came here (July 1st), stock men were feeling a little blue over the dry weather, but we have had rain on an average of four days per week ever since, and the grass is growing fine, and every one is in good spirits. The company had just finished the best and most complete set of yards here that are to be found in the state. There are seven shoots for loading, with two pens to each large enough for one car of cattle; also six large pens that will hold ten car loads apiece, and back of that a large yard that will hold 500 head. An alley 15 feet wide runs around the whole yard with gates opening from each pen into it. There are also gates from one pen to another, and well fixed so as to be very handy. The small pens next to the shoots are floored with two inch plank. Eight men can load from 150 to 200 cars per day.
>
> To one never having seen them it is quite interesting to watch a lot of these wild Texas long-horns loaded. First a herd of perhaps one thousand head will be driven in within a short distance of the yards and stopped. Now stopped with a herd of Texas cattle is far different than with natives. You get a herd of the Texas running in one direction, there is no more use in going in front to stop them, then before an engine running without an engineer, as in either case – as the boys say – 'you are liable to get killed

at any minute.' The only way to break into the side and get them partly turned, and then follow up the advantage thus gained until you get them to going round in a circle, or as the Texas men say, get them to "milling," when once started in this "milling" process they will sometimes "walk around" for three or four hours. Then they go to work "cutting out." Two or three men ride in and drive one out, and start him off away from the herd, then another, and so on until 22 or 23 – a car load – are out, when they are driven to the yards. It takes a large amount of experience and skill to handle them successfully. If they get the least mad or willful – which is often the case – you have to let them have their own way for the time being and work by strategy. (3)

"CUTTING OUT."

Cattle selected to be sold were "cut" from the herd making horses especially suited for the task desirable. Illustrated by Professor Henry Worrall
- Historic Sketches of the Cattle Trade by Joseph McCoy.

Proper promotion was of utmost importance to the success of the new Ellsworth railhead. The uninitiated investor contemplating the stock business often did not recognize the many levels of commerce available to them in the cattle industry. Drovers Cottage owner Moses B. George was well versed in the tier system existing in the livestock business. He recognized the great potential of attracting cattle buyers of diverse backgrounds to the new Ellsworth cattle market. He had after all, seen how the intricate workings of the Abilene market had brought prosperity to the city and to individuals who managed wisely. He had just recently marketed a total of eleven thousand head of cattle in four separate transactions at the Ellsworth market. The dealings reflected different tiers of the market with fat cattle going to feed reservation Indians, big steers to graze one more season on Kansas ranches and young cattle to a ranch near Pueblo, Colorado. George set out to educate potential investors with a letter to the *Reporter*.

97

There are now in the vicinity of this place more and better cattle then at Abilene at any one time in its palmist days, and large numbers of them are being selected every day by buyers from Iowa and Illinois, who are getting pick of herds ... Cattle this year are in finer, more healthful and thrifty condition than I have seen them in years, owing largely to the unusual fine feed and large supply of pure water about Ellsworth.

George continued his glowing account of the profits of wintering cattle, never calling to mind the most recent disaster of the 1871-1872 winter. He quoted prices for various classes of cattle and closed by observing, "I would like to see this matter agitated throughout the State and see our people on hand as early as those from other States. There is more money in wintering Texan cattle than anything I know of." (4)

The cattle season of 1872 was shaping up to be a rousing success, but to Ellsworth's dismay the very man the town had counted on to give them an edge over competing railheads, especially the new market at Wichita, had written a letter to the Wichita *Eagle* throwing a bad light on the cow camps in the Smoky Hills around Ellsworth. Editor Marsh Murdock used Pierce's observation that the Ellsworth range was "very short of moisture," to draw cattlemen to the Wichita market. That fact had been true in the early months, but as the correspondent for the Manhattan *Nationalist* had pointed out, recent dependable rains had caused the range to flourish.

For the most part, fears of cattlemen turning away from the Ellsworth market were unjustified. Words printed in newspapers were not enough to sway experienced range men. The prairies filled with cattle and Ellsworth filled with cowboys.

The onslaught of trail cowboys, gamblers, adventurers and women of easy virtue undoubtedly created anxiety for the Ellsworth City Council. No one on the council was willing to return to the wide open days of Ellsworth's youth. The townl needed a tough man to keep the lid on the daily celebration. Ed Hogue had performed well since his temporary appointment as chief of police, but his fiery disposition left the city fathers uneasy. In light of available candidates the city council held its breath and officially designated Hogue as Ellsworth City Marshal August 26, 1872. Brocky Jack Norton was retained as Assistant City Marshal. (5)

While the town was coming to grips with the question of law enforcement, an unexpected difficulty set citizens against one another. The political season was upon them as politicians tempted voters with pledges for the future. But the political contest was about to take an unexpected turn.

Ellsworth's original plat separated the business district along two main streets paralleling the railroad. By that action the Ellsworth Town Company quite unintentionally caused a natural division that by 1872 progressed to a jealous competition between the proprietors of South Main and those of North Main. Ellsworth *Reporter* Editor George Atwood had been in town just a little over three months. His initial impression of Ellsworth had led him to believe that the town's promoters were benevolent toward one another, especially in their efforts to shape a successful Ellsworth, but upon reflection he was forced to concede that there were many differences of opinion as to Ellsworth's future.

When we located in Ellsworth we supposed, this being a new town, that there was no dissention or rivalry between people. But by degree we have found out that this was not the social Eden we pictured it in our first *Reporter*. According to different men Eden must be North or South of Main Street. During the rebellion we refused to acknowledge less than all the States as our Union, and we shall not recognize less than the whole of Ellsworth as our town. We have no jealousies in our home – indeed, we should heartily rejoice if south-main street extended west through the city limits and through one or two additions. In that event we should have lots of job work and advertising. We can hardly wait for the county to get large enough to support an eight column paper which we are anxious to print. As for the court house, we kept out of that fight. – To have 'waded in' would have been exceedingly impolite. We understood with many others, that the house would be built on the "Court House Square," and looked for lots up there, but the men who had the power, put the house on Main street and there it will be built, on the foundation nearly completed ... And now politics are getting demoralized! It is difficult to say just who is to blame for it all, Horace Greeley, or Court House, or Phillips or Strickler.

Political dissention was not just a local phenomenon. The Republican party was in shambles. At the national level Horace Greeley had broken with the Republican Party to form a new party.

The whole political system seemed disrupted all the way down to the state and local tickets. Atwood's reference to the new Ellsworth County Court House and Jail was an exceedingly sore subject, not only in Ellsworth but throughout the county. The city was anxious to build a fine building to represent county government but rural residents were almost unanimously against it. Farmers were suddenly pitted against city businessmen.

The town had been plated with a "Court House square", reserved for county government north of the business district. That square was designated on the east side of today's Douglas Avenue between 2nd and 3rd streets and is the present site of the Ellsworth Elementary School.

Arthur Larkin, an 1867 founding businessman, was building a new hotel at the corner of North Main Street and E Street (Lincoln Avenue). Larkin owned lots on the corner east of his hotel, designated on the old plats as D Street (Court Avenue). Quite naturally Larkin recognized the benefits of having the courthouse near his hotel and offered the D Street property free of charge to the County Commissioners. They took him up on it. However the offer was made in "confidential negotiations," The public knew nothing of the arrangements until they had been agreed to. Investors of the property next to the long designated "Court House Square" were left holding land intended for development based upon its location next to the supposed seat of county government. To say that there were hard feelings would be an understatement.

The whole thing spilled over into the local political arena. Republican Congressman Col. W. A. Phillips of Salina was being challenged by S. A. Strickler, a Republican from Junction City. Each man was backed by representatives of the opposing factions within the Republican Party concerning the Ellsworth County Court House. Ellsworth politics were in complete disarray.

Atwood ended his comments with a hopeful, "But let us not despair. We are all in favor of 'longhorns.' We all want a big city. After a little jealousies of the present will be forgotten in the endeavor of each to do his most to build up Ellsworth. Hail happy day!"

Atwood was doing all he could to put a good face on the turn of events but his statement that, "We are all in favor of the longhorns." exposed his continued incomplete understanding of the discord within his county. The growing legion of farmers were a force to be reckoned with as their numbers found the longhorns to be a financial menace they were more than happy to do without.

Arthur Larkin was one of the first businessmen in Ellsworth. He was a great promoter of the town, establishing several businesses including the Grand Central Hotel.

Courtesy Ellsworth County Historical Society.

Even as tensions were straining to the breaking point, the newspaperman did not allow the civic dissention to entirely consume him. Being new to buffalo country, Atwood accompanied friends on a grand "Buffalo Hunt". Nothing could have prepared him for what he was about to experience. "Here was abundant opportunity to shoot, but not the least anxiety to do so. I had such a view of buffaloes as I never could have expected, never would enjoy again. This was all sufficient for me. I stood and studied the host with devouring eyes, while my horse snorted and pulled at the bridle in a passion of enthusiasm. Yes, there, beyond the peradventure, in my plain sight, grazed the entire buffalo army of Southern Kansas. As far as the western horizon the whole earth was black with them. The desire to shoot, kill, and capture utterly passed away. I only wished to look, and to look till I could realize or find some speech for the greatness of nature that silenced me." His silence was deafening, for all too soon the grand "buffalo army" would be gone.

Nature was giving way to the advancing culture of an insatiable nation. Armies had come in opposition to the "greatness of nature" and, upon accomplishing their desire, moved forward seeking new conquests. Fort Harker was slated to be abandoned. The sale of government property at the fort attracted Ellsworth's Mayor, M. C. Davis. Ever mindful of the advancement of his community, Davis acquired a much needed hook and ladder apparatus to fight the dreaded fires that were a continual threat to the security of the town. The purchase was the last act performed by Davis in service to the town he held so dear. Continued battling over the location of the courthouse turned out to be more than Davis could stand. He resigned his position as mayor, put his property up for sale and made plans to immediately move to Clayton, Illinois.

The dramatic exit of M. C. Davis seemed to have little effect on the community. For the time being, the dance would continue. The Nauch, outside Ellsworth's city limits, carried on nightly while more respectable couples formed the Ellsworth Dancing Club. Their first dance was to be held Friday evening, September 6th. Farrell & Stebbins even went so far as to buy M.C. Davis' business house with the intentions of renovating the building for dancers, "if the dancers will promise to use it."

Culture was coming to Ellsworth in spite of itself, and with culture, ideology soon gained recognition. Seventy-two subscribers, including several saloon men were posted in the *Reporter* in support of building a new Catholic church, "to cost not less than twelve hundred dollars." (6)

Culture was coming, but Ellsworth's immediate future lay with the cattlemen. One such example was Colonel O. W. Wheeler. The Colonel was well known as the man who first drove cattle from Texas to Abilene over the famous Chisholm Trail. His marketing transactions in the fall of 1872 made big news. "Col. Wheeler has already shipped this season from Ellsworth 28 cars of cattle, and still has 67 car loads to ship from that point. He has also shipped 47 cars from Abilene, and 8 from Junction City, besides 300 head of stock driven to the vicinity of Manhattan and other points east of Abilene, for the purpose of wintering them. Altogether Col. Wheeler has already sold during the present season over 4000 head of cattle – 3000 of which were bought by Mr. Hunter of Kansas City, the largest sale made by any dealer in the market." The sale to Hunter was reported by McCoy to have amounted to one hundred and twenty-five thousand dollars.

The leaders of the cattle industry became familiar figures on the streets of Ellsworth. Thousands of dollars changed hands daily. Perryman & Lytle sold to Mabry & Millett. Col. J. J. Myers sold to Powers and Company. John Good bought cattle from George Hill. Bennett & Sheidly purchased cattle while James Ellison and One-Armed Jim Reed sold cattle. The partnership of Hittson, Goodnight, Weaver and Chesholm sold out a herd of cattle that had spent the previous winter on the plains of eastern Colorado. Hittson was a swashbucking hombre who had fought the Comanche war chief, Quanah Parker. In his working clothes he was described as, "… wearing two Navy Colt pistols and carrying an 1866 rimfire, .44 caliber Winchester (Yellow Boy)."

Charles Goodnight had forged the Goodnight-Loving Trail with his partner Oliver Loving. Chesholm was none other than "Jinglebob" John Chisum, known for his particular practice of slitting the ear of his longhorns, allowing the lower half of the ear to flop in manner that left no doubt as to who the owner was. At the end of the trail that led to Ellsworth, Kansas, the cattle kings of the west were making the deals that fed the rest of the country. Ellsworth had achieved its long held dream. (7)

An Ellsworth resident by the name of William B. McClellan made the kind of news in early September that reminded everyone of the not so distant past. The Ellsworth *Reporter* bluntly recorded, "Judge Lynch shot dead Donovan, the horse thief, confined in the jail at Hays City. McClellan was in the same room at the time and had a narrow escape. He is under a strong guard at the Fort and it is quite likely that he will be acquitted."

Six weeks earlier, July 21, 1872, Pony Donovan and his gang raided a railroad camp thirty miles west of Fort Dodge. The camp was made up of a crew employed to grade the roadbed in advance of laying track for the Santa Fe Railway. The thieves stampeded twenty or thirty mules. A pair of soldiers heroically chased Donovan and his gang but soon found themselves captured. The gang had great fun stripping the soldiers of everything, including their clothes. The soldiers were told that if they were caught at anytime in the future they would be killed. The unfortunate posse was finally released while the gang hurried away with the railroad mules.

Donovan grew bolder than ever. He was "King of the Horse Thieves," but his overconfidence would be his undoing. The bandit leader was recognized on the streets of Hays City and arrested. His timing was unfortunate.

McClellan had just been jailed for killing Jack Wright over the affections of Nettie Baldwin. McClellan and Baldwin were no strangers to Pony Donovan. All three were associated with the Sanderson ring of horse thieves out of Junction City and Ellsworth. Nettie had been one of Ellsworth's popular girls at Lizzie Palmer's Nauch.

McClellan's victim, Jack Wright had many friends in Hays City. After being notified that McClellan was in danger of being lynched, Kansas Governor James M. Harvey sent an urgent message to General Pope, Commanding at Fort Hays. Pope ignored the message. McClellan was housed in the basement of the Ellis County Courthouse, chained to a supporting post in the room; the same room that held Pony Donovan.

That night vigilantes crept close to the courthouse, shoved rifles through the basement windows and opened fire with a hail of bullets. Pony Donovan was killed.

McClellan was not hit. The next day McClellan was moved to the guardhouse at Fort Hays. Donovan was interred on Hays City's Boot Hill. (8)

The Ellsworth County countryside churned with turmoil throughout the 1872 cattle season. Indignant farmers and stockmen joined forces to make a shambles of Ellsworth County's Republican Party. Their political tactics viciously split the party, pitting rural voters against urban voters.

Senatorial candidate John H. Edwards, on September 26th, weighed in on the opinion that the Texas cattle trade was Ellsworth County's greatest asset. Two days later settlers held a convention in Ellsworth to reorganize a Farmers Protective Association. The effort was headed by W. M. King and a minister, Dr. Abraham Essick. King's opinions ranged to the extreme in radicalism. He went so far as to denounce many of the very men needed to form the association by declaring that the domestic stockmen were worse than the Texans, "in letting their stock run free to commit depredations and then disclaiming ownership when they did.

Dr. Abraham Essick had only recently come to Ellsworth County. He was pastor of the York Street Church at Gettysburg, Pennsylvania, and witnessed the horror of the great Civil War battle. Essick recalled, "During the early part of the day, I watched the movements of the armies from the steeple of the church, which stands next (to) the parsonage - saw the wounded and dying constantly brought in ... On Monday morning we moved to the battled field and saw sights which I cannot describe. Dead men and horses already far gone into decay, muskets, knapsacks, broken caissons, and cannon, etc etc. lay everywhere ... My church was occupied for a hospital and it was several weeks before it could be used for religious services. For many weeks after the battle there was a stench filling the air, which was almost unendurable. This caused a great deal of sickness. I was taken down with fever and was unable to perform ministerial duties for about two months." Essick performed the funeral service for one of his congregation, twenty-year-old Virginia "Jennie" Wade. Killed by a stray bullet, Jennie Wade is believed to be the first woman to die as a result of military action during the war.

Essick arrived in Ellsworth County with intentions of entering into the stock-raising business. He immediately accepted a leading role in the protective association. The association voted to petition the county commissioners for a herd law requiring drovers to stay with their cattle and keep them from damaging settler's property. To underscore the association's resolve the members established the motto, "Protection we want. Protection we must have!"(9)

Settlers on the prairie were not the only ones struggling to survive. Fire was a dreaded enemy to municipal development on the Kansas frontier. Many of the buildings in Ellsworth were frame wooden structures, often unpainted and tender dry. An uncontrolled fire could wipe out an entire town in less than an hour.

The town's worst fears became reality when the call of "Fire!" echoed throughout Ellsworth early Sunday morning, September 29, 1872. The one o'clock a. m. fire began "... no bigger than a man's hand and the observer thought he could extinguish it." But it soon turned into a blaze that wrapped the complete Sanderson & White Livery Stable in flames. The livery was an essential element of the syndicate of horse thieves loosely organized by the Sanderson brothers. The firm was one of Ellsworth's earliest businesses established on the banks of the Smoky, "... when

Ellsworth was a baby ..." The livery could fit a traveler with a good horse or a wagon train, "... good for 100 tons ..."

The fire spread so quickly that very little could be saved. A few saddles and some harness were hauled from the fire. Five horses were lost. One horse was saved but was so severely burned that it had to be "put down." Only two of the horses belonged to Sanderson & White, "... the others to different parties ... The nearest buildings were only saved by great exertions, the heat being so intense on the roof of Mr. Kidder's house, as to blister his ... hands while he was protecting his home."

The same issue of the *Reporter* stated that Kidder, who had been a partner with Ira Phelps in the grocery business, had gone into the cattle business and presently had a herd on the trail to Ellsworth.

The same issue of the *Reporter* featured a lighter element as the editor quipped, "Ellsworth is rather quiet now: trade has not subsided so much in the city as in Nauchville. The sound of the harp has died out, the violin ceases its vibrations and the feet of the dancing maidens have taken themselves to Sherman and other places.

Perhaps his observations were only wishful thinking for cattle were "being shipped in large quantities daily." Another account in the same issue of the *Reporter* noted that thirty-nine cars of cattle were shipped on Tuesday.

Where there were cattle there were cowboys and where there were cowboys plenty of "dancing maidens' could be found. Instead of quiet, the activity reported in the paper would indicate a bustling community. A fire company was being organized. The Catholic Church was under construction and in an article entitled, "Hurra! Hooray!" G. A. Atwood triumphantly announced the opening of the bridge for traffic.

> The Iron Bridge across the Smoky is completed. Teams began crossing over it Tuesday. (October 1, 1872) We give due notice to the inhabitants of Kansas that the Ellsworth Smoky River Iron Bridge is ready and able to bear 1,000 tons "over the river." The bridge is 300 feet long, consisting of three spans of 100 feet each. The company warrants the bridge to bear 10 tons to the foot which makes one thousand tons to the span. The bridge stands twenty feet above the river bed – on iron piers of secure foundations. It is a handsome structure costing $15,000, and we invite all Kansas to go and see it.

As though railroad news had become humdrum a note in the *Reporter* impassively noted, "Ellsworth is going to have another railroad – Developments will be given in due time." (10)

While rural settlers continued to agitate the political climate, the city of Ellsworth walked a tightrope of continuing to provide gainful diversions for the insatiable Texas cowboy while maintaining law and order for the safety of its citizens. The brothels and dance halls outside the city limits helped keep the revelry to controllable limits. But civilization was definitely in the eye of the beholder.

Dance halls were perhaps the most notorious of hangouts in any western town.

The King Iron Bridge & Manufacturing Company of Cleveland, Ohio, built the first bridge to span the Smoky Hill River in 1872.
Courtesy Ellsworth County Historical Society.

Joseph McCoy had seen plenty of celebration while in Abilene. His eyewitness observation of the typical frontier dancehall is the next best thing to being there and the revelry that he saw was repeated in every major cattle town in Kansas.

> The cow-boy enters the dance with a peculiar zest, no stopping to divest himself of his sombrero, spurs, or pistols, but just as he dismounts off of his cow-pony, so he goes into the dance. A more odd, not to say comical sight, is not often seen than the dancing cow-boy; with the front of his sombrero lifted at an angle of fully forty-five degrees; his huge spurs jingling at every step or motion; his revolvers flapping up and down like a retreating sheep's tail; his eyes lit up with excitement, liquor and lust; he plunges in and "hoes it down" at a terrible rate, in the most approved yet awkward country style; often swinging "his partner" clear off of the floor for an entire circle, then "balance all" with an occasional demoniacal yell, near akin to the war whoop of the savage Indian. All this he does, entirely oblivious to the whole world "and the balance of mankind."

Within Ellsworth's city limits saloons carried on "round the clock" celebrations of life as railroaders, cowboys, and wagon masters were encouraged to share hard earned pay with one and all.

"DANCE-HOUSE."

A day away from camp found the "cow-boy" in search of a "jolly" time which could certainly be found in an Ellsworth dance house. Illustrated by Professor Henry Worrall
- Historic Sketches of the Cattle Trade by Joseph McCoy

Ellsworth was as tough a town as any at the end of the trail. Councilmen were well aware of the fact that a tough town needed active lawmen, but Marshal Ed Hogue's style of aggressive peacekeeping was stifling business. The city council replaced Hogue with Brocky Jack Norton on October 8. Brocky Jack's experience under Wild Bill Hickok at Abilene may have helped him in dealing with the Texas cowboys. The council hadn't lost all faith in Hogue though. He was retained as a deputy on the force. (11)

G. A. Atwood continued to promote unity to his divided readers.

> Now ... is the time to look out for the future of our town and county ... Ellsworth must make itself a city that can live with or without the cattle trade. If the effort is made, this city may become the great cattle market of Kansas, where the West will come for herds and where the East will come for beef.
>
> But we should go on and work for other things regardless of the cattle trade. Roads must be built; mills must be built; railroads must be built; farms must be built; the town and country must be built up permanently.

Atwood took on the role of a captain steering his ship through dangerous waters as he addressed what could well be the undoing of the community.

> Now if there are any jealousies between our citizens they ought to be forgotten. All are equally desirous of a large city. Certain work has got

to be done before we can have one. If we are not agreed that work may fail. Ellsworth will fall behind, there will be no home market for farmers produce. Almost primeval quiet will reign over the prairies and buffalo grass will grow in our streets.

... So then we say every man should do his duty. Ellsworth is now in an embryo state, when it may live or die, according to the will of her citizens.

All wish for good times coming but they will only come by willing it. (12)

The November election reflected the turmoil found in the Republican Party, which made up the majority of Ellsworth County voters. The slate offered a balance of rural and city candidates. On its surface, the newly formed political alliance between rural and urban leaders should have resulted in a sweeping victory for Ellsworth County Republicans. However, the tremendous divide between rural Republicans and the businessmen within the city brought catastrophic defeat to the leading political party in the county. "The town's Republicans, it turned out, had failed to support rural members for the slate and the countrymen refused to vote for the townsmen ... In short, rural-urban hostilities cut so deeply into the local social fabric that a temporary political alliance could not mend the gap."

The *Reporter* responded to the failure of the Republican Party with an admonition. "Now let us go to work and see if we can't do something for our town and county. Election is over. Bury your hatchets for a few months and over your pipes of peace consider what we shall do to make Ellsworth one of the best counties in the State."

Atwood could be hopeful that Ellsworth would be able to progress beyond its bitter divisions. Remarkable changes could be seen looming on the horizon if, as Mr. Atwood counseled, the town's leaders could work together for the good of the whole community. However, the frontier was not far from the consciousness of the robust society that had shaped Ellsworth's character. That character produced a whole bevy of individuals who were fascinating in their own right. One of Ellsworth's most interesting attorneys Harry L. Pestana traveled west to Hays City. Pestana fit right in with the frontier crowd. When Hickok was wounded and run out of Hays City in 1870, the famous gunman was said to have hid out at Pestana's Ellsworth home until tempers cooled. This time Pestana had been retained by the man who had survived the Pony Donovan courthouse killing, William B. McClellan. McClellan was an Ellsworth man and a known member of the Sanderson horse thief crowd.

Horses continued to be a favorite form of commerce in Ellsworth. Trading horses was for the most part a legitimate activity but no matter how honest a horse trader professed to be, the occupation almost always conveyed a questionable reputation to the partaker of the profession. The *Reporter* attempted to set such men straight with the words of a syndicated philosopher.

Advise to Hoss Jockeys

Never swap hosses with a deaken – not if yu belong tew the same church as he duz. If yu hav got a hoss that yu ask $200 for, and are offered $75 for

107

him, alwuz sell him: don't spile a good hoss trade for $125.

If you should, bi acksident, get hold ov a sound hoss, git shut of him as soon as you kan, for you won't be happy with him.

If in swopping hosses, you get cornered and kan't lie, postpone the trade until the next day.

Nobody expects tew buy a hoss without gitting cheated; therefore if a hoss jockey don't lie, he loses one ov his blessed privileges.-Josh Billings (13)

The *Reporter* carried an article in the November 14, 1872, issue reminding one and all just what could happen in an end-of-trail town. Newton, Kansas, posted one more Wild West moment before giving up the trail business to other towns. Justice of the Peace, George Halliday entered the Gold Room to partake of his morning dram. A tough by the name of Pat Fitzpatrick approached the Judge and asked that he set up a round of drinks. The Judge was evidently in no mood to do so and informed Fitzpatrick as to his thinking on the matter.

Taking offense, Fitzpatrick drew his pistol, fired and announced. "I've had it in for you anyway." Judge Halliday was killed instantly. Fitzpatrick stepped over the Judge's body and demanded a drink from the bartender. He then turned to the door and ambled his way into the street singing as though nothing out of the ordinary had just happened.

City Marshal Jack Johnston, who had only been on the city payroll for a couple of weeks heard the shot. The marshal grabbed a rifle and headed into the street. At the city well he laid the rifle down, waiting for Fitzpatrick as he brazenly walked along the street singing a song. When Fitzpatrick crossed the street opposite Marshal Johnston, the marshal called out, "Halt, stick 'em up!" and reached for his rifle. Fitzpatrick laughed as he pulled his six-gun. The marshal's rifle was quicker. There was only one shot. Pat Fitzpatrick reeled from a bullet in the forehead. Newton added another man to Boot Hill. The *Reporter* declared, "Great excitement prevailed. Farmers came into the town armed with rifles, and uniting with the better citizens of Newton, paraded the streets and closed all the saloons by force and virtually put the town under marshal law. This shows what may take place where saloons and dance houses are regarded as evidence of prosperity." (14)

The barbaric display of violence may have been appalling to Ellsworth *Reporter* editor, G. A. Atwood, who had not lived through Ellsworth's own violent inauguration, but Ellsworth's founders were well aware of what might take place. They had a competent police force in place and were ready to deal with the occasional violent outburst. As Atwood had so often pointed out, the city's main concern involved forging a stable economic future.

That future could well make Ellsworth a hub city if planners had their way. Rumors of new railroads filled the air all across Kansas in 1872. Ellsworth was giddy over the potential of the Memphis & Ellsworth Railroad, the King City & Ellsworth Railroad and the Ellsworth & Zarah Railroad, purported to be all coming to Ellsworth. Wild estimations of an Ellsworth with a population of ten thousand people in "… less than ten years, probably in five," were thrown about. Atwood used every prospect to urge Ellsworth leaders to work together for the common good of the community.

The sound of the hammer continued to echo across town as both the Catholic

THE FIRST COURTHOUSE
ELLSWORTH 1873

The location of the Ellsworth County Courthouse on the corner of South Main & Court Avenue ignited controversy that severely divided the community. An unknown artist sketched this interpretation of the building.
Courtesy Ellsworth County Historical Society.

Church and the Ellsworth County Court House were being roofed. The courthouse was already becoming the meeting place for citizens as the paper announced a railroad meeting at seven o'clock Saturday evening, December 7th. "We want to see every citizen of Ellsworth present, as all are alike interested in our railroad enterprise. Rev. Dr. Sternberg will be present and others from the country." Perhaps the prospect of railroads centering their businesses at Ellsworth could at last break the fierce division that had taken hold of the town.

The resources of Ellsworth County were put forth as fine examples for prosperity. Ellsworth County boasted an abundant supply of water from streams and free flowing springs. Coal could be found in a number of places and in response the Ellsworth Coal Company was formed. A water driven flouring mill was being contemplated for erection on the Smoky Hill River near town. Ellsworth was poised to leap forward into the future with eyes wide open.

Each new week brought news of fortunes looming on the horizon. Those fortunes could well be within the grasp of Ellsworth's citizens if only they could join together to overcome differences. With every turn of potential prosperity, division kept Ellsworth at odds with itself. It seemed as though a great specter from the town's violent past was holding Ellsworth in its grasp, imparting a spirit of conflict that could not be shaken.

Ghosts of the not too distant past haunted the town even as its leaders labored to throw off the chains of madness they had inherited from the days of '67. One of those madmen from Ellsworth's past made the papers.

"Curley Marshall, a desperado of considerable note, recently departed this life peacefully in his bed at his home in Wichita. He used to live in this city and killed at least one man here. Last summer he made Newton his headquarters. One day a stranger came into a saloon wearing a "stovepipe" hat. The wearing of such a hat was sufficient provocation for Curley Marshall to shoot him, which he did without hesitation.

Curley's reputation brought him even more notoriety than he deserved. He had been a government scout, and as many who had sprung from that profession, Curley lived fast and loose. He was famous for opening the First Chance-Last Chance Saloon at the Kansas State line on the Chisholm Trail. Indian Territory was dry as far as alcohol was concerned. Curley's place was the first place a cowboy could get a drink after days on the trail through "The Nations." Of course it figured that the very same saloon was the last place to legally quench the desire for stimulating spirits before crossing the line back into the territory.

The newspaper report of Marshall's shooting of the man in the "stovepipe hat" had mistaken Marshall for another man by the name of Mike McCarty. It was a drunken McCarty, not Marshall, that killed the merchant Doc Anderson when his aim for the "stovepipe hat" failed him.

Curley Marshall was actually away from his saloon at the time of the shooting, rounding up prostitutes to work in his dance hall. George Freeman recalled, "Marshal's extensive acquaintance with the class of people who were known to frequent the dance hall and visit the houses of prostitution, assured him that his business would be profitable in various ways. He also sold whiskey of the vilest kind to his patrons and friends."

Marshall's brand of frontier entrepreneurship turned out to be too excessive even for men who were used to living on the edge. The people of Caldwell found good reason to shun the First Chance-Last Chance Saloon. Feeling unwelcome, Curley Marshall sold the saloon, moved to Wichita and according to Freeman, "… died by disease brought on by his intemperate habits and life of debauchery." (15)

As 1872 drew to a close the town had many reasons to celebrate. In spite of its divisions, the business district was more prosperous than it had ever been. The Drovers Cottage stood prominently along the west end of South Main Street. The new courthouse had deeply divided the community, but Ellsworth could point with pride to the new building as an enduring symbol of self government. The Catholic Church was finished and Arthur Larkin was about to complete the Grand Central Hotel just in time for the Catholic Festival and Ball.

All day the Grand Central was alive with the noise of preparation. Extra hands were called into service. The new furniture, the new crockery, the new silverware were unpacked, the eight walnut extension tables were drawn out, the tapestry carpets were put down. The hall was decorated and the kitchen was the scene of important culinary operations. By noon people from the country began to come in. All the afternoon there was hurrying to and fro – men and women carrying frosted cakes and other kinds of cake to add to Mrs. Larkin's large supply. At 8 o'clock the Grand Central was full; and 10 o'clock it was crowded and if the snow did keep any away it was well for the comfort of all. This city turned out almost en masse, and the country had a large number of representatives present. Brookville did nobly; Lincoln county had some delegates present and would have had more if it had not been for the snow; Russell contributed to the number of Festivalers and we presume other counties.

Dancing commenced at about nine o'clock. Bradshaw, Parkhurst, Hank and Hagerman furnished excellent music. About ninety couples were present and all of course could not dance at once but as the ball lasted till the full orbed monarch of day presented himself through the east windows, all had as much exercise as they could desire. A little after 12 o'clock supper was announced. The tables could only accommodate a third of the company at once. The feast was a most bountiful one … The meats were good, the cakes were good, the sauce was good, everything was good and the new silver forks did good duty in carrying away the supper.

Following the grand feast participants were encouraged to cast a monetary "vote" for various categories such as "handsomest young lady". Prizes included a cane, set of silver spoons, gold bracelet, smoking cap, and a watch.

"After all this was over the dance was renewed. Those who could not dance enjoyed looking on. There were handsome ladies dressed elegantly and it was a pleasure to watch them go through the mazes of the dance, their light feet keeping time to Bradshaw's music."

The divided town may have resisted political unity. Farmers and stockmen could passionately disagree. North Main establishments quite possibly held jealousies over the vigorous business along South Main. But they could all agree on one thing. The Catholic Festival and Ball in the new Grand Central Hotel was a grand success and a most memorable night. (16)

Ellsworth closed out the year on a high note regarding the flourishing cattle trade. The Kansas Pacific stockyards shipped a total of forty thousand one hundred sixty-one head from Ellsworth during the 1872 season, compared to seventy thousand six hundred head for Wichita. Those numbers appeared to give Wichita the edge, but observations from the Kansas City cattle publication, *The Cattle Trails*, found only fifty-six thousand head of cattle on the range at Wichita, none at Great Bend, and one hundred thirty-five thousand head at Ellsworth.

The important difference between competing railheads was that a far greater percentage of cattle were used for stocking local ranges, and many more were driven to other destinations. As much as anything, the cattle towns were just a stop on the road north and Ellsworth had secured the major share of that business in 1872. (17)

Arthur Larkin's Grand Central Hotel at the corner of South Main and Lincoln Avenue.
The Ellsworth *Reporter* office is next door to the east.
Courtesy Ellsworth County Historical Society

Chapter Eight

THE LONGHORN METROPOLIS

Severe snow storms and frigidly cold weather persisted throughout the winter of 1872-1873. Monday evening, December 30, 1872, Maggie Weir was going from one room to another at Mollie Brennan's house, one of the dancehalls in the brothel district of Nauchville. Conditions were ripe for tragedy. The kerosene lamp that she carried suddenly exploded in her hands. The burning fluid abruptly flashed over her face, breast and arms. Although severely burned she had the presence of mind to run out into the snow and extinguish the flames. The house was soon engulfed in flames and deemed a total loss. Just as Lizzy Palmer had done before her, Mollie set about to rebuild and reopen. There was no time for sentiment on the Kansas frontier.

The winter was unusually cold. Storms blew in quickly and often caught people out in the open. Mr. Godfrey, "an intelligent young lawyer" was found near Great Bend so badly frozen that both his feet, his right arm and left hand were amputated. A Mrs. Cooper was found under a railroad bridge east of Ellsworth in serious condition. While attempting to cross the bridge she fell through and injured her spine. By the time she was found the unfortunate Mrs. Cooper had been lying unable to move for three hours. She was expected to survive.

Mr. Sanday and his two sons were in the process of building a dugout on "Oxhide" Creek, with plans to move to their new land in the spring. While attempting to return to Fort Harker during a storm he lost his way. In his wanderings he happened onto a neighbor's home but not before his hands and feet were frozen.

His oldest son, Charles, was not so fortunate. He had also left the safety of the dugout to return home but soon became lost in the storm. The wind and snow covered his path so that he could not retrace his steps. Seeking the only shelter available, Charles dug a hole in the snow and covered himself up.

The next day his mother went to look for him along the "Oxhide". She found him, "...near the new adobe creeping on his hands and knees endeavoring to make his way home."

The boy was taken to the home of Mr. Jewell where his father was also sick in bed. Speaking of young Charles Sanday, a friend of the family, Mr. T. Ferrell described, "His feet have turned black and are very much swollen, the skin has come off from his hands and wrists. His face was also frozen – He lies in a delerium...and it is thought he cannot live but a few days." The *Reporter* continued, "Mr. Ferrell has visited the family and he represents the suffering of the son as indescribable. We who slept safe and warm through the terrible night of January the 4th, can well afford to contribute something to help along the poor family." A postscript announced: "Later – Charles Sanday died at six o'clock Tuesday morning."

The storm that caught Mrs. Cooper and the Sandays was typical of Kansas blizzards. Monday, January 4th began with favorable weather.

> The forenoon was mild and the snow melted from the roof. About 2 p.m. it snowed in the peaceful New England style, the snow flakes being large and feathery. About 3 p.m. there was a sudden change. The wind blew furiously in every direction whirling the snow in clouds; one could not see across the street and several men who were in town who started home were forced to return being unable to proceed. The weather was fearful though the thermometer was not below zero.

The snow dominated news items in the January 9th, *Reporter*.

> There are some good sized snow banks in town. The railroad snow plows were kept busy Saturday and Sunday clearing the track. Between Ellsworth and Fort Harker a drift sixteen feet deep was shoved off the track by a "double header." ... Several teams have been stopped by snow-banks. Sleighing is tolerable but sleighs are few.
>
> The eastern bound passenger train Saturday was forced to halt over night at Fort Harker. It was Sunday noon before the snow-plows opened a passage for it.
>
> Saturday the western train was about two hours late; it was escorted by a snow plow and an extra engine. The train stopped opposite the Grand Central (Hotel) when the passengers ran through the pelting storm to hot coffee and a warm supper.

However treacherous the weather, Ellsworth's residents endured as though life were one continuous festival. On New Years Eve revelers serenaded those who had locked themselves away from the night.

> Oh! The deliciousness of being waked from slumber by the charm of a midnight serenade! The one we received New Year's night surpassed anything we were ever favored with before. We caught intimations of its approach afar. Long before the seventy-five musicians stepped lightly on the piazza we knew a serenade was coming. It was "Sweet Home," rendered in a variety of pitch, time and expression, with an accompaniment of mouth-organs, bones, whistling, some loud exclamations, running up and down stairs and the shuffling of feet. It appeared to us in our drowsy condition as if "Sweet Home" was out on a 'spree,' but that may have been all imagination. After singing, three cheers were given for the *Reporter* office for which compliment we will now make our bow. Our little girl

sleepily inquired if they wouldn't make their "froats sore." By appearance next day we concluded they must have been laid up with a sore throat.

The winter months were a time for merriment. Balls were grand social affairs that drew the community together. The Masonic Festival and Ball at Major Gore's Drovers Cottage was predicted to be "crowded to-night with the elite of the county ... Mrs. Gore will spread a feast to-night at the Cottage that will tempt the fair and gay to indulgence ... Two large halls will be used at the Cottage to-night by the dancers so that all can 'trip the light fantastic toe' together."

Grand Balls were a pleasant distraction, emphasizing proper society. Not to be outdone by their neighbors in Ellsworth, the soldiers of the 6th Cavalry at Fort Harker also held a grand ball. As reported in the Ellsworth *Reporter*, the evening was most memorable.

A ride on the Kansas Pacific of a few minutes brought us at the fort. Lt. Kingsbury conveyed us in an easy-going wagon to his comfortable quarters. His room looks more like a study than a soldiers' camp. Major Chaffee, commander of the post, called in and we were happy to meet him.

On arriving at the ballroom, we found members of the two companies well dressed, soldierly, gentlemanly young men, the hall handsomely decorated, everything in order and the three musicians with bows drawn ready for the grand march.

"There were a goodly number of ladies present and the large hall was occupied by the company until 1 o'clock when supper was announced. The supper was excellent and there was plenty. After one or two more dances the company separated. Lt. Kingsbury and Capt. Curlett bundled Bradshaws and our folks and sent us home in a coach and four. The evening was delightful and we with our escort of cavalry under command of George Seitz enjoyed the short ride.

Let the wind blow and the snow fly. Frontier fortitude would not let the weather dampen the revelry of wintertide festivities.

1873 marked the beginning of the end for the great buffalo herds that had once ruled the Kansas plains. In western Kansas hunters spread both north and south in ravenous plunder for hides. The *Reporter* announced, "It is estimated that the buffalo are being killed off at the rate of 1500 a day." (1)

Sadly, Maggie Weir who was severely burned in Mollie Brennan's house on December 30, 1872, took a turn for the worse. The paper reported that Miss Weir was supposed to be getting well, but she died suddenly Thursday night, January 16, 1873. She was said to be formerly of Bloomfield, Iowa. "One more unfortunate, weary of breath, rashly importunate has gone to her death. Her remains were interred in the cemetery north east of this city." (2)

The "sporting" crowd lived a fast life, for no one knew what tomorrow might bring. The dance halls outside of town were a tinderbox set to explode without

115

warning. In March of 1872, Taylor DuBoise jealously killed George Palmer while Palmer and his wife Lizzie were reconciling their marriage. Lizzie was the madam of The Nauch, Ellsworth's most notorious brothel. DuBoise fled Ellsworth but was apprehended by Sheriff Chauncey Whitney and eventually sent to the Salina jail for safe keeping. Tuesday, January 21, 1873, DuBoise escaped from the jail. He was never heard from again. (3)

Winter continued into spring. Early grass failed to materialize creating a hardship for cattlemen already on the trail north. But the weather didn't delay the buyers who by late March were enthusiastically arriving in Ellsworth. In addition cattle owners were arriving at the railheads in advance of their herds. Colonel Jacob J. Myers, "… the extensive stock dealer has bought the 'Powers' Ranche' for $25,000.00. He has a large herd of longhorns on the way." The firm of Armstrong and Burton reportedly established a ranch near Myers, seven miles east of Fort Harker on the north side of the Smoky Hill River.

However, the open range that had once served the Texans for summer cow camp was rapidly being settled. Farmers were settling beyond eastern Ellsworth County into areas west of Ellsworth. New settlers meant new calls from for a herd law. A confrontation was in the works.

Be that as it may, the great longhorn parade was already well advanced in a steady march from Texas to Kansas. Henry Beverly wrote from Texas to grocer I. W. Phelps that drovers who drove to Wichita last year, "will drive to Ellsworth this year." The great battle for the cattle trade was rekindled once again between Ellsworth and Wichita.

Wichita would not be happy with only a portion of the Texas cattle trade. City promoters began an aggressive campaign to secure even more drovers by printing up five thousand promotional circulars addressed to drovers in southern Texas. An agent was sent down the trail to personally solicit drovers during the months of April and May.

For its part, Ellsworth recognized that the old Park City Cutoff was still too close to Wichita. They hoped to alleviate that problem with a new trail proposed in the Kansas Pacific "Guide Map" referred to as Cox's Trail, William M. Cox was the general livestock agent for the K. P. Drovers were urged to take Cox's Trail to avoid trouble with settlers in Sumner, Sedgwick, and Reno Counties in Kansas.

Near Ellsworth tragedy struck Ellsworth County's well-known Faris family for the second time in two years.

> Last Friday (March 14, 1873), Mrs. Irwin Faris, while milking, was run over and so severely hurt that she lived but a short time. She was the widow of Irwin Faris, who died last summer. Mr. and Mrs. Faris were the first settlers of Ellsworth county, most worthy people, and the unfortunate circumstances that took Mr. Faris away last year, and Mrs. Faris last week, are deeply regretted by the whole county.

Irwin Faris and his brother Henry arrived in what would become Ellsworth County in 1860. They operated a ranch on Clear Creek, trading with travelers and Indians. Irwin died of hydrophobia, the result of a skunk bite while hunting buffalo June 5, 1872.

One week after the announcement of Mrs. Faris' death, another relative was in the news. "Mr. E. P. Faris while on his hunting expedition killed a white buffalo. He brought the hide home with him and exhibited it to several of our townsmen. He refused $20.00 for it." The rare occurrence of sighting a sacred white buffalo, let alone killing one, seemed to mark the passing of an era.

Only a few short years had passed since great herds of unlimited numbers of buffalo grazed over the land. Not even their bones were allowed to return to the earth that had nurtured them. "The country around Ellsworth is being cleared of bones. Goldsoll has shipped 15 carloads of buffalo relics this season." Goldsoll was Mayer Goldsoll, whose Old Reliable House served Ellsworth as a general mercantile business. His business was favored by drovers and farmers alike offering groceries, clothing, blankets, trunks, boots and shoes, hats and caps, jewelry and just about anything else that one's heart could desire. Bold letters in his weekly advertisement in the *Reporter* also announced "CASH PAID FOR HIDES, FURS & PELTS." Buffalo bones were not excluded from his trade and by May 1st he had shipped a total of two hundred fifty tons.

Bones were being collected from the western prairie as fast as they could be collected. Ten car loads of bones passed through Ellsworth on railcars in mid-April. The *Reporter* providently asked, "Where is the flesh that covered the bones? And Plato would ask, where are the souls of the buffaloes and cattle that once roamed over the prairies." (4)

The new cattle trail to Ellsworth was heavily promoted. Knowing that cattlemen were already arriving ahead of their herds, the *Reporter* featured the Kansas Pacific Railway's table of distances from a guide map that was being circulated to drovers. The table listed campsites along "The Great Texas Cattle Trail" from the Red River on the north Texas border to Ellsworth. A well-known location on the old Chisholm Trail was selected as the turn-off for the new trail. "Trail leaves the old trail at Huffaker's and Sewell's store on Pond Creek- N.W. toward head of Bluff Creek then North to Raymond. Experienced Guide on the trail."

The new route passed such locations as the Ninnescah River, Salt Creek and Rattlesnake Creek. Raymond had been the ford for the Arkansas River in 1872. "The company will provide a boat at this point for the accommodation of drovers. Good camping grounds south side of the river. Best ford on the river." However, by 1873 so many setters were established along the Arkansas River at Raymond that the crossing had to be closed. The trail was shifted west to Ellinwood where an excellent crossing over the Arkansas River could be utilized. From Ellinwood the trail crossed Cow Creek and Plum Creek before arriving at Ellsworth, three hundred fifty miles north of the Red River. Other shipping facilities available to drovers were located at Brookville, Bosland (Wilson), Bunker Hill, Russell and Ellis.

Col. Robert D. Hunter, superintendent of the K. P. stockyards confidently informed the *Reporter* that he would be dealing in stock through a commission firm he had gained an interest in, that of Hunter, Pattison and Evans. The commission house was not only established at Ellsworth but Chicago, St. Louis, and Kansas City.

William Cox, Titus Buckbee, and Hunter's brother were making arrangements to travel south on the new trail to meet herds on their way to Kansas. Buckbee was one of "the boys" that stampeded the buffalo through Ellsworth in 1868. The paper proudly spoke of Ellsworth's Titus Buckbee, "… known of all men as one of the best boys in all the West … He is a good man for the place and will do good for Ellsworth … Ellsworth will stand by you Titus."

As cattle herds began to arrive on the Kansas plains the Ellsworth *Reporter* announced that, "L.B. Harris of San Antonio opened the new trail to Ellis - The L. B. Harris Trail." Two weeks later on May 1st, the paper reported that Harris was holding five thousand head of cattle near Ellsworth while other reports mentioned him at Wichita. (5)

A correspondent calling himself, "Occasional" predicted Ellsworth to be the headquarters of the 1873 cattle season. Citing "letters received almost daily from Texas," "Occasional" boldly predicted "150,000 to 200,000 (longhorns) to come here the present season." His listing of drovers on the trail to Ellsworth was a virtual Who's Who of the trail driving industry, including J. D. Reed, L. B. Harris, J. J. Myers, Dillard Fant, Doc Burnett, Choate & Bennett, Bill Butler, J. L. Driskill, Mark Withers, and a host of others.

Captain Eugene Bartlett Millett followed the cattle trade wherever cattle were needed. He sold thousands of head to Indian agencies in the Dakotas. When miners in Nevada and Idaho needed beef he fattened them in the mountain valleys and drove them to the mining towns. Millett and Major Seth Mabry partnered for years on the trail making the name Millett & Mabry one of legend on the cattle trail.
Courtesy Ellsworth County Historical Society.

It was only the first of May and twenty-eight herds of cattle, ranging from two to ten thousand each, were reported on their way to Ellsworth. The largest herd of ten thousand was owned by W. S. Perryman & Co., while Allen and Bennett drove eight thousand, J. J. Meyers was on the road with six thousand and Millett and Mabry partnered for another six thousand longhorns. Captain Eugene Millett arrived by way of the new trail which he liked, "first rate." 1873 was proving to be one of the largest cattle drives to date.

Captain Millett's approval was significant. From the early drives to the hostile Missouri border to Idaho and the Dakotas Millett was a veteran of the trail. He and his brothers, in partnership with various leading cattlemen annually drove several herds to northern destinations. The Millett operation was known as a "tough outfit," able to shoot its way through a dangerous situation if need be. As the Captain of the outfit Millett knew men, cattle, horses and trails as well as any man in the business.

Besides treating the founders of the American cattle industry on the streets of Ellsworth the President of the United States Ulysses S. Grant could be glimpsed as he passed through town in his presidential railcar. From the platform the President, "... lifted his hat and bowed his acknowledgements in answer to the hearty cheers that were given him."

The same issue of the *Reporter* brought news of the death of one of Ellsworth County's pioneers. Presidents may receive accolades from far and wide but the author of Robert Campbell's "In Memoriam" knew the true worth of a man.

The number of good men who pass away, whose virtues were only known to the little neighborhood in which they lived is greater far, than those whose virtues are "Trumpet tongued" to the world, and over whose graves are raised polished marble, and the chiseled record of their fame. To the former class notably belonged Robert D. Campbell, of Thompson Creek. One of the pioneers of the county, enduring with patience, all the evils imposed by a frontier life, persistently maintaining his position amid all the difficulties which beset the settler in this portion of the State in 1867-68, he lived to partially realize the consummation of his ideas in relation to Ellsworth county, and went down to the grave full of years and honor. Men with such a determination of purpose in settling a new country, when they die, deserve something more than a passing notice, for it is to the emulation of such we owe all that our country is today. If they upon the first appearance of difficulties had left the state in her early and troublous times, where would now have been our boasted progress? Truly the character of our pioneers inspired the motto upon our state banner, "Ad Astra Per Aspera." Mr. Campbell was essentially a pioneer through all his life, following the verge of civilization from his own door in Pennsylvania where he was born in 1795, through Ohio, Indiana, Iowa and Missouri, to Kansas where we find him in 1866. He was a peaceful neighbor, whose counsels were sought, and advice followed, a kind father, and charitable to all. He died in the seventy-ninth year of his age., on the Septennial anniversary - to the hour – of his arrival on the creek, and with deep regret we have laid him on the quiet hillside in sight of his former home." MEMENTO MORI (6)

119

The signature was meant to remind the reader of his own mortality. "Remember you are mortal" is a sobering adage for all who breathe the breath of life, be they of humble roots or of towering heritage. Memento Mori was right about Ellsworth County's beginnings. Indeed it was men like Robert Campbell that made the development of Ellsworth possible, allowing others to find a future in a land that had been primitive only a few short years before.

David W. Powers was a pioneer in his own right, yet prospered from the combined efforts of the early settlers. Powers brought a new banking concern, The Bank of Leavenworth to Ellsworth in early May. A portion of the Nunamaker Jewelry store was rented for the innovative bank. Originally established at Salina, Kansas, in 1870, the bank specialized in livestock loans, dealing heavily in the Texas cattle trade.

Having experienced the devaluation of Confederate paper money, Texans were naturally leery of any form of transaction that involved paper. But as the cattle trade matured, money transfer became more complicated. Because the Powers family understood cattle from David's extensive experience in both the freighting and ranching business they soon earned the trust of the cattlemen and profited from an honest understanding of both men and cattle. Besides David W., the principle owners of the bank included James W. and David B. Their move to Ellsworth established the Powers bank as the first banking institution in Ellsworth. The elder David listed his home as Leavenworth, Kansas. James W. was in charge of the bank in Ellsworth.

Businesses tended to come and go throughout Ellsworth's early years. However as 1873 unfolded the town evolved into a stable commercial center. A snapshot of the business district at the beginning of the summer season found three blocks of lively business houses on the south side of the Kansas Pacific Railway and two blocks of business on the north. The stock yards were just at the west end of North Main, commencing at the corner of I Street (North Colorado Street).

One block east on the west corner of H Street (South St. Louis Avenue) and across the tracks from the stockyards, Drovers Cottage stood as though overseeing both the cattle business at the stockyards and the spirited businesses of downtown Ellsworth. Drovers Cottage proudly displayed the American flag flying above its famous edifice of eighty-four rooms with a laundry and livery attached. The Star Clothing House of R. Jacks and Co. displayed a "Big Star" across the street east of the hotel. Beyond that was D. L. Beach's Blacksmith and Wagon Shop and John Mueller's Boot Shop. Mueller established his boot shop in the old Biart Drug Store, with the sign of the "Big Red Boot" on the front of the store.

Jacob's Drovers Store and Reuben & Sheek's Clothing Store were next along the street. Nathan Schloss of Leavenworth occupied a portion of Reuben & Sheek's with cigars and tobacco. Next door was Nunamaker's Jewelry Store, also the home of the Powers' Bank.

Clothing merchant Joseph Ringolsky of Leavenworth returned each cattle season to operate Drovers Headquarters just east of Nunamakers. Perry Hodgden, an entrenched Ellsworth man was next door operating a general store. East of Hodgden, Ira Phelps provided a complete line of groceries for camp and home.

David Powers, Leavenworth, Kansas, found the freighting business profitable enough to open a banking concern. D.W. Powers and Company provided much needed credit to Texas cattleman during the 1870's.
Illustrated by Professor Henry Worrall - Historic Sketches of the Cattle Trade by Joseph McCoy.

Historic Sketches of the Cattle Trade by Joseph McCoy.

D. W. POWERS & CO.,

BANKERS,

Ellsworth, Kansas.

Transact a General Banking Business.

Particular attention given to the accommodation of Merchants, Stock Dealers and the Texas Cattle Trade.

Collections from

Banks, Bankers & Merchants

RECEIVE OUR ESPECIAL ATTENTION, AND REMITTED FOR PROMPTLY ON DAY OF PAYMENT, AT CURRENT RATES OF EXCHANGE.

Refer to our Correspondents:

DONNELL, LAWSON & Co., Bankers, No. 4 Wall Street, New York City
ALLEN, HOFFMAN & Co., Bankers, St. Louis, Mo.
UNION NATIONAL BANK, Chicago, Ills.
FIRST NATIONAL BANK, Leavenworth, Kansas.
FIRST NATIONAL BANK, Kansas City, Mo.
MASTIN BANK, Kansas City, Mo.

South Main Street looking east from the Stockyards. The open plaza was originally reserved as railroad property with North Main Street built very close to the tracks.
Courtesy Ellsworth County Historical Society.

Popular South Main businesses - Mueller's boot shop was known for the sign of the "Big Red Boot." Jacob's "Drovers Store" is next door. Ruben & Sheek's general merchandise can be seen on the far left.
Courtesy Ellsworth County Historical Society.

All of the previous buildings were frame structures in the tradition of the false fronted stores seen in most frontier towns. But the next two businesses along South Main Street were established in an attractive brick building at the corner of F Street (South Douglas Avenue). Bell's Great Western Hardware Emporium occupied the main floor while Minnick and Hounson's Drug Store could be found on the second floor. Dr. E. G. Minnick also kept an office for his medical practice at the drug store.

Various businesses were found along F Street (South Douglas Avenue) leading south to the river. The old Marshall House, famous from Ellsworth's most notorious days was just south of the Bell's hardware. Lou Boyd and Annie Roaker operated a millinery shop near the Marshal House. Across the street "Judge" James Miller kept an office as an agent for the sale of Kansas Pacific lands and properties held by the National Land Company. Sanderson and White's Livery was located south of Miller's office at the end of F Street next to the Smoky Hill River.

Continuing east of Bell's hardware, along South Main Street, on the corner of F Street and South Main Street, was Jake New's Ellsworth Billiard Hall. The American House Hotel operated by John Kelly was next. Mayor Goldsoll's popular general store, "The Old Reliable House" was next. Goldsoll operated out of St. Louis while making Ellsworth his home during the cattle season.

Nick Lentz, who hailed from Wuertenburg, Germany, operated a unique business which offered herbal baths in the bath rooms at the back of the saloon. Valentine Hank conveniently located his barber shop next to Lentz' bath house. Hank was described as a "fashionable barber" with two first class barbers from Chicago in his employ. Hank was also a musician; one of several instrumentalists who provided music for the dances held about town. (7)

Beebe's Hardware provided groceries and provisions in the next building east of the barber shop. Next door was a saloon operated by Irishman Joseph Brennan. Brennan's saloon was a favorite of the professional gamblers and was also known by the nickname, "Gambler's Roost." Brennan's wife was 'Mary', not the notorious 'Mollie' Brennan who operated a brothel in Nauchville.

Across an empty lot stood Thomas Dowd's Delmonico Restaurant and Saloon. Most businesses in Ellsworth sold alcoholic refreshment of some kind, whether they called themselves a grocery, a drug store or a restaurant. Cramer & Wilson's Meat Market was on the corner of E Street. Across the street and in the middle of the block was Whitney and Kendall's Furniture and Undertaking store and next to them on the corner of D Street was August Bayers' Blacksmith and Wheelwright shop.

Nauchville was just a short block south of Bayers' place, just outside the city limits. Lizzie Palmer and Mollie Brennan both ran dance houses along a single street designated Bayers Street. A complete tally of businesses operating in Nauchville, sometimes referred to as "The Bottoms" is unknown. The Ellsworth Theatre became one of its most popular attractions for music, dancing and stage performances as well as sensual amusement. Nauchville even boasted a race track with a steady run of the horses which also provided for a vigorous exchange of wealth.

123

The *Reporter* felt compelled to offer a bit of advice to stockmen arriving in Ellsworth, "… you will find places of amusement and places of abusement." The season was only beginning.

North Main had its own compliment of frontier business houses commencing with the Ellsworth County Court House on the corner of D Street (Court Avenue). The Ellsworth *Reporter* was just west of the court house with Arthur Larkin's brand new red brick Grand Central Hotel on the corner of North Main and E Street (Lincoln Avenue). The hotel was erected at a cost of twenty-seven thousand dollars. The manganese limestone sidewalk in front of the Grand Central cost four hundred dollars, making it the finest walk west of Kansas City. Z. Jackson's general mercantile was just to the west and across the street from the Grand Central. Jackson was also the postmaster. Stage coaches from the U. S. Express Company arrived regularly.

West of Jackson's the business houses continued with Davis and Son's Restaurant and Ice Cream Saloon. "Albert Prime makes it good!" Arthur Larkin's general mercantile was next. The Ellsworth City Council held its sessions above Larkin's where attorney Ira E. Lloyd also kept an office.

The Redman & Sutton Meat Market was next, followed by Albert Beede's old saloon, which only recently had become the Empire Saloon operated by Hopkins and Company.

J. C. Veatch operated the popular City Hotel. Veatch posted a grand sign at the top of his hotel, "Welcome Texas". Three saloons could be found west of the City Hotel. Hopkins & Cook's saloon, the U. S. House, formerly operated by Rowdy Joe Lowe, and Leo Hertzig's saloon were sure to attract a steady crowd of customers. In fact there were so many saloons in Ellsworth that the *Reporter* was prompted to testify, "Whiskey is an antidote against snake bites. With eight saloons in town there is no danger to be feared from snakes by our people." Ellsworth City Attorney, Harry L. Pestana could be found upstairs at the U. S. House. He later moved his office to a room above Larkin's, where the other city offices were located.

Andrew Schmidt's shoe and boot shop was next. George Seitz's "Phoenix" Drug Store, "the oldest drug store in western Kansas" was on the corner of North Main and F Street (North Douglas Avenue). Doctor William Masterson Duck, Ellsworth County Coroner, kept an office above Seitz Drug.

Ferrell & Stebbins, carpenters and contractors kept a shop across the street to the west. David Nagle had previously operated the City Livery. John Kelly purchased the livery to provide a full service to his customers at the American House Hotel. A few unidentified businesses filled the lots west, leading back to the Kansas Pacific stock yards at the corner of North Main Street & I Street.

Reporter editor G. A. Atwood was interested in advancing Ellsworth to a first class city.

> The other morning we took a walk up the hill north of Ellsworth. Our city looks well from there, but it is too contracted. It does not make the show by half, that it would if our people lived as others do, have dwellings separate from their business houses. Most of our business men live over their stores or in the rear of their shops, and Ellsworth is larger than it looks to the casual observer. This contraction will be remedied in time." (8)

The Plaza viewed from the east. The Grand Central Hotel is on the far right.
Drovers Cottage can be seen in the distance left of the depot. R. Renecke Photograph.
Courtesy Ellsworth County Historical Society.

The Kansas Pacific Stock Yards in 1873. Minimal building had been accomplised north of
the Plaza. The new schoolhouse can be seen in the center of the picture.
R. Renecke Photograph.
Courtesy Ellsworth County Historical Society.

Events began heating up by mid-May. The *Reporter* carried a story of a disturbance between a Mr. Taylor and a Mr. Edwards. It seems, "Taylor attempted to pay off a grudge he owed Edwards with a revolver. The ball went through Edwards' leg without injuring it much. Taylor swam across the river and escaped. A Cheap Ridance."

The Smoky Hill River Bridge that had brought so much pride to the community in October of 1872 suddenly became an embarrassment. Fastened to each end of the bridge was a sign. "THIS BRIDGE IS UNSAFE FOR HEAVY LOADS." A letter in the Ellsworth *Reporter* expected answers.

> ... Who is responsible for the state of things? Either the King Bridge Company, the township offices or County Commissioners. Who rises to explain? Don't all speak at once, gentlemen! The first large drove of cattle driven over it from appearances would precipitate the entire structure into the river! This is not what the tax payers bargained for. Light is wanted on this most extraordinary transaction and must be forthcoming soon and thus save an unpleasantness.

No explanation was offered. (9)

The King Iron Bridge & Manufacturing Company of Cleveland, Ohio, was founded in 1858 by Zenas King. The company was among the first to move bridge building beyond a local craft to a national industry. Instead of using local materials the company manufactured the iron components and shipped them to the building site. King organized a network of sales representatives, known as "pitch men" to sell the product out of offices in New York, Boston, Philadelphia, Iowa, Missouri and Texas. The pitch men often underbid local bridge builders to get the jobs. In Ellsworth's case the King Bridge Company did not construct the bridge to meet the requirements necessary for the commercial traffic of heavy freight and cattle.

The quick solution to the problem was a new ford on the river just east of the bridge. The ford matched up with E Street (Lincoln Ave). Cattle formerly driven down F Street (Douglas Avenue) were diverted one block east.

The political conflicts of 1872 softened somewhat over the winter. Perhaps the pleasant social atmosphere of almost weekly festivals and balls brought rivals to an understanding that they must put the whole of Ellsworth first if they were all to prosper. The courthouse no longer seemed to be a stumbling block. Civic leaders even found a way to utilize the abandoned courthouse square for the benefit of the community. A new brick school house was to be built on the square at a cost of nine thousand dollars. The proposed building was described as two stories high, thirty-four and one half feet by forty-five feet. The design, "drawn up by one of the best architects in Leavenworth," included four large school rooms with closets and a teacher's room. Ellsworth was slowly developing a polite social society in spite of itself.

A certain amount of frontier temperament could still be found on the streets and in the businesses of Ellsworth. Some of that temperament naturally spilled over from other towns like Hays City, where frontier justice was still the standard rule of behavior. To say that frontier justice was often imprecise would be an understatement. The story of George McClellan is a case in point.

McClellan's steady paramour Nettie Baldwin was often at the very "heart" of trouble in both Ellsworth and Hays City. Nettie had survived an Ellsworth shooting in January of 1870 in which she was shot in the stomach and breast. She worked for Lizzie Palmer at the time and in the 1870 census identified her occupation with the provocative description, "Squirms in the dark." In a fight allegedly over Nettie, George McClellan killed Jack Wright at Hays City in 1872. George was arrested and tied to a post in the basement of the Ellis County Courthouse along with horse thief Pony Donovan. When vigilantes appeared at the lower windows of the courthouse the quiet assassins may have been looking to kill McClellan, but when the dust settled from a barrage of bullets, Pony Donovan lay dead while McClellan survived.

McClellan was moved to the guardhouse at Fort Hays for safe keeping and eventually was sent to the Saline County Jail. Because of a change of venue the case was brought before the Ellsworth County district court on May 1, 1873. By that time McClellan posted bail, but he failed to appear. One would think that a warrant for his arrest would have been issued. Perhaps it was, but the Ellsworth *Reporter* heralded the former fugitive in its May 29th issue. "McClellan who was reported killed last winter is going into business in our city." The business was a bit of an upscale brothel with theatrical performances known as The Ellsworth Theatre.

Apparently, after posting bail McClellan was allowed to wander as he pleased. On June 5th the *Reporter* noted that McClellan raced a horse against a man by the name of Gentry for a one hundred dollar purse in Brookville. Gentry's horse won. McClellan and a man by the name of Freeman were touted as leading citizens of Ellsworth as they prepared to open the Ellsworth Theatre. The June 12th issue of the *Reporter* announced, "Ellsworth has a theatre. How is that for the 'Longhorn Metropolis'?"

At the height of the cattle trade, Ellsworth County became one great pasture for Texas cattle. An estimated 170,000 Texas longhorns grazed over the Smoky Hills in 1873. Illustrated by Professor Henry Worrall - Historic Sketches of the Cattle Trade by Joseph McCoy.

The Longhorn Metropolis certainly was earning its name. The May 29th edition of the Ellsworth *Reporter* reported that one hundred thousand longhorns had arrived on the Ellsworth range; on June 5th the number was placed at one hundred twenty-five thousand; and a week later it was increased to one hundred forty-three thousand five hundred. By July 10th the *Reporter* documented over one hundred seventy thousand head grazing the surrounding prairie.

Ellsworth was reveling in its success to draw the drover to town in great numbers. In anticipation of trouble, the Ellsworth City Council beefed up the city police force. Marshal John W. "Brocky Jack" Norton boasted four deputies early in June. The men included John "Happy Jack" Morco, John S. "High Low Jack" Branham, and John "Long Jack" DeLong. Although not a "Jack", Ed Hogue completed the "hand". The *Reporter* referred to him as "Short Jack" but since his name wasn't John or Jack the cowboys had another name. The police force dealt a strong hand on the streets and with obvious reference to sporting cards, the set of officers were comically known as "Four Jacks and a Joker".

A few Texans figured to give the Jacks some trouble the night of June 10th. A young tough by the name of Billy Thompson and a couple of friends were lubricating themselves freely and making a public spectacle of their intoxication. Expecting trouble, Marshal Norton made his way to the brothel district outside of Ellsworth known as Nauchville. There he, "occupied quarters in the dance hall where a dance was in progress. The Texans tried to gain admittance but were kept out by the marshal." The carousing Texans turned away from the dance hall and walked down the street, shooting at wooden clocks, signs and just about anything that would make a target. Marshal Norton and his deputies chose to let the boys blow off a little steam for the rest of the night.

The *Reporter* was quick to demand action.

> It sounded very much like the 4th of July yesterday morning. Firing shots at sign boards had better be suspended. The authorities should enforce the ordinance prohibiting any shooting in the city limits. In order to have good government it is necessary to commence right.

As *Reporter* editor Atwood was penning his advice to "authorities", Norton was in the process of arresting Billy Thompson in his bed at the Grand Central. Deputy Hogue found the other two men, S. A. Fine and J. W. Ford in a similar hung-over condition, arrested them and brought them before Police Judge Vincent Osborne. Fine was charged five dollars and paid up. Ford was fined fifteen dollars and also paid. Billy Thompson was singled out as the ringleader and fined thirty dollars. He refused to pay and was jailed. Thompson was held a week until he finally paid his fine and was released June 18, 1873. (10)

The new cattle trail to Ellsworth was well received by drovers, which was undoubtedly distasteful to Wichita promoters. An attack by Osage Indians on drovers along the trail did not go unnoticed by the Wichita paper. The editor "unselfishly" shared the article with as many papers as possible. The *Reporter* filed its own response.

128

In several daily papers we have read a sensational dispatch sent from Wichita giving an account of "Indian outrages" … "on the new Ellsworth trail." – The telegram states that a party of fifteen Osages attacked Messrs Chambers, Earl, and Trailor, while watering their horses at a branch in a ravine. Mr. Chambers was killed and scalped and the other gentlemen barely escaped with their lives. Earl turned and killed one of the savages. The Indians did not rob the body of Mr. Chambers as his watch and purse were found upon him. The Indians were pursued but escaped … These disturbances occurred on the new Ellsworth trail, and will cause cattle to be driven to this point.

We are informed by Mr. Perkins who was present at the time of the above occurrence, and who assisted in the burial of Mr. Chambers that the event happened just twenty miles from Wichita, the nearest point in which cattle can be driven to that town. And furthermore that the murder was committed out of a personal spite to Mr. Chambers which is proved by the fact that he was not robbed, that the cattle were not stampeded, and that no other outrages were committed. It would appear as if Wichita had formed an alliance with the Osages to work against Ellsworth, but of course that city will not resort to such an extremity! There is no danger from Indians on the new Ellsworth trail and Texans are driving over it with thousands of cattle every day for Ellsworth, but the Indians, the mosquitoes, and other savages are stampeding all the cattle from Wichita.

Champ Traylor (correct family spelling) was driving cattle for his father Josiah. According to Champ the cattle had stampeded the night before. "… The next morning all hands were out trying to round up the herd." Champ and Chambers rode past some Indians who began shooting at them. Chambers was killed. Champ always loved fast horses and he was riding one at the time. He outran the Indians but later said that when the Indians were shooting at him the horse seemed to run the slowest. As soon as the cowboys got together they rode back to the scene of the attack. They found Chambers dead and scalped where he had fallen from his horse.

The Western Stock *Journal* of Pleasanton, Texas, noted the "considerable rivalry" between Wichita and Ellsworth.

An agent has been sent from Wichita to meet the advance herd of the grand cattle army that are moving in solid phalanx in that direction, with instructions to use every effort to induce Drovers to take their herds to Wichita, and ship from that point. – While at the same time agents of the K. P. R. W. have established camps at salt fork of the Arkansas, on Pond Creek, and are working like tigers for their company. It is said that every available object on the route is covered with posters, setting forth the advantages of Ellsworth as a shipping point … Judging from the great number of cattle that are now on the road for those points, it would seem that both places would soon be jammed and crammed to their hearts content. (11)

The office of Ellsworth city mayor was unexpectedly vacated by William H. Brinkman at a most crucial time, requiring a special election on June 21st. Judge James Miller received ninety-four votes over Major James W. Gore's eighty-six votes. The Topeka *Commonwealth* declared, "One of the old fort men is the present Mayor" of Ellsworth. Mayor Miller met with the city council for the first time addressing them "… on the necessity of preserving good order." According to Robert Dykstra, author of *The Cattle Towns*, many businessmen, especially saloon owners thought the city lawmen were too heavy handed in their enthusiastic efforts to preserve order. (12)

Business at the end of the trail depended heavily upon contented customers. Most of those customers found contentment in the distractions provided by sporting crowd. Fast women, fast horses, good beer, fine wine, theatrical performances, billiards, dice and cards kept the money flowing.

One of the most popular games was Spanish monte. Monte had its origins in the Mexican American War. The game was played with a deck of forty cards, discarding the tens, nines, and eights. A card was drawn from the bottom of the deck and another from the top. The bet was made on the next card turned up from the bottom of the deck. If that card matched the suit (heart, spade, diamond or club) of one of the two cards originally played, the dealer (known as the banker) paid all bets. If the card did not match; the banker took all bets. Sometimes called "Monte Bank," Spanish Monte inspired great emotion. Monte was a popular game with the Texans and could be found in all the end of trail gambling halls. The game even drew the attention of the Ellsworth *Reporter*.

> In the gambling halls … you see groups around the tables betting on their favorite game "monte" with a recklessness that would astonish the old eastern fogies. 'Tis said that the presence of gamblers is an indication of prosperity in a Western town. If such is the case, this place must be very prosperous. Nearly every saloon is a gambling house and runs from two to ten tables, where any kind of a game can be had.

Excitement reigned on the streets of Ellsworth. The *Reporter* announced, "Horse racing every night!" The courthouse was the center of attention as the town prepared to celebrate the 4th of July with a grand ball in the new county house, even though it was not yet completed. Ellsworth's favorite string band made up of W. S. Bradshaw, Valentine Hank, Dr. Fox and George Parkhurst were slated to provide the music. The Ellsworth County Courthouse also housed the county jail. The *Reporter* wryly observed, "The most comfortable place in town is the new jail. It is now ready for use. Too many should not crowd in it at once."

That didn't stop a man by the name of Fletcher from placing himself squarely on the wrong side of the law. He reportedly took a gun from another of Ellsworth's carousers, which attracted the attention of an unnamed police officer. Fletcher was ordered to relinquish the gun but refused. Not to be denied, the officer shot Fletcher in the thigh, gaining possession of both the gun and Mr. Fletcher.

A correspondent for the Leavenworth *Commercial* commented, "The Ellsworth police are considerate for the lives of people. If a man is troublesome they only put a ball through a leg or arm. This has a tendency to quiet him, and saves the city the burden of funeral expenses."

The celebration continued day and night. Nauchville was outside the jurisdiction of city police officers, but that did not leave it without law enforcement. "Sheriff Whitney is keeping order at the Theatre. No danger of any disturbance there."

A correspondent from the Kansas City *Cattle Trail* offered up a glowing assessment of facilities at Ellsworth.

> We arrived in Ellsworth at 3 p.m. Put up at the Drovers Cottage; were refreshed spiritually and otherwise by Mr. Gore. After supper Mr. R. D. Hunter accompanied us to the Stock Yards of which we made a thorough inspection. They were arranged under the management of Mr. Hunter. There are seven chutes and one in course of construction. Each chute has double accessory pens, can hold two car loads of cattle for separate cars at one time, the dividing pens in centre with lane running clear around them by a nice arrangement, these massive gates either open or shut, and are never out of use.
>
> A pleasant evening followed by a bright morning with a southerly wind and cloudless sky which was proclaimed as a hunting morning, the boys were up and away while the sun (in) the east was adorning. At five a meeting was called in the barroom of the Drovers Cottage by the people to exchange opinions on the great topic of the day, and also to return our thanks to Mr. Cox, Maj. Gore, Col. R. D. Hunter, and the citizens of Ellsworth. Maj. Gore considering our demonstration hostile, opened a bombardment on the boys with champagne corks, but finally was compelled to succumb to superiority of numbers although he held the position and fought right manfully, for some time. – The homeward train shortened our toast to an "Ostrich." Ellsworth would not even allow us to pay our wash woman. May that ocean of prairie food be nutritious forever, and Ellsworth the shipping centre. (13)

It is hard to imagine the level of activity on the streets of Ellsworth in July of 1873. Cowboys filled the streets, tourists tumbled off of passenger cars, and gamblers eyed pilgrims with greedy confidence. The Ellsworth Theatre established itself as the pinnacle of entertainment with the sensational appearance of Miss Kitty Leroy. The *Reporter* could hardly contain its adoration. "Her dancing is excellent and her appearance without fault. Indeed, she is an actress who would be encored at the Boston Theatre."

Ellsworth was riding on a crest of exhilaration that it had never known. A correspondent from the Kansas City *Journal* enthusiastically anointed Ellsworth as the seat of a cattle market that "surpasses the world." The *Reporter* boasted, "We have it from reliable authority that Ellsworth presents a busier aspect than her big sister, Wichita. Ellsworth takes the lead this year in the cattle trade."

"Nobody killed yet," the *Reporter* announced at the top of its July 3, 1873, LOCAL NEWS column. But with so much celebration, trouble was bound to boil over.

131

Robert D. Hunter, a veteran of the cattle trail switched to managing the stockyards at Ellsworth in 1872. That experience led him to invest in the commission business. Hunter & Evans became one of the largest commission houses of the time. Illustrated by Professor Henry Worrall - Historic Sketches of the Cattle Trade by Joseph McCoy.

Saturday night, July 5, 1873, the cauldron erupted. The cause for the trouble may have been a fight. The *Reporter* only calls it "a little disturbance." What ever lit the fuse resulted in an amazing display of courage.

> Sooner than you can imagine about a thousand men came forth to see "what was the matter." We can compare this human swarm with a hive of bees. Get up a little disturbance about the hive and how quick the noted workers rush forth, armed and loaded for battle. But there is rarely any one hurt in our crowds. Law is master, and an officer in the discharge of his duty is not molested by the thousand lookers-on."

Nevertheless, the *Reporter* felt compelled to add to those comments in another column of the paper. "We never shall forget the display of bravery in the discharge of his duty that Ed Hogue performed last Saturday in making an arrest.

One more note could be found within the pages of the July 10, 1873 paper. "We always feel like commending our present police force. They are each and all worthy of their stars, and some of them have earned golden ones in other and bloodier fields. Where all are worthy, it would be partiality to individualize."

All seemed to be moving in Ellsworth's favor. Even the unfortunate miscalculation of size for the Ellsworth County Courthouse was dealt with in an uncharacteristic laissez faire attitude. When it was found that the building was too small to accommodate all of the offices for county government, the space allotted for the jail was turned into an office. Plans for a new building built to specifically to house the sheriff and his "guests" were begun without hesitation.

> The room in the new court house that was designed for a jail is now occupied by the Treasurer and it makes a very suitable room for his office. We always did think it a poor plan to build a jail and court house under one roof. Now that the court house is occupied it is easy to see the foolishness of using one of the six rooms on the first floor for a jail ... After all the controversy, and recrimination on this building it gives an air of permanency to this city, and reflects advantageously upon the stability of the county, and will fully meet all the requirements demanded, until the further development of Ellsworth county calls for a more extensive building which we hope is not in a very remote future. The court house is the coolest place in the city, and our officers have pulled off their coats in good earnest to bring up the records to a standard which the times require ... (14)

But just what did the standard for the times require of Ellsworth? From its original germination through the seedling's early life, Ellsworth had found itself baptized in blood. "Nobody killed yet," the *Reporter* proclaimed; as if to say our "trial by blood" is yet to be fulfilled. Whether intended or not, the enigmatic forecast was about to unfold.

Chapter Nine

BLOODY SEASON

The cattle season of 1873 was wildly exciting for anyone associated with Ellsworth. Thousands of strangers walked the streets and frequented the businesses. Without fail, the celebration prevailed well into the summer.

Reminisces of old drovers can be found in *The Trail Drivers of Texas*, a collection of letters compiled by the Old Time Trail Drivers Association in San Antonio, Texas. To hear them tell it, nothing of note ever happened at the end of the trail.

Dick Withers told of stampedes and swimming rivers on the trail. But like most cowboys, when he spoke of arriving in Ellsworth, Kansas, in 1873, all he said was, "After crossing the Arkansas at Great Bend I pulled on to Ellsworth, where I found brother Mark with the front herd, and we delivered our cattle, sent our horses back to Texas and returned home by rail."

E. A. "Berry" Robuck barely mentioned Ellsworth and certainly didn't tell the whole story. "I met Mac Stewart, Noah Ellis, Bill Campbell and several other old Caldwell County boys in Ellsworth, Kan., on one of my trips … After meeting this bunch in Ellsworth, a number of us returned home together with the saddle horses." No one would every suspect that Ellsworth was any more than a place to deliver cattle, collect your money, and go home. (1)

But the reality was just a bit more rowdy than the old trail drivers would have one to believe. Surprisingly, the first half of 1873 had been relatively calm, as least in terms of violence. Normally a town filled with wild cowboys would have seen daily occurrences of gunplay, if only for fun, but Ellsworth's lawmen kept a lid on the festivities with uncompromising efficiency.

A young lawyer by the name of Ira E. Lloyd arrived in Ellsworth that memorable summer of 1873. Lloyd lived all his former life in quiet law abiding communities. Recalling his introduction to Ellsworth, he described himself as, "in every way a tender-foot." His observations soon left little doubt as to his opinion concerning the character of Ellsworth's city lawmen.

Lloyd described Brocky Jack as, "a tall man killer." According to Lloyd, Brocky Jack "was a cold blooded, calculating villain, with several notches on his pistol, but none, in my opinion, gained in a fair fight. At heart he was a coward. Brave when he had the drop on another. Under a mask of silence he posed as deep and wise. His few words were esteemed oracles."

Assistant Marshal Happy Jack Morco was five feet ten inches tall, weighing about two hundred pounds. "He wore a slouch lightish colored hat. He was a born criminal and fled from a western territory for an un-named crime. Happy Jack was a drunkard, a brawler, and brave where there was not danger. Assassination to him was a trade. He had a certain amount of courage when drunk and when he thought the fear of him made it safe to bluster and brag."

Lloyd found Ed Hogue to be, "a supple time-server, brave when well backed - - - quick to make terms, if odds were even or greater. He was the stabilizer on the force."

Lloyd continued, "The other members of the police force were just ordinary scoundrels. Every man on the force was a bribe-taker and a villain. Every man on the force would kill on the slightest provocation, if he felt his hide was safe in doing so. Every man on the force in those days would not hesitate to commit any crime, in order to satisfy his passions or his revenge."

According to Lloyd the efficiency of the police force resulted in five to thirty arrests on a daily basis. Not all were prosecuted but according to Lloyd, most were arrested "with an idea of blackmail," which the lawmen utilized against the cowboys and prostitutes to "steal from the weak and timid."

As anger turned to indignation, a state of war developed between the police and the Texans, who were of course supported by the gamblers and prostitutes; all victims of the "lawless police force." The fines levied supported the city government, and what Lloyd termed as blackmail, was the officer's "cut" for making the arrest and gaining a conviction.

While Nauchville was located outside of town, it was not immune to the influence of Marshal Norton and his policemen. Lloyd described the collection of dance halls and brothels in equally negative terms.

> ... Abode to the worst female characters that had ever lived in the dens of vice in Kansas City and other cities ... These disreputable women patronized the saloons as freely as the men, wearing high heel shoes, fancy stockings and often shapely feet which they displayed on the rail footrods in front of the bars. At about seven o'clock every evening, these painted creatures, dressed in gaudy clothing would parade the principal streets of Ellsworth, attracting as much attention to their charms as possible.

Lloyd detested the entire proceeding, but fate changed his opinion of the worth of the dregs of society who were being victimized by the police. One of the women of "blemished repute" asked Lloyd to represent her in court. The young counselor's first response was to say no, but he hesitated, asking her to return an hour later. For that hour Lloyd wrestled with the question. "Could I conscientiously take a case for such a creature? I had an abhorrence to act for her. Yet, suppose she were ill, would not the doctor give her attention? ... did she not have rights, and was it wrong for an attorney to assert such rights for her? ... Also, I needed money. So I decided I would take her case."

His action would set him at odds with Marshal Norton and his police force. Happy Jack called upon Lloyd in his office prior to his second case. Lloyd had won the first case and was about to come between Marshal Norton and Happy Jack and their well laid plans for blackmail. Happy Jack didn't mince words as he advised Lloyd, "to be careful what I said or did, and that if I was not careful, his pistol held a bullet for me."

Lloyd's client was convicted and ordered by police judge Vincent Osborne to pay the fine, plus court costs. But Lloyd was not done. "I with all my energy, hate and force, defied the court and its officers to dare to execute the judgment of the court by committing the defendant, for non-payment of fine and costs." The young attorney was threatened by one of the town thugs as he left the court room and bluffed a friend of Happy Jack's with an empty revolver.

His next move was to apply to the city council to cancel the fine. Being inclined to favor the Texans, the council chose to hear Lloyd's argument. Lloyd revealed "the villainies of the two policemen." Ellsworth City Attorney Harry Pestana made his case. Lloyd's remarks to the city attorney were even more bitter. Happy Jack was so incensed at Lloyd's argument that he jumped up and drew his revolver. Several spectators jumped to Lloyd's defense and calmed the riled lawman until he finally regained his seat. Lloyd resumed his argument only to come face to face with Happy Jack once again; his hand on his pistol. Again the angry deputy was persuaded to sit down. Lloyd's condemnation of Marshal Norton and the complete police force so disturbed the members of the city council that they adjourned without taking action. "The excitement was intense."

The council room was upstairs above Arthur Larkin's general mercantile store. Lloyd's office was in an adjoining room. J. Charles Brown, who would later become a well-liked officer, stopped Lloyd as he was preparing to leave his office. "for God's sake go back, Happy Jack is waiting to shoot you as you come down the stairs." Returning to his office Lloyd stepped out on an overhanging porch. The unseasoned boards had shrunk, leaving large cracks. Through one of the cracks Happy Jack could be seen, "gun in hand, watching the stairway."

Lloyd spent the night in his office with a revolver at the ready. Voices from below echoed threats to "kill the s-o-b," but Happy Jack was finally persuaded to give up and go home. Lloyd knew his life, "was not worth a rush." Any excuse would be used to kill him. For that reason he refused to carry a weapon. Any sudden movement of the arms could be interpreted as a threatening action and so Lloyd made a point of keeping his thumbs in the armpits of his vest, or his open hands resting on his chest when near any of his avowed enemies. (2)

Whether corrupt or not, city officers kept violence to a noticeable minimum. Trouble could erupt at any hour, day or night. Marshal Norton and Happy Jack worked the early morning hours of July 15, 1873, on the trail of three thieves in the vicinity of Fort Harker.

Police Items - John Smith and another man whose name we did not get were arrested about sunrise Tuesday morning, for breaking into Davis' store. Smith had a preliminary trial yesterday, and will have some more today. It is reported that he has been engaged in extensive steals in the Territories. Smith was captured by "Brocky Jack" and "Happy Jack," at Fort Harker, after a careful, determined chase and search on horseback. It is supposed that Smith's companion escaped, and that the second man arrested will be discharged. (3)

136

The city council moved to reduce the size of the police force two days later on July 19th, Happy Jack Morco and High Low Jack Branham were relieved as deputies. Ten days later a citizen's petition demanded that Happy Jack be reinstated. The council capitulated and Morco was rehired. The vote of public confidence only served to bolster Happy Jack in his zeal to arrest offenders of the law, especially if they were Texans. (4)

The evening following Happy Jack's reinstatement Calvin G. Beach filled up on too much Ellsworth whiskey. For some reason the drunken man found himself in front of the home of livery man James White. Besides operating the well-known Sanderson & White Livery, White and Sanderson had for nearly a year joined with Evander Light in the wood and tie business. Light employed crews to cut ties from the earliest days that the railroad first built through the state. The previous winter the company put up one thousand three hundred cords of wood and only just commenced a new contract to supply Fort Hays with nine hundred cords of wood and nine hundred tons of prairie hay.

The drunken Calvin Beach attempted to break into James White's home. White ordered him to leave, but Beach continued his assault. White fired through the door, "and sent a small Smith & Wesson bullet through Mr. Beach's body."

The *Reporter* described the bullet as, "passing through his right side, above the hip, coming out at the abdomen, inflicting a severe but not fatal wound. He is under the care of Dr. Duck and is doing well."

A Reporter from the Topeka *Commonwealth* gave a more complete accounting of the incident. The *Reporter* had been introduced to Calvin Beach by Arthur Larkin, proprietor of the Grand Central Hotel, in which place Beach had a room. The correspondent visited Beach several times, "once with the city Marshal, Mr. Norton."

The *Commonwealth* correspondent was in Ellsworth the night Beach was shot.

> In this town where so many men have 'died with their boots on' the signal of an attack on a man, or on his home or place of business has always been ground enough for the person attacked, the owner of an assaulted home to place himself on the defensive and save his life if possible. For any hesitancy his life must surely pay the forfeit ... I asked him for the truth that I might correctly report it ... His laconic reply was, "I cannot blame Mr. White, he did not know me; he thought me a burglar, no doubt. I would have done the same. Do not print anything until I'm dead or well."

Predictions for Calvin Beach's survival were premature. His conditioned worsened throughout the week and he breathed his last breath near midnight Saturday night, August 2, 1873. "... The first tragedy of this memorable place and memorable season ..."

Judge James Miller preformed the Episcopal burial service at the grave in the Episcopal Church cemetery. (5)

As summer drew on, cattlemen began to notice an alarming trend. Eastern buyers were slowing their purchases. Cattle continued to arrive on the overcrowded range with fewer and fewer buyers making offers. Cattle covered the prairie like locusts from a plague while cattlemen settled in, bided their time, and hoped for an enlivened market in the fall. The saloons filled to capacity night after night. Gambling concerns raked in stacks of money. The "carnival of sin" carried on around the clock.

The Ellsworth *Reporter* carried on its pages the prospect of yet another form of entertainment. A large ad promoted "John Robinson's Great World's Exposition." The circus advertised two thousand men & horses, one hundred male performers, twenty beautiful lady performers, forty-two cages of wild beasts, fifteen sun-bright tents, forty musicians, all adding up to three miles of solid procession. The John Robinson Circus, one of the largest shows in the country, had its own railroad cars, and boasted the largest collection of wild animals of any circus in America.

A special police force was hired for the circus, but nothing of note happened to warrant their presence. The *Reporter* wondered, "Perhaps the extra police was put on to watch the lion." (6)

Saloons ran seven days a week, consequently Sundays at the end of the trail were not exactly quiet and peaceful. The John Robinson Circus had just left town; another reason for celebration. The record doesn't state the time of day, but Sunday, August 10, 1873, Brocky Jack became intoxicated. The disturbance that he created couldn't be ignored.

Ira Lloyd learned of the disturbance from a gambler and gunman, A. M. Campbell. Lloyd immediately set out to lay a trap for the rogue lawmen. "Campbell was straight. That is as straight as a gambler could be." Campbell told Lloyd that he was in Nauchville when Marshal "Brocky Jack" Norton, Deputy Happy Jack Morco and another unnamed policeman shot out the lights "and performed similar other tricks" in one of the dance halls.

In the meantime the city council relieved one more officer of his duties on August 12th. They continued to be concerned over the negative effect anti-Texan sentiment in the police force was having on business. Unfortunately, Marshal Brocky Jack Norton was given discretion as to who should be dismissed. Norton chose to fire the only man with any kind of rapport with the Texans, "Long Jack" John De Long. Even Ira Lloyd adopted a "strong liking" for Long Jack, who was actually a Texan with "actual and not counterfeit southern chivalry."

Like a pair of matching pistols, Norton and Happy Jack were two of a kind, holding power over Ellsworth. With fiery Ed Hogue added to the mix, Texans would find reason enough to loathe Ellsworth lawmen.

Lloyd convinced Campbell to swear out a complaint against Norton. Campbell was broke and would do it only if he could leave town because "they would kill him." Lloyd gave Campbell ten dollars and after filing the complaint, Campbell caught the first train for Kansas City. (7)

While the intrigue of battle between Marshal Norton and attorney Ira Lloyd played out, the community continued to strive for a future of principles and decency. The corner stone for the new school was dedicated, Tuesday August 12, 1873. The event was accompanied with "becoming ceremonies." The completion of the foundation was noted with the observation, "It ought to hold up the brick walls and allow the scholars to jam themselves full of knowledge." Recognizing the importance of the occasion, "Copies of the *Reporter* and other articles were deposited and sealed up, to be opened perhaps a thousand years hence."

The brick construction was to be done by J. H. Kinear who had come to Ellsworth in 1872.

> The results of his coming are seen in the handsome Grand Central, in the two brick stores, in the new Court House, and before cold weather comes again, we hope to chronicle the building of a handsome school house and other buildings. Mr Kinear is a good brick builder, and ought to be kept busy laying them in place.

Kinear would definitely be busy. A vote for bonds to build a new Ellsworth County Jail was cast with a majority voting to build the jail. The *Reporter* noted, "Kinear will probably burn 500,000 more brick. It will take a few for the jail." (8)

A. M. Campbell's complaint, backed by the determined Ira Lloyd was taken seriously by the city. Friday, August 15th, Marshal Brocky Jack Norton found himself in the awkward position of standing before Judge Vincent Osborne's court with little evidence to defend himself. Campbell's complaint alleged that Brocky Jack, "… was disturbing the peace and did unlawfully shoot off and discharge a pistol and was unlawfully drunk and disorderly". Court records document, "Defendant appeared to answer Complaint read and plea of Guilty to being drunk and disorderly but claims that said pistol was discharged accidentally.

I do find the defendant guilty of being drunk and disorderly.

V.B. Osborne   Police Judge" (9)

That very day would become one of the most notorious days in Ellsworth's history. The situation was a tinder box waiting for the spark. Billy Thompson was once again on a wild streak. He had been drinking heavily and anyone who knew him knew that there would be trouble. Considering the state of affairs, Brocky Jack was in no mood to temper the situation. A large crowd had gathered at Nick Lentz' Saloon. Brocky Jack was content to withdraw into the rogue's congregation and let the chips fall where they may.

Throughout the summer of 1873, the gambling halls of Ellsworth witnessed a literal tempest of activity.

> Every night four or five tables in almost all the saloons were occupied by gamblers and their victims - - - The Texas cattlemen and cowboys - - - - who were fleeced and robbed in a way they did not understand.
>
> At certain seasons of the year, thousands of dollars were piled upon the tables … drinking and swearing and the stench of liquor and tobacco, often made the rooms reek and the air thick enough almost to cut.

The most popular gambling resort was Joe Brennan's saloon, dubbed "Gamblers' Roost" by the sporting crowd. Dick Clark dealt faro at Brennan's saloon. Clark was one of the most well-known gamblers of his day. He had a reputation as a "square" gambler and was sure to take a hand in any "big money" poker game. A Topeka correspondent wrote of Clark, "He is widely known and has the reputation of being one of the best hearted and cleverest poker players in the country. His face, while engaged in play, is one of the most passive I ever saw."

139

Gamblers may have made their bread and butter from fleecing the unschooled cowboy or sightseer, but they often found themselves facing one another. Just as billiard champions defended their skills with the cue and ivory, gamblers won and lost reputations as lady luck bestowed her charms upon her latest beau.

One legged Jim Goodwyn was a regular at the Ellsworth tables. Jim Moon was described in the Topeka Daily *Commonwealth* as, "a well proportioned, athletic man, with brown hair and mustache." He carried himself with, "a style of a New York gambler …" Emma DeMar became his companion at Ellsworth and they remained together as they moved on to other towns. Years later, in Los Angeles, California Jim Moon married Emma according to her own account, "at the point of a pistol."

John Sterling hailed from Indiana. He had a reputation as a "good-natured, warm-hearted man always ready to help the needy or skin a sucker." (10)

Texan Ben Thompson arrived in Ellsworth intending to establish a gambling hall of his own. He had been a partner in Abilene's Bull's Head Saloon with Phil Coe. Coe was gunned down by Hickok in 1871 while Thompson was away in Kansas City.

Thompson was in a class of his own. Not only was he a very successful professional gambler, he carried the reputation of being one of the best gunmen in the west. While in Abilene he and Hickok both recognized the wisdom of keeping their hands close to the vest when in one another's company.

That summer of 1871, Thompson was involved in a very serious buggy accident in Kansas City in which his wife was seriously injured. The accident required his immediate return to Texas at a particularly dismal time in his life. He remained in Texas during the cattle season of 1872, suffering from a bout of depression.

By the time Thompson arrived in Ellsworth in 1873 the gambling halls were already overdone. Thompson chose to establish his headquarters at Gamblers' Roost.

Ben's brother, Billy Thompson, was almost always on a tear. While Ben had the air of a professional gambler, Billy associated more closely with the cowboy crowd. He had come up the trail with a Millett & Mabry herd and tended to blow off steam in the typical cowboy way, which was often unrestrained. When Billy went wild the whole world was his oyster. It was best not to get in his way.

Billy was somewhere in the crowd as the knights of the green cloth contested their skills. The tables at Gamblers' Roost had been busy all night and into the next day, Friday August 15, 1873. A game of Spanish monte stole the show with unusually high stakes. The "banker," Neil Cane could not cover a bet and asked Ben Thompson for help. Not wanting to risk the bet himself, Thompson looked up John Sterling who was more than happy to put up the money. In fact, he was so appreciative that he told Thompson that he would share any winnings made on the bet.

Sterling won one thousand dollars, but instead of splitting his winnings with Ben Thompson he stuffed the money in his pocket and walked out the door.

By the time Thompson was aware of Sterling's departure, Sterling had disappeared into the street. Thompson went looking for Sterling that afternoon and found him two doors west in Nick Lentz' saloon.

Thompson confronted Sterling, asking for his share of the winnings, but the drunken Sterling boldly slapped Ben Thompson! Both men were unarmed in accord with the "No Gun Law." Sterling was obviously out of his senses for no man in his right mind would slap the notorious Ben Thompson. Thompson lunged forward but was halted by Happy Jack Morco and two threatening pistols. All Thompson could do was demand that Happy Jack take Sterling out of his sight. Happy Jack then gathered up his friend and the two of them walked out onto the walk. Once outside they turned west toward Jake New's Ellsworth Billiard Hall at the end of the block.

Once Thompson regained his composure he left Lentz's saloon and returned to his "Gamblers' Roost" gaming tables in Joe Brennan's saloon. Thompson was in the midst of recounting the events to Cad Pierce when Morco and Sterling passed by the open door of Brennan's saloon; Happy Jack with two drawn pistols and Sterling wielding a shotgun. "Get your guns, you Texas sons-of-bitches and fight!" echoed through the hall.

Enraged, Thompson asked several Texans in Brennan's saloon to loan him a "checked" gun from the collection at the back of the saloon. Ben's guns were at the end of the street in the Ellsworth Billiard Hall. No one was willing to give Ben a gun. If he wanted one he would have to retrieve his own.

Within moments Ben was running down the back alley to the back door of the Ellsworth Billiard Hall. Ben walked out the front door with his pistol on his hip and a sixteen-shot Henry rifle in hand. Billy soon joined him. A challenge to Ben was a challenge to them both, even if Billy could barely stand up from the effects of alcohol.

Ben immediately noticed that Billy was carrying a prize shotgun given to Ben by cattleman Captain Cad Pierce. Both barrels were cocked and Billy was being very careless with the weapon. Suddenly one of the hammers dropped. A shot tore through the boardwalk at the feet of cattlemen Captain Eugene Millett and Major Seth Mabry. Ben took the shotgun from Billy but before he could unload it someone called. "Look out Ben here they come with guns!"

Ellsworth County Sheriff Chauncey Whitney was alerted by the shot. Whitney, known to his friends as "Sandy", had been informed earlier in the day of Billy Thompson's drunken condition by John Montgomery of the Ellsworth *Reporter*. The sheriff was probably aware of Ellsworth City Marshal Brocky Jack Norton's disposition over his drunk and disorderly conviction. If there was going to be trouble, Brocky Jack would most likely stay out of it. Sheriff Whitney sent his wife to a picnic southeast of Fort Harker and waited at the restaurant in Veatch's Hotel for trouble.

So it was that Sheriff Whitney walked out to the railroad depot in the middle of the plaza where Ben and Billy Thompson were standing. The location provided better visibility and the hope of an open fight with Happy Jack and John Sterling. The Thompson's were hailing their opponents to come out into the open and fight when Whitney approached from the north side of the plaza. Whitney was friends with the Thompsons and readily convinced them to return to the saloon and lay down their arms. Whitney assured the Texans that he would take care of Happy Jack and Sterling. It appeared that once again, "Sandy" Whitney had reversed another deadly situation. The men walked casually to Brennan's Saloon to take a drink.

Inexplicably, Happy Jack and Sterling suddenly appeared running down the boardwalk. Happy Jack had one pistol drawn and his hand on the other in its holster. Sterling followed with a shotgun. Billy and Sheriff Whitney had just entered Brennan's saloon. Taken by surprise, Ben called out to Happy Jack, "What are you doing?" But the deputy pressed forward without an answer. Ben raised his rifle to shoot, alerting Happy Jack of his danger. Ben fired. As Happy Jack dove through the doorway of Beebe's hardware, the bullet splintered the door casing.

As Whitney returned to the street he demanded "What does this mean?" In the confusion Billy, with shotgun in hand, stumbled through Brennan's doorway. Just as he had done earlier, Billy accidentally triggered the shotgun. Sheriff Whitney called out, "I am shot!" Buckshot had entered Whitney's side and chest. Whitney whirled around twice but remained on his feet. Still standing, he called for his wife.

Ben cried out, "My God Billy you have shot your best friend!" Accounts differ as to Billy's response but eyewitnesses agree he answered something to the effect, "I know it. I am sorry." Rumors were circulated and even printed in the *Reporter* that Billy responded by saying, "that he did not give a d__! that he would have shot if it had been Jesus Christ." Years later, witnesses at Billy's trial did not verify hearing those words.

Whitney responded saying, "He did not intend to do it, it was an accident, send for my family." Friends quickly rushed to his side to support him. Whitney was carried to his home at the northwest corner of Lincoln Avenue and 1ˢᵗ Street.

Meanwhile, the town exploded in rage as the Texans gathered in front of the Grand Central Hotel in a classic standoff. Billy mounted his horse and rode to meet Ben in front of the Grand Central. The two exchanged guns. One of the Texans shoved a roll of bills into Billy's pocket as he turned south and escaped onto the prairie. Ben, now armed with his favorite shotgun and backed by an army of Texans held his ground. Marshal Norton refused to act. A virtual standoff existed between Ellsworth's citizens and the Texans for a full hour in which Ellsworth lawmen seemed to have disappeared.

Sixty-three-year-old James Miller, the mayor of Ellsworth, was infuriated at his inept police force. He approached Ben Thompson to negotiate a cease-fire. Thompson insisted that the assassin-prone policemen must be fired from the force and disarmed before any Texans would disarm. Miller considered his options and put his faith in Ben Thompson. The entire police force was fired on the spot. Once accomplished, Miller returned with Ed Hogue who, as Assistant County Sheriff was the only lawman left to receive Thompson's arms. Thompson handed over his guns and accompanied the mayor to his office where he was charged with shooting at Happy Jack Morco. The powder keg had been defused, at least for the moment.

The hour being too late for an "examining trial," Thompson suggested that he give bond for his appearance the following day. Miller insisted on a ten thousand dollar bond. Several supporting Texans offered to deposit the money. Miller was still unsatisfied with the arrangements until "Seth Mabry and Captain Millett deposited the amount to the credit of responsible citizens, procuring their signatures ..." Thus Thompson was released through the efforts of Mabry and Millett, backed by the word of Ellsworth men that Miller trusted. By the terms of the bond Thompson was required to appear in court the following morning to answer the charge.

Chauncey Belton Whitney served Ellsworth as a lawman in one capacity or another from 1867 until his death on August 18, 1873. Courtesy Rick Mack Collection.

A posse was finally formed and struck out onto the prairie in search of Billy Thompson. The Texans ridiculed the citizen posse. Cad Pierce jokingly offered one thousand dollars for the arrest of the pursuing party.

Mayor Miller called a special session of the city council to gain approval of his executive decision of firing the police force. He was met with disapproval. After lengthy and heated consideration, a resolution to approve Mayor Miller's actions was barely approved by a three to two vote. Miller asked that John DeLong be instated as city marshal, but that failed. Miller then appointed Ed Hogue to the position, which the city council approved. Amazingly, Miller reappointed Happy Jack as deputy, along with John DeLong and Ed Crawford. Again the council approved the appointments by the vote of three to two.

Billy Thompson lived the cowboy life, never
quite taming the demons living within.
Courtesy Ellsworth County Historicical Society.

Famously, Wyatt Earp has been given credit for bringing calm to Ellsworth that
tragic day. However, no evidence exists to support this story, which is largely the
creation of Earp's biographer, Stuart Lake. No witness testified as to the presence
of a person by the name of Wyatt Earp or the actions that are ascribed to him. A
report published in the Winfield *Weekly Courier* identifies J. (James) C. Earp as the
author of a letter describing events during the bloody season of 1873. The report
says that, "Mr. Earp was present and witnessed the shooting of Whitney and Pierce
…" Interestingly no mention is made of any Earp actually taking part in the fracas,
which only supports the notion that Wyatt Earp, a young unknown, did not tame
Ellsworth on August 15, 1873. Ellsworth was in fact brought back from the brink
of anarchy by sixty-three-year-old Mayor James Miller. (11)

While the mayor and the Ellsworth City Council were hashing out the details
of the new police force, Ben Thompson chose to attend the Ellsworth Theatre in
Nauchville. The 1773 comedy stage play, "She Stoops to Conquer" was being
performed. George McClellan's frontier theater was set in a "low one-story
building, seventy-five by twenty feet."

144

Texan Ben Thompson was described as fearless,
cool, and resourceful under trying circumstances.
Courtesy Ellsworth County Historical Society.

... The doors opened at nine in the evening ... Talent was provided
from St. Joseph, Missouri, Kansas City, and St. Louis ... Patrons were
enticed inside by orchestra music produced by violin, violoncello, guitar,
and cornet. What it lacked in harmony it made up in volume and spirit.

The room itself was unplastered and unpainted except for the
proscenium and the drop curtain. The stage was opposite to the entrance.
Plain pine benches afforded a seating capacity for one hundred fifty
patrons. At the right of the entrance was a bar for dispensing "cholera
medicine." At the left of the entrance stood a monte gambling table.

To the left of the stage was the box which extended outside like a
bake oven. The capacity of the box was usually twelve, made up mostly of
"ladies," though a long-haired gallant from the sunny south was frequently
seen sandwiched between the gaily decorated and dashing "ladies."

The drop curtain of the stage is ornamental as well as suggestive. A
gay and chivalric cattle herder, dressed in the style of a Spanish don, with
a crimson jacket trimmed with gold lace, and a huge plume flowing from

145

his grand Castilian sombrero, with ponderous spurs protruding from his boots, is mounted on a furious and awe-inspiring horse. A fiery untamed member of the long horned species has just been lassoed by the valorous herder, and is making desperate efforts to get released, but the herder is invincible and holds the lasso with toper-like tenacity. Between the herder and his victim is a mammoth lone, illuminated with golden and silver colors. To the valiant Texan, upon whose patronage the proprietors of the theatre mainly rely, the scene is sublime and inspiring.

On a typical night there were fifty patrons - - young men mostly - - on the pine benches. Seven or eight "ladies" giggled, monte players cursed, orders for cigars and drinks were unceasing, and the singing, dancing, and theatrical performance progressed.

There was a "green room" back of the stage. To certain patrons this was the sacred realm. Here scores of herders drank wine and liquor and indulged in familiar pleasantries with the stage girls.

It is the acme of a herder's ambition to obtain accession to the 'green room' and crack a bottle of wine with the girls. The visits to the green room frequently cost a dozen head of steers, but Texas is able to stand the damage and don't care for the expense." (12)

Ben Thompson was completely absorbed in the play, allowing the actors to take him away from the treachery of the day. A tap on his shoulder brought him to the realization that a friend was speaking to him. He leaned back as the incredible words were whispered that Billy was in town. Ben could not have been more surprised, "… had a thunderbolt out of a clear sky struck him." Billy was waiting near the Grand Central Hotel.

Just being in Ellsworth was amazing enough, but Billy's story of his "escape" from the posse was incredible. Ben later related just what happened to Billy after he rode out of town.

… He went out in the prairie and layed down and went to sleep; that he was drunk and that he slept until about 9 o'clock that night. He did not know where he was; that he got up and wandered around an hour or so until he saw the lights of the houses in Ellsworth about 11 o'clock in the night. When he came in he had no money with him and had lost his pistol.

Evidently the posse that rode out after him didn't try very hard to catch their man. They rode out on the trail perhaps ten miles before giving up and returning the Ellsworth.

Billy was badly hung over and generally feeling pretty blue over the day's events. At the time, Ben thought that Whitney would recover. Ben told Billy that the sheriff was not badly hurt and that he would go see him and square things for Billy. In the meantime, Ben advised his brother to go to one of the cow camps outside of town and wait till the situation in town cooled down. Billy left town with a herder by the name of Jack who worked with the McGehee outfit. Billy made a point of sending word of his safety to Ben every day.

Chauncey Whitney was in greater danger than Ben Thompson had supposed. He was suffering intensely. Buckshot had struck the unfortunate sheriff in the chest, shoulder, and arm. Dr. Fox and Dr. Gregg worked around the clock in an attempt to relieve his pain. The wounds were beyond their capabilities, but the doctors held out hope that a surgeon could save him.

Major Gore, proprietor of Drovers Cottage, put up fifty dollars and guaranteed the expenses to bring Dr. William Finlaw from Junction City. He arrived as quickly as possible by train, but upon his examination it was discovered that some of the shot had passed through Whitney's lungs and had lodged in his backbone. There was nothing that Finlaw could do. Ellsworth County Sheriff Chauncey Beldon Whitney mercifully died following three dreadful days of suffering on August 18, 1873.

The community was devastated. The Ellsworth County Commissioners voted to, allow payment to Whitney & Kendall Furniture & Undertaking, the sheriff's own place of business, for "one coffin for Sandy" at a cost of thirty-three dollars.

"Mr. Whitney was a member of the Masonic order, and he was attended to by his brothers in Masonry at his bedside, and buried by them in the Episcopal church yard."

Dr. Levi Sternberg preached the funeral service before a very large crowd of friends and mourners. The services at the grave were described as "impressive." "Dust was rendered to dust; safe from the storms, free from cares, in the bosom of mother earth, rests the body of our late Sheriff C. B. Whitney."

Ellsworth's old vigilance committee soon found reason to exact its own authority over Ellsworth's affairs. Undesirable persons were identified among the transient crowd and offered a chance to leave before things got worse. If a man was handed a white slip of paper, a "white affidavit," he knew that leaving town was a good idea.

Two days after Sheriff Whitney's death three Texans heard rumors that they would soon receive white affidavits. John Good, Neil Cane and Cad Pierce approached Marshal Ed Hogue. Pierce wanted to know if there was anything to the rumor. Hogue replied, "There was no such thing ..."

Policeman Ed Crawford approached and began to argue with Pierce. Pierce stepped back, shifting his hand behind his back. Crawford drew his pistol and opened fire on Pierce, who retreated toward the doorway of the Beebe's hardware store. Crawford chased him, shooting again as Pierce entered the door. Pierce fell to the floor just inside the store. Crawford continued his attack, pistol whipping Pierce until his brains spilled out on the floor. Pierce was unarmed.

Neil Cain narrowly escaped being shot down by deputy "Happy Jack" Morco, who drew down on him with both his six-shooters. This time Marshal Hogue intervened to prevent another tragic shooting. Cane saddled up and left town.

Cad Pierce was well known on the cattle trail. His death was reported in the Nebraska City *Press*. "of Capt. Cad. Pierce we can truly say a more perfect gentleman, since we have been acquainted with him, would be hard to find in any city or state." The paper published accounts of events in Ellsworth in two separate editions noting, "Pierce's body was brought to Junction City last night, attended by 50 Texans, on its way to Texas. Pierce was the owner of 7,000 head of cattle. The

Texans are breathing vengeance and threatening to burn the town. Lively times are looked for. All is now quiet in Ellsworth."

The Texans were in no mood to be shoved around. An entire army of them could be recruited from the surrounding cow camps. A gang of gunmen rode into town just to show their contempt for Ellsworth and its white affidavits. The men boldly rode through the town for about twenty minutes, informing all who could be found that Ellsworth would be burned to the ground.

Citizens formed themselves into a squad of "protectors." Checked guns were seized and a dozen or so additional men, deemed "hard cases" by the vigilance committee, were ordered to leave town.

Kansas Governor Thomas A. Osborne issued a proclamation with a description of Billy Thompson and offered a reward of five hundred dollars for his arrest and conviction. The Governor telegraphed Mayor Miller, directing him to call on the State Government for aid if he could not maintain peace. He then sent Attorney General Archibald L. Williams to Ellsworth to "look over the situation."

Billy Thompson returned to Texas by way of the cattle trail with some of the men who had had enough of Kansas. Ben Thompson boarded a train for Kansas City. Ellsworth officials heard rumors that Ben was about to return with arms to equip the Texans for a war with Ellsworth. Trains were searched as they arrived from the east in Salina, but Thompson did not attempt to revisit Ellsworth, instead he returned to Texas by way of St. Louis and New Orleans.

A correspondent for the Topeka *Commonwealth* wrote of the mass departure of the rough element from Ellsworth.

> That class of persons commenced looking after their carpet bags, and the next train east on the K. P. was freighted with more infamy than is usually transported in one day. The 21st of August will be remembered in Ellsworth for the exodus of he roughs and gamblers.

The *Reporter* assured Texans that honorable drovers were still welcome to the advantages of the city and county. After all, there was still the business of selling cattle to be dealt with, and as a cattle market Ellsworth was unsurpassed. (13)

The market of 1873 was severely glutted with cattle and the market was depressed. Major George W. Littlefield recognized the advantages of the Ellsworth market. In a letter to his nephew, Shelton Dowell, Littlefield stated that he was seeing opportunity in the depressed cattle market. Littlefield lived by his own creed, "I have only one rule in business: When everybody is wanting to sell, I buy; When everybody is wanting to buy, I sell."

In his letter to Shelton, Littlefield emphasized the urgency of the moment.

> This is our Place. This is the Place, and this the winter, for you & I to make a rise in the world – I say, if I can buy 1000 head of cattle cheap on one years time next month at Ellsworth ... Bring all the money you can control of ... Here we meet LIVE energetic men ... one year from now we will have made at least $6,000.00 in cash ... cattle will be lower this fall than we will ever see them again ...

Littlefield rightly discerned the character of the 1873 cattle market. If big money was to be made from the 1873 season it would probably be completed in 1874. (14)

Meanwhile, the Ellsworth City Council had another powder keg on its hands. The entire police force was once again fired on August 27, 1873. Ed Crawford and Happy Jack were invited to leave town. Richard Freeborn was appointed city marshal and given authority to hire his own deputies. Freeborn selected J. Charles Brown and John DeLong. Charley Brown was the man who had warned Ira Lloyd of Happy Jack's plot to assassinate him. DeLong was the one man from the "Jacks" that could deal effectively with the Texans.

Ed Crawford and Happy Jack traveled east to Salina, but Happy Jack was arrested by Salina lawmen on an order from Ellsworth. Deputy Charley Brown and Texan John Good traveled to Salina in an attempt to regain a brace of ivory handled six-guns that allegedly were taken from Good while Happy Jack was performing his duties as an Ellsworth policeman. They received no satisfaction, but warned Happy Jack not to return to Ellsworth. The thought of being thrown out of town infuriated the former policeman all the more. Upon his release from the Salina jail Happy Jack determined to return to Ellsworth in spite of the warning, saying "he was good for all his enemies up there."

The disgruntled former policeman arrived back in Ellsworth on September 3rd. The next day he proceeded to make a spectacle of walking the streets, openly wearing Good's pistols. Deputy Charley Brown met Happy Jack in the street and advised him to "check" the guns according to city law. Marshal Brown's advice was ignored, bringing about a second admonition to put the guns away. A third meeting between the men became heated. Happy Jack went for his guns but Brown was too quick. Two rapid-fire shots dropped Happy Jack with a bullet in his heart and another in his forehead. He was dead before he hit the street. Happy Jack was buried in the old cemetery on the hill east of Ellsworth.

In one of those classic "believe-it-or-not" scenerios, Happy Jack's former wife just happened to be in Ellsworth touring with a theatrical troupe. She refuted his claim of killing twelve men in Oregon.

> ... It was four men he killed - - that he used to get drunk and abuse her
> - - that one time she called for help while they were living in Portland and
> that Jack shot four good citizens who came to her relief. He was put in jail
> but managed to escape. It was at this time that he had his arm broken. Jack
> and his wife had not met for several years, and she was three days in town
> before he recognized her.

The death of Happy Jack appeared to bring some resolution to the recent weeks of violence. Citizens returned to their normal daily life while the Texas cattlemen who remained waited for the stagnate market to improve. (15)

The new Ellsworth County Jail captured the limelight as plans drawn up by Major Henry Inman were unveiled. Instead of brick, stone was proposed. "The railroad company would probably furnish the stone at cost of freight and quarrying from their mine in Ellis County, but there is good stone in this county and we hope it will be used." (16)

Sheriff Chauncey Whitney's widow, Nellie Whitney was eighteen years old, with a one-year-old daughter, Mary Elizabeth. Chauncey and George Kendall had opened their furniture store with credit. They hadn't paid for anything. The lumber for the little one room house that Chauncey built for his new bride was not paid for. Years later, Nellie wrote of her distress in a letter to her daughter. "The only thing we owned was a horse – not even my sewing machine was paid for but we would have come out all right had he lived ... We bought a lot – but did not pay for it." She was penniless and deep in debt.

The businessmen, saloon keepers, and gamblers all contributed "a couple of hundred dollars" to Nellie to help her through. She rented her house and moved back into her parent's house. She, her mother, and her sister took in sewing while Nellie studied evenings to become a teacher. The renter of her home was one of the physicians who first tended to Chauncey. She doesn't name him but according to Nellie he charged her the first six months rent as his fee, then lived in the house another six months finally leaving in the night without paying the rent. As the house was furnished he had worn out her "few things." As Dr. Fox remained in the community, the scoundrel that took advantage of a poor widow with a young baby must have been Dr. Gregg. (17)

Plans for the new Ellsworth County Jail were moving steadily forward. On September 18, 1873, the *Reporter* announced that J. H. Kinear and Chauncey Whitney's old partner, George Kendall, obtained the contract to build the new stone building for four thousand six hundred dollars. The "house" was expected to be finished before cold weather. One week later, local stone had evidently been found as ground was broken and stone was being hauled. (18)

As the season slipped deeper into September large numbers of cattle were still grazing lush Kansas prairies. Cattlemen who sold early in 1873 were the winners in the long run. The glutted market pushed trading activity into the doldrums as cattlemen waited for a hopeful improvement. Instead, the market collapsed on September 18, when the financial empire of Jay Cooke and Co. of New York City closed its doors. The Panic of 1873 devastated the cattle industry. Cattlemen began to sell herds for any amount of money, hoping to scrape enough money together to start over next year.

Just as Major Littlefield had foreseen, tremendous opportunity developed in the cattle market in the fall of 1873. Cattle could be purchased at rock bottom prices. One-Armed Jim Reed and his old partner, Shanghai Pierce, were two of the cattlemen who were in a position to invest. The men bought seven thousand head of cattle to winter over with plans of selling them on the early market in the spring.

Many cattlemen were not so fortunate and were forced to sell at ruinously low prices. The majority of drovers were still indebted for the cattle that had originally been purchased in Texas. Notes were due in October amounting to one and a half million dollars. Drovers were faced with the unthinkable. Either they could sell to buyers for less than cost or they could ship their cattle to the eastern terminal markets. But there they were subject to receiving checks that quite possibly were worthless. According to a correspondent at Wichita, "cattlemen, as well as cattle, are slaughtered every day." (19)

The panic was even affecting Ellsworth County's new jail as stated in the October 23, *Reporter*. "Owing to the panic, our jail bonds have not been sold. But the work is going on in building." Saloon owner and steady booster for Ellsworth, Leo Hertzig advanced money to keep the project on track. (20)

Just as Happy Jack had been forewarned not to return to Ellsworth, Ed Crawford also ignored the warnings saying he, "was not afraid ..." even though friends of the murdered Cad Pierce, the man he had killed earlier were still in town. Crawford arrived in town November 2nd and proceeded to make the rounds of the sporting houses. He was reported "full of whiskey ..." on the 6th and on the 7th "considerably under the influence." At Lizzy Palmer's dance hall he barged in on Suzie Hart and an intimate customer just as several Texans entered the dark hallway leading to her room. Suzie ran from the room as the men closed in. Suddenly six shots rang out and Ed Crawford lay dead on the floor of Suzie's room. No one was ever brought to justice for the killing. At the coroner's inquest John DeLong testified that someone in the crowd stated the "Putnam" had shot Crawford. "I also saw Putnam with a Pistol (a Navy Pistol I think)."

Charley Brown also testified that he had heard the remark "made by several in the crowd that Putnam had shot Crawford." Putnam was a brother-in-law to Cad Pierce, the man Crawford had killed following the Whitney shooting.

Alice Chambers was working in Lizzy Palmer's dance hall the night Crawford was killed. She was no stranger to violence. She had been Phil Coe's girl in Abilene when Coe was killed by Wild Bill Hickok. Alice testified in court.

> I heard her talking to someone in her room I do not know who it was. Crawford had made the remark that he had "Sugar" and wanted a girl to sleep with him. Crawford went down the Hall to Suzie Harts room and immediately after I heard some man say to Crawford "go away" – I do not know whether Crawford had a pistol or not. As soon as I heard a noise in Harts room I was afraid and run out of the house, - I do not know any of the men that was in the room at the time.

Suzie Hart verified that she was talking with a man when Crawford tried to enter her room. "I should not know the man that was in my room again if I saw him." Suzie became frightened and ran from the house to Molly Brennan's house. "After I left the room it appeared to me that all the men in the house made a rush for the Hall towards my room ... I never saw so many men in the House at one time."

Lizzy Palmer weighed in with a lengthy description of events but did not know the names of any of the men involved. She did see "Put" with another of the girls, Annie Lee, that afternoon. "I do not remember seeing him there after that."

No one was arrested for the murder. Apparently some kind of conflict developed between newly appointed Ellsworth City Marshal Richard Freeborn and his deputies, Charley Brown and John DeLong. Both resigned following the death of Ed Crawford. Marshal Freeborn resigned November 18th. The Ellsworth City Council wasted little time. Charley Brown was appointed Ellsworth City Marshal the same day.

Mollie Brennan sold her house and all its belongings to Ellsworth City Attorney Harry L. Pestana, November 10, 1873. Mollie spent a considerable amount of time with Billy Thompson while he was in Ellsworth. She may have followed Billy, but whatever her reason for leaving, she never returned to Ellsworth.

Ellsworth had seen the best of times and the worst of times all in one year. While the celebration continued, money changed hands at an incredible rate. Gamblers and prostitutes got their share but groceries, liquor, clothing, jewelry, and watches were all in demand. There were many commercial businesses often stocked to the ceilings with similar merchandise. Mayer Goldsoll's Old Reliable House, while a very popular establishment, was nevertheless just one of many commercial houses on the streets of Ellsworth in 1873, which makes his sales all the more remarkable. Several of Goldsoll's busiest months averaged thirty thousand dollars in sales while his total sales for the year were one hundred and fifty thousand dollars! Ellsworth in 1873 was truly unimaginable.

The wildly dramatic year of '73 ended symbolically with the completion of the new Ellsworth County Jail. The *Reporter* noted that, "The building presents a fine appearance." The bloody season was at an end. As for the Texas cattle trade, Ellsworth and the Kansas Pacific finished the year shipping thirty-thousand five hundred forty head by rail while Wichita and the Santa Fe logged over fifty-five thousand head. The figures did not represent the total numbers of cattle traded. Great herds were driven beyond Ellsworth to the vast cattle ranges of the Dakotas and Wyoming.

Ellsworth had actively denounced a large number of Texans through vigilante action. But many continued through the disastrous panic to make Ellsworth their headquarters. Promoters could only wonder what 1874 would bring.

The Ellsworth County Jail was built after county officials discovered they had not allowed enough room for county offices in the Ellsworth County Courthouse. The jail in that building was converted for use by the Ellsworth County Treasurer. Courtesy Ellsworth County Historical Society.

Chapter Ten

RELUCTANT TRANSFORMATION

The American Cyclopaedia: A Popular Dictionary of General Knowledge began publication in 1873. It had been many years since an updated "cyclopedia' had been published in the United States. The sixth volume, published in 1874, covered subjects from "DEMPSTER to EVERETT" and referenced "ELLSWORTH, a central county of Kansas, intersected by Smoky Hill river; area, 7:20 sq. m.; pop. in 1870, 1,185. The Kansas Pacific railroad passes through it. The chief productions in 1870 were 2,175 bushels of wheat, 12,167 of Indian corn, 4,393 of potatoes, and 1,604 tons of hay. Capital, Ellsworth." Four-year-old statistics were nearly the equivalent of a lifetime on the leading edge of civilization, known as the Kansas frontier. (1)

By 1874, two thousand people received mail from the post office in the city of Ellsworth. The community boasted a new county courthouse, a new county jail, and a new schoolhouse described as, "an ornament to our county."

A combination of railroad business, cattle trade, and farm settlement helped to swell the business community to an extent found only in much larger cities. Ellsworth at the beginning of 1874 had much to look forward to. (2)

Economically, the previous season had been more than anyone could have imagined. Most of the stimulus came from the great herds of Texas longhorns marketed at Ellsworth.

Farmers initially scorned the cattle trade. Cattlemen often made little effort to compromise with settlers, making the already hard life of farming even harder by allowing wild cattle to trample crops and devour haystacks. Farmers organized against cattlemen and demanded a herd law and quarantine, but overwhelming numbers of powerful cattlemen in 1873 virtually silenced the farmers for the season. Former opponents of the cattle trade actually joined the cattlemen; buying, grazing, and selling cattle to their own benefit.

By late winter of 1874, Texas cattlemen were few in number on the Kansas prairies. Most were back in Texas planning another drive that would begin as soon as weather warmed and new grass began to flourish.

New voices began to oppose the cattle trade. Dairyman D. B. Long noted in a February 5, 1874, letter to the Ellsworth *Reporter* that the county was quickly settling up. Wheat farmers were moving into the southern portion of the county. Ellsworth badly needed a flour mill and although a stockman himself, Long observed that the Texas cattle trade could only last another year or two. "It is high time our attention was turned to something that will be of permanent and lasting benefit to the county."

The editor of the *Reporter* raised the ire of one farmer when he openly invited the Texans to return to Ellsworth County. A letter posted to the *Reporter* reflected the opinion of many Ellsworth County farmers.

It is too plainly known that farmers do not want any of the work of last year. In the first place, where do you get your authority to ask them here? You know, and we all know that they do not come here before the 1ˢᵗ of March, and too, you know that we have no herd law in force. More than that, you know that our farming must be done without fences until we can grow them. You have already admitted that ... Texas cattle cannot be held during a storm. The law says plainly; they must not come here, and if you take the side of "Texas Cattle Trade" in opposition to the farmers, you may find there will be two sides to the question.

If you will but take the trouble to look over these hills, you will find there is no room here for Texas cattle without seriously interfering with our rights, aside from the law. We want settlers not Texas herds. It is a very questionable advantage to the settler to be compelled to picket his own two, three or four head of stock and give up all the range to parties who come here with no other intention than to fatten their stock on the grass that properly belongs to us. If you have the welfare of the county at heart – go on with the good work of helping fill all our vacant sections with "tillers of the soil." Invite them to bring stock and you will find there will be no police force necessary to take charge of their revolvers when in town trading. Help us to build up the county and we will not let the town go down by any means. We came here for peace, not war, and it means war when our crops are destroyed by stock that are brought into the State contrary to law.

Believing that our interests are identical – that the town needs the country support and vice versa, I hope and trust that you may not get too far estray. More again, if I have not trampled on your rights too severely.

IN EARNEST (3)

Perhaps there were too many distractions at the time but considering his service to the community, the death of the Ellsworth County Coroner Dr. William Masterson Duck on February 3, 1874, was barely mentioned by the *Reporter*. Dr. Duck died in Leavenworth. A former partner, Dr. Fox was appointed to the county coroner position. His office was in George Seitz' Drug Store.

A February issue of the *Reporter* extolled the virtues of the new Ellsworth County Jail, saying it was, "... the best jail in the Western part of the state, but not a prisoner in it." The county soon gained a "boarder" but the prisoner elected not to yield an extended stay as reported March 5ᵗʰ.

J. M. Greider escaped Saturday night from the new jail. The sheriff saw him at eleven o'clock safe in the jail, but with the help some of his friends he was got out after that hour. The lock to the iron doors was broken, and as the prisoner was not confined in a cell, he walked out without any further trouble. The sheriff is not at all to blame for this escape as the building is not fully ready for prisoners.

Perhaps the jail was not ready for prisoners, but it was certainly ready for a dance. Ellsworth citizens were always ready to "tip the light fantastic toe." The same issue that reported Greider's escape announced, "The new jail will be 'dedicated' tonight by a dance in the large rooms in the second story. Every one is going." A later edition reported that approximately forty couples attended the dance, but the rooms were found "too small and cool," so the dance was "adjourned to the Drovers Cottage." The dance reportedly lasted until a late hour with Bradshaw playing some of his best music.

Business houses in frontier Ellsworth were constantly in a state of flux. Not only did enterprises come and go frequently, but buildings were commonly moved to new locations. One case in point was the old Marshall House, one of the earliest hotels in Ellsworth. The hotel was established on the west side of F Street (South Douglas Avenue). F Street was perhaps the most active street in town during 1867. Most commerce was at that time associated with the freighting business leading to Santa Fe. The southern end of F Street approached the wagon ford across the Smoky Hill River.

Fires were a constant threat to frontier towns. South Main Street had seen several large fires. Mr. Joseph Anderson, proprietor of the Marshall House, reckoned that the open lots across the street on the east side of F Street were more secure from fire. The site also provided more light and more room for his customers. Accordingly, he moved the Marshall House, lock, stock and barrel, across the street. Rousing times called for prompt and confident decisions and Ellsworth businessmen in 1874 were quick to adjust to perceived trends. (4)

Spring was on its way and with it, the new grass. Drovers were already making up their herds in south Texas with plans to take to the trail by mid April. The *Reporter* quoted the Gonzales (Texas) *Enquirer* writing that the grass in Texas was fine and the cattle in splendid condition for driving. Several drovers were about to begin the drive, "among whom are Gus Walker, who will take from 1500 to 2000 head, and the Messrs. Houstons 4000 to 5000 head." Before long, Texans would be arriving in Ellsworth with new herds of cattle and pockets bulging with money to spend.

The Kansas Pacific made ready for the coming drive by publishing the *"Guide Map of the Great Texas Cattle Trail from Red River Crossing to the Old Reliable Kansas Pacific Railway."* The pamphlet carried several illustrations representing scenes at Ellsworth and included a map of the trail. The company purposely misrepresented the quarantine line for Texas cattle placing it far west of Wichita. The implication was that Wichita was excluded from trade with "through" cattle from Texas. The "Ellsworth Cattle Trail" was labeled "The Best and Shortest Cattle Trail from Texas." For its part, Wichita would not be shy in promoting its advantages and also finding plenty of fault in the Ellsworth market. The fight for the cattle continued.

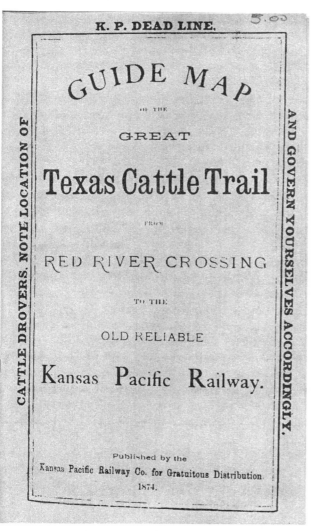

Meanwhile a large and enthusiastic crowd gathered at the Ellsworth County Courthouse on Monday, April 20, 1874, for the express purpose of raising money to promote the cattle trail to Ellsworth. A committee of businessmen was appointed to collect subscriptions, which by the next morning amounted to one thousand dollars. Texas Cattleman Shanghai Pierce was employed to work on the cattle trail "in behalf of Ellsworth." The Kansas Pacific hired another respected Texan, James Elliott to act as their representative on the trail. The two men headed directly for Pond Creek, Indian Territory, where the Ellsworth Cattle Trail turned northwest from the Chisholm Trail. Wichita was not to be outdone and soon had its own representatives, Peyton Montgomery as the Santa Fe agent, and Texan Jim Bryden who had successfully represented Wichita since 1872. Through their representatives, Wichita and Ellsworth argued for the cattle trade with oncoming drovers at Pond Creek. Some drovers were bribed in hopes that other drovers would follow. (5)

157

Herds began to cross the Red River into Indian Territory in mid-April. One trail boss was just a teenager. Sol West was only seventeen years of age when the firm of McCutcheon & West employed him in 1874 to boss a herd from Lavaca County, Texas, to Ellsworth, Kansas. Even at such a young age, Sol was anything but a novice at the business. He had been on the trail since 1871.

The weather was gorgeous the day Sol and his men drove the herd into Indian Territory. Sol described a splendid drive with clear, open, spring weather. Suddenly, on April 8th, 1874, the weather turned bad. Drovers and cattle marched forward in a cold mist that turned to light snow. The chuck wagon well ahead of the herd setting up camp and the men were anxious for the day to end.

The camp was at a place called Hell Roaring Creek, on the old Arbuckle Trail in what is today southern Oklahoma. As the snow began to grow heavier the herd came into sight of the wagon. They were almost there, perhaps one hundred yards from camp, when the wind turned to a gale and a full-scale blizzard was upon them.

The cattle turned their heads to the south and began drifting with the wind and snow. Every man in the outfit was under twenty years of age. The test of manhood was upon them as they fought nature's fury to hold the herd together.

The cold, wet day chilled both man and horse. The blizzard brought them to exhaustion. Horses began to falter. One by one each horse went down, breathing its last in shivering agony. Sol ordered the dismounted men to return to camp as smaller and smaller numbers of cowboys strained to hold the herd. Sol's was the final horse to go down. He and two of the last men to loose their horses held the herd as best they could on foot throughout the rest of the night. Their hands were so cold that no one could retrieve the box of matches that each man had in his pocket. Even if a match had been secured ice-brittle fingers would not have been able to strike a light.

During the early morning hours one of the three men with the cattle spotted a light in the distance. An hour or more later the grounded cowboys stumbled into the two-room dugout of rancher, Jim Taylor. The frozen drovers were fed and put to bed.

When the storm cleared Sol and his men set out for the camp. Jim Taylor and about fifteen of his men followed and arrived at the camp to help in any way they could. Sol traded some of his cattle for three of Taylor's horses and one mule. Sol then sent two men to find his surplus horses, referred to by cowboys as the remuda. Sol's remuda of sixty-five horses was large enough to allow each horse plenty of rest during the long drive to Ellsworth.

Sol had placed two men in charge of the horses before the storm hit. They were found on foot about eight miles south of the camp. The wranglers told of being caught out in the open in the driving blizzard. Every one of the horses died from exposure, even though they had crowded together to stay warm. The two wranglers found a grove of blackjack timber and saved their own lives by building a fire and keeping it going all night. The cattle were held in place for a few days while Sol traded with local Indians for horses. Once his men were all mounted, the drive was continued to Ellsworth.

Kansas Pacific Railway,

The old Established and Popular

Texas Stock Route.

GRAZING GOOD, WATER PLENTIFUL,, SHIPPING FACILITIES
PERFECT, YARDS FREE, RATES LOW.

Two Fast

STOCK EXPRESS TRAINS DAILY

FROM

Ellis, Russell, Ellsworth, Brookville,

Salina, Solomon and Abilene

TO

Kansas City and Leavenworth,

Connecting with the following Roads:

ST. LOUIS, KANSAS CITY & NORTHERN; MISSOURI PACIFIC;
CHICAGO, ALTON & ST. LOUIS; CHICAGO & ROCK
ISLAND; TOLEDO, WABASH & WESTERN;
HANNIBAL & ST. JOSEPH,

AND

KANSAS CITY ST. JOE & COUNCIL BLUFFS.

The only route by which Shippers have the choice of the following Markets :

DENVER, COLORADO. RUSSELL, ELLSWORTH, LEAVENWORTH
KANSAS CITY, QUINCY, ST. LOUIS AND CHICAGO.

Drive to the KANSAS PACIFIC RAILWAY, and avoid hauls over new roads of 300 and 400 miles
without transfer or rest.

THE KANSAS PACIFIC RAILWAY

Offers from Denver and in connection with its newly completed branch—ARKANSAS VALLEY RAIL-
WAY—from LAS ANIMAS special inducements in the way of low rates and quick time to shippers of

Colorado and New Mexico Stock.

Call upon S. R. AINSLIE, Las Animas, or G. LYMAN, Denver, for rates.

EDMUND S. BOWEN,   T. F. OAKES,
    Gen'l Supt.   Gen'l Fr't Agent.

The first trail herds to hit Ellsworth in 1874 arrived on May 6. There were seven new herds that day. Bill Butler out of Karnes County, Texas, had the largest herd with one thousand two hundred head. Six more arrived ready for market the next day, totaling eight thousand eight hundred head for the thirteen herds.

Many towns made an effort to gain the Texas cattle market in 1874. That same year Joseph McCoy published *Historic Sketches of the Cattle Trade of the West and Southwest,* in which he described "… a comfortable resting yard at Ellis, midway distant between Denver and Kansas City." Cattle were already being shipped from New Mexico and Colorado over the famous Kansas Pacific Railway. Richard King of the massive King Ranch of south Texas drove cattle to Ellis and shipped large numbers out of the yards described by McCoy.

Great Bend didn't openly court the cattle trade, but the cattle came anyway. Cowboys did what cowboys did at the end of the trail. The Great Bend *Register* dated May 30, 1874, reported, "On Monday evening a little shooting affair occurred near the Depot. It seems that during the day a couple of parties 'got away' with 15 or 20 dollars of a cow boy's money in some game of chance." (6)

159

By now, cattlemen had been grazing the Kansas prairie long enough to appreciate its advantages. The potential for ranching on the lush grasses attracted drovers with the idea of establishing local headquarters for year-around grazing. Ranches developed along the rivers, provided the best grazing and protection. Making permanent residents of the transient cattlemen made sense to the Ellsworth *Reporter* and other advocates of reasonable development of the plains.

An Ellsworth Ranch

We find the following description of Powers' ranch in this county, furnished by P.K.Y. to the Journal of Commerce:

While writing about farmers and stock-raisers, we will mention the ranch of D. B. Powers and Bro., of the firm of Rogers, Powers & co. commission men in your city. This farm or ranch, as they call it out west, is without doubt, the finest body of land in the Smoky valley. It is in a bend of the Smoky Hill river, about thirteen miles east of this place, and contains 2,160 acres; about 2,000 acres of this is rich bottom land that cannot be surpassed in the state. Surrounding this bottom is a high rolling prairie covered with rich grass that gives an unlimited range for stock and is well watered by a never-failing stream called Bluff Creek. For a stock ranch, Mr. Powers has all that could be desired. 1,400 acres are enclosed with a good board and wire fence, 300 in one field which is used to raise corn and millet to feed his stock, while the balance of this 1,400 acres is used as a pasture for his fine blooded stock, which numbers among his herd some of the finest bulls and cows in the state. - Although the Powers Bros. are among the heaviest dealers in Texas cattle, yet they show their business tact by investing in the pure blood, also. Ellsworth may be proud of these enterprising gentlemen.

The same issue of the Ellsworth *Reporter* noted:

The first cattle shipment ever made from Kansas City to Boston direct was made yesterday by Messrs. Rogers, Powers, & Co. It consisted of thirty-eight head of beeves for another party, and thirty-two of which they sold themselves to a Boston man who was yesterday at the yards. This lot averaged 1300 lbs., and sold for $5.25. Messrs. Rogers, Powers & Co. deserve credit for the sale for the best that anybody else would offer for them was $4.87 ½, but they found a buyer willing to pay $5.25. - Journal of Commerce.

The Powers made their reputation on preparations for winter feeding and the subsequent storms that often crippled central Kansas. Joseph McCoy noted these practices in his *Historic Sketches of the Cattle Trade of the West and Southwest*, "... with such facilities and good preparations their wintering operations are uniformly a success, and heavy losses by storms comparatively unknown." McCoy reported that Hungarian grass is raised and fed, keeping "... Texas cattle thriving and in good heart during the worst winters known in Kansas."

Facilities at the ranch were minimal. Cowboys were housed in "dugouts." Again, Joseph McCoy observed the managerial qualities of David W. Powers.

> Mr. Powers's business, as may be inferred, is large and varied, and requires a good business man to successfully manage it; this he has shown himself to be. He has engaged in almost every branch of business pertaining to live stock, as well as every manner of handling it, having cornfed, grazed, ranged, shipped, and packed cattle; besides, for one or two years has fed the Lo family on the upper Missouri river country. (7)

While Ellsworth seemed to have much in its favor, the Texas cattle trade provided only a fleeting solution to the town's future. The growing outcry from the farming community was about to overcome the drovers. The simple act of taking up claims and closing the open range would soon force the drover from the county.

An event unfolding in west Texas was about to herald a new age for trail driving. John T. Lytle and Thomas M. McDaniel boldly planned to drive a herd of cattle across uncharted territory in route to northern range.

Frank Collinson recalled that the outfit had its hands full as the cattle stampeded every few days. One particular stampede began with a streak of lightning. "... Every steer jumped to its feet and was away on the run. The entire herd seemed to move like one huge animal.

"Finally, when they were herded there was water standing everywhere, and it was difficult or impossible to bed them again." The entire crew of drovers, wet to the bone, stood guard throughout the miserable night.

Singing to the cattle usually helped to calm them but, "... it took a brave lad to sing under such conditions."

The herd reached Fort Dodge in June. Nearby Dodge City was "... a typical Western rag town" according to Collinson.

John T. Lytle successfully guided his herd on a route that would soon become the most traveled cattle trail in history, the Western Trail. In the not too distant future Dodge City would become a far cry from the typical "Western rag town" of 1874. For the time being, there was no market or even a small set of stockyards at Dodge City. Lytle continued his drive north across Kansas to Fort Wallace, then to Sidney, Nebraska. From there the cattle were delivered to an Indian agency at Fort Robinson, Nebraska. (8)

However promising the new trail may have looked to those early drovers of the Western Trail, the primary focus of 1874 was the "Great Texas Cattle Trail." As far as Ellsworth promoters were concerned, Ellsworth was the only railhead of significance that mattered. By early June drovers were arriving daily and the celebration was once more in action.

Horse racing began June 1st "on the fine track north of the city." A six hundred yard race with a one thousand dollar purse saw the large crowd place "considerable money" on a black horse owned by McCune and Scutch, and a bay owned by Arthur Larkin. The black beat the bay by eight feet. Other races that day held the crowd until a thundershower dispersed them to their "homes and camps." Another race was scheduled for the next Saturday. Sam Johns operated the races. Good order was expected to be maintained.

Johns was perhaps more typical of the folks drawn to Ellsworth than history has recognized. He knew horses and mules about as good as anyone. As a young man he was drawn to the Colorado gold rush in 1859. He later became connected with the Central Overland California and Pikes Peak Express Company and the celebrated Pony Express to California. Johns enlisted in Company E., First Colorado Infantry when war broke out between the states. He served in the quartermasters department and was present when Confederate forces were defeated at Glorieta Pass in 1862. The unit was later mounted and redesignated the First Colorado Cavalry. He lived for a time in Denver following his discharge from service before moving to Leavenworth where he operated a dray service.

Johns arrived in Ellsworth from Leavenworth late in 1873. He immediately rented Arthur Larkin's Livery Stable. Sam Johns was a frontiersman who felt very much at home in Ellsworth, Kansas. (9)

As is oft to happen in a frontier town, unexpected incidents tell a story that rarely receives historical recognition.

City Marshal Charley Brown was kept busy taking care of poor unfortunate souls. A young Englishman was found in a lifeless state of exhaustion lying in a freight car on the railroad. The marshal took him to the jail building "not as a prisoner, but to be provided for." The next morning he had gained strength but was still unable to stand on his own, "but for the help and food furnished by our authorities might have perished by this time."

In another incident a young girl "from one of our neighboring cities" was traveling alone. She intended to apply for employment at one of Ellsworth's hotels. "On the way to the city she fell in with a fast young man who, under the promise of protecting her and conducting her to the hotel, took her to one of the houses in the addition (Nauchville)." When one of the residents of the house interviewed the girl she "who might have been deceived herself ... promised to save her at the peril of her life, if need be. She took her to her room and in the morning informed the City Marshal of the presence of the innocent stranger."

Marshal Brown at his own expense, assisted by others in the community, returned the girl to her home while the *Reporter* commended the unfortunate courtesan for her act of charity.

> Let it stand to the credit of the "unfortunate" who was ready and brave to rescue virtue and honor, that she did nobly, and though unfortunate herself, is still a woman, and the friend of woman's virtue. The scoundrel who sought the ruin of the unsuspecting girl was ordered to leave the city and was glad to get himself away alive. (10)

The scoundrel may not have been arrested for attempting to steal away the virtue of an innocent young woman but another young man did run afoul of the law after stealing a saddle from Sam Johns. The saddle was recovered and "The prisoner awaits the decree of the District court."

Young men who endeavored to acquire the property of others, especially when it pertained to horses, were wise to heed the advice of the June 18, 1874, Ellsworth *Reporter*. "It may be necessary to hang a few horse thieves to teach the reckless thieves a lesson – that horses are not common property like the antelope that belong to one who catches it."

Dutch Henry Born was one of those horse thieves that was causing trouble. He carried out a vendetta against both the Indians who had stolen his horses, and against the army who would not help him recover his loss.

Bill Tilghman met Dutch Henry in the spring of 1874. Tilghman was visiting Johnny and Gus Williams, two German boys from Ohio living south of Ellsworth in a dugout. As the young men were finishing breakfast, Dutch Henry and his brother, John rode in. The Born brothers had a herd of horses grazing just up the creek, freshly stolen from a band of Kiowa Indians. Tilghman was in need of a good horse. When he looked them over he recognized a prize race horse that had previously belonged to a chief by the name of White Deer. Tilghman purchased the horse and named him "Chief". Tilghman later recalled that Chief was "the best horse I ever owned … I kept Chief till he died, and I shed tears when I buried him."

Dutch Henry's exploits made him a wanted man. Ellis County Sheriff Alex Ramsey showed up in Ellsworth June 15, 1874, with a United States warrant for the young horse thief. Apparently, Dutch Henry had stolen government stock at Fort Hays.

Ellsworth County Under-sheriff John Stephens was called up to assist Sheriff Ramsey. Dutch Henry and his brother lived in a dugout on Oak Creek north of Ellsworth. The two lawmen set out to arrest the horse-thief. About five miles north of Ellsworth, a man was seen riding horseback over the prairie. It was Dutch Henry. The chase was on. Sheriff Ramsey called to Dutch to surrender, but a raised revolver was his firm answer.

The officers reined in their horses. They quickly dismounted and fired, but Dutch Henry wheeled his horse and galloped out of range.

The bottoms along Oak Creek were covered with heavy brush that provided Dutch Henry with safe refuge. Going into the brush after a desperate man was too dangerous, especially for only two men. Surveying the situation, Ramsey ordered Stephens to return to Ellsworth for more men and guns.

Ramsey stayed a safe distance away, keeping an eye peeled for any attempt at escape. Under-sheriff Stephens located City Marshal Charley Brown and Sam Johns. Johns did not normally serve as a lawman and may have been specially deputized for the occasion. He certainly had the background to rise to the occasion.

When the men returned to Sheriff Ramsey's position on Oak Creek they moved in to take their man. A cave was located and evidence inside the cave indicated Dutch had been there. Evidently the officers' delay led him to believe that he could make his escape. He was tracked up a ravine and located hiding in some tall grass.

Sheriff Ramsey called to Dutch Henry to surrender as the three other members of the posse set about to surround the outlaw. With no answer, Ramsey fired his revolver. The echo of three rifles being cocked sounded across the ravine. Shots were fired. Dutch wisely surrendered.

When he was taken it was found that he had suffered a slight wound to his face from the shot fired by Sheriff Ramsey. Two other wounds also proved to be slight.

Dutch Henry Born was the most famous horse thief of his time. He and his brother, John Born, lived for a while in a dugout north of Ellsworth on Oak Creek. Courtesy Mable Bennett Collection.

As the victorious posse rode into town with the captured Dutch Henry a "... great crowd of men and boys gathered at the jail to see the prisoner." There were two jails in Ellsworth at the time, the City Jail and the Ellsworth County Jail. The County Jail, built in 1873, would have most likely been the probable place of overnight confinement. One would think that being housed in the Ellsworth jail would have been a safe haven for the suspected horse-thief. But only two years before, Pony Donovan had been shot to death by vigilantes as he rested in jail at Hays City. Considering the admonition by the *Reporter* that "it may be necessary to hang a few horse thieves ..." Dutch Henry was most likely heavily guarded through the night.

The next morning Sheriff Ramsey and his man boarded the 10:35 train for Hays City. Oddly enough, no account of them arriving at Hays has been located. Dutch Henry was a cunning individual and became famous for his uncanny ability to escape from captivity. It would appear that he somehow escaped from custody between Ellsworth and Hays City.

He certainly made good time on his get-away. Ten days later, on June 27th, 1874, he was at a lonely buffalo hunter's camp in Texas called Adobe Walls. The Texas panhandle was familiar surroundings for Dutch. It was the same country that he had first ventured into to steal horses from the Indians.

Dutch Henry was surrounded by his friends. Among the hunters on the "staked plains" were men with Ellsworth connections, such as Billy Dixon and Hi Bickerdyke. Dixon helped build Fort Harker in 1867. Bickerdyke was the son of "Mother" Bickerdyke, the noble woman who nursed so many soldiers during the Civil War.

Adobe Walls was a complex of stores established to support the buffalo hunters that had moved into the area. The ruin of an old adobe trading post from the 1840's was just a mile south which gave rise to the name of the new "town" of Adobe Walls. The town contained a total of three sod buildings.

Before sunrise on June 27th, the hunters were awakened in Jim Hanrahan's saloon by what they believed to be the sound of a support pole breaking in the roof. Everyone was up and dealing with the structure when, just at day-break, hundreds of Indians descended upon the camp.

Various accounts differ, but there were approximately twenty-eight men and one woman in Adobe Walls that morning. Throughout the day the hunters held off the attackers with deadly accurate shooting from the big buffalo guns. In the afternoon the Indians backed off to the hills to lay siege to the beleaguered group of hunters and merchants. Billy Dixon took a shot at one of them seven-eighths of a mile away. The men waited. The Indian fell from his horse. It was one of the longest shots recorded with the big buffalo guns.

On the third day, five cowboys rode into Adobe Walls. They were gathering scattered bands of stray cattle that grazed the lush grass of the staked plains, but Indian troubles had forced them to "give it up."

One of the cowboys was Bill Tilghman. Dutch Henry welcomed him enthusiastically, wondering out loud how the men had evaded the Indians. The Indians had given up the fight. The surprised cowboys saw no sign of Indians as they approached Adobe Walls. The siege was over. Dutch introduced his friend Bat Masterson. "Bat, here's Bill Tilghman and I bet he can beat you shooting." The two plainsmen instantly hit it off and became lifelong friends. (11)

Despite Ellsworth's extensive efforts to attract the cattle trade, nature took its own course in the matter. Spring rains did not developed. The grass was in poor condition. Drovers moved to other parts of Kansas where their cattle could improve in condition before selling in the fall. Ellsworth settled in for a long summer.

To add insult to injury, the Rocky Mountain Locust swarmed down on Ellsworth County July 1, 1874. From there the grasshoppers spread to every county in the state. Through the month of August they continued, "... like storms of rain to almost deluge the land." The sound of their chewing was described as "like the working of thousands of scissor blades." In one hour the deadly scourge of locusts could turn a pleasant summer scene into one of bleak despair. Crops were decimated. John M. Muscott described the invasion into Rice County.

165

For the first three days after their appearance, the whole heavens were darkened with their presence and the earth with their bodies. They covered every tree and plant, and every green thing -- the prairie and water courses. They flew like hail in the faces of men, dashed themselves against every object, animate and inanimate, and as they rushed through the air or near the earth, and struck an opposing object, the rattle of their contact resembled the sound of a hailstorm on the roof, or the clashing of sabres in the scabbards of a squadron of cavalry at full gallop. Like the frogs and the locusts in Pharaohs time, they were everywhere.

When this scourge had fairly settled down upon us, the stoutest hearts quailed before it, and gloom was depicted on every countenance. The plow was left standing midway in the furrow, and for a while all farm labor was virtually suspended. The most gifted pen and the most eloquent tongue are inadequate for the task, for language is too poor to paint the scene of desolation wrought by the grasshoppers of 1874. (12)

Editor and co-owner of the Ellsworth *Reporter*, George Atwood, published his last words to Ellsworth in the July 20, 1874, edition of the paper.

We have sold our interest in the *Reporter* to Major H. Inman, who will from this date occupy our place as editor. Mr. Inman is well favorably known to many of our readers as an able, brilliant writer, as an earnest, outspoken man. We feel sure that he will achieve honor and success as a journalist, and that under the new proprietorship the *Reporter* will do a vast work in the development of Western Kansas. John Montgomery, our worthy partner for a year, retains his interest in the paper. In thus ending our co-partnership it is a pleasure to feel that there has never been the least disagreement between us, and it comes hard to break off our relationship. May it ever prosper. (13)

A chapter of the National Grange was formed in Ellsworth County early in 1874. The National Grange was formed in the years following the Civil War to unite private citizens in an effort to improve the economic and social position of the nation's farm population. The Grange was not only an organization of like-minded supporters of agriculture, but also a fraternal organization known as the Order of Patrons of Husbandry.

Dry conditions worsened as the summer wore on. Prairie fires plagued the state. A particularly devastating fire, driven by a fierce windstorm, swept through Wilson's rural neighborhood. Grangers efforts were confined to assisting affected farmers and gaining the cooperation of the Kansas Pacific to equip their locomotives with "spark traps." (14)

Poor range conditions unquestionably damaged the 1874 cattle market at Ellsworth. The numbers were drastically reduced from previous years. Wichita closed the shipping season firmly in the lead as the cattle shipping center of Kansas with fifty thousand two hundred fifty-three head of cattle loaded onto Santa Fe cars. Ellsworth, suffering from drought, tense relations with the Texans, and homesteading settlement shipped eighteen thousand five hundred. Great Bend came in third, but proudly proclaimed themselves more successful than the leaders, considering the town invested no effort to attract the drovers. A little more than sixteen thousand head of cattle shipped at Great Bend added up to three thousand seven hundred more than the year before. The failure to bring Texans to Ellsworth on the heals of the wildly exciting year of 1873 was devastating to Ellsworth's merchants.

As the 1874 season drew to a close the sad news of Colonel J. J. Myers' death was relayed across cattle country. Col. Myers was attacked at Omaha, Nebraska, by robbers who chloroformed him to get his money. He survived the attack but returned to his home in Lockhart, Texas, suffering from the effects of the chloroform. Col. Myers died December 10, 1874, at the age of fifty-seven.

In 1867, Myers advised the young Illinois cattle dealer, Joseph McCoy, that his idea of a cattle depot in Kansas, far away from the settlements of Missouri, was a good one. The Colonel promised his own herds to support the project. From that advice the cattle railhead at Abilene was born. Myers was one of the major drovers on the trail, never driving fewer than four thousand head. He reportedly bought the Powers Ranch in eastern Ellsworth County for twenty-five thousand dollars, however, records do not show a transfer of the land to his name.

Ellsworth County farmers were not interested in large cattle interests taking up tracts of land. The farmers were gaining momentum in their efforts to restrict open grazing of Texas cattle in Ellsworth County. The quarantine or "dead line" on Texas cattle only restricted their presence during the summer. Wintered cattle were not subject to the quarantine and wandered over the entire county until cattlemen were ordered to "herd" their cattle. However the law lacked proper protection of settler's rights. A call for a new "Herd Law" echoed across the county. (15)

Reverend John Jellison represented the farmers in the Wilson area. He ran unopposed for a seat on the Ellsworth County Commission. The settlers west of Ellsworth were united in their opposition to unrestricted grazing and voiced their opinion in a letter to the *Reporter*.

> We all know what we want and let us be in earnest to get it. We want a herd law twelve months in the year; we want the dead line moved from where it now is far enough west so that we shall not be troubled with Texas cattle crossing our county.

Major Henry Inman, formerly a Texas supporter, now editor of the *Reporter* praised the benefits of a modified herd law with its "objectionable features" removed. "At last a majority of the people of Ellsworth county including our leading merchants, have opened their eyes to the fact that the basis of our wealth, and prosperity, lies in the proper advancement of our agricultural interests."

Not only advancement of agricultural interests, but survival was on the minds of those who had endured the drought and grasshopper plague of 1874. Crop failure left many setters destitute.

The drought only confirmed what some political leaders thought of the Great Plains. General H. H. Hazen wrote of its inhospitable climate in the *North American Review*. The General observed in an article entitled "The Great Middle Region of the United States, and its Limited Space of Arable Land," that a line defining the eastern boundary of that forbidding land could be drawn from north to south beginning "... on the British border near Pembina and run near Yankton, Dakota; Ellsworth, Kansas; and by Wichita through Texas." The land west of General Hazen's imposed line was assumed, according to his professed knowledge of the plains to be worthless for farming except in Kansas and even then he refered to the land west of Fort Hays as "desert lands."

There were few in 1874 who could argue that western Kansas was an agreeable place to live or that farming could become a sustainable practice in a land of harsh variations in climate. Yet proponents held to the state's creed, "To the stars through difficulty" as though it were a mere initiation to justly become a Kansan, and as Kansans they would all face that initiation together.

The *Reporter* addressed the problem of destitute farmers, not only recognizing their immediate concerns, but those of the coming season.

> ... it should be borne in mind, that aside from the fact that these unfortunate people have nothing to eat, and no clothes to wear, there is a "seed" time as well as a harvest. That without seed there can be no harvest. And that unless these people are furnished with seed for the spring time, their condition will be as deplorable then as now.

Major Inman called on those able to donate seed to contribute in order to put "our sufferers in a position to help themselves ..."

Former *Reporter* editor G. A. Atwood was appointed by Kansas Governor Osborne to oversee distribution of clothing donated by the United States government. Overcoats, blankets, shoes, boots, stockings, drawers, shirts, dress coats and cloth for sewing were distributed at Wilson, Ellsworth and Fort Harker. (16)

Warm coats and blankets were undoubtedly welcome gifts as the holiday season turned thoughts to winter festivity. There would surely be more dances in Ellsworth as members of the community gathered to celebrate their common bond. For all the differences that had come between them, they were family and as it is with all families, they would make the best of living in this place called Ellsworth.

The season of good cheer was begun with a grand Christmas Eve Ball at Drovers Cottage. If ever a community knew how to come together against the dark days of winter it was Ellsworth. As the celebration was beginning at Drovers Cottage, a few intimate friends and relatives gathered at the home of Marcius and Mary Henry to celebrate the marriage of their daughter, Abbie M. Henry to John Montgomery. The Reverend Dr. Levi Sternberg "officiated at this quiet little wedding, which in simplicity and good taste may be taken as a model, in contradistinction to the ostentation, extravagance, and foolishness that usually characterize the modern fashionable marriage."

Miss Henry was the sister of Sheriff Chauncey Whitney's widow, Nellie Whitney. John Montgomery had been the printer of the Ellsworth *Reporter* from its beginning, being the one who gave the paper its name. From its founding the paper had seen three editors, while Montgomery continued as its printer. He became a co-owner in 1873. The report of the marriage was written by the *Reporter*'s latest editor, Major Henry Inman.

> The ceremony was short, but was made doubly impressive by the presentation to the bride, by her father, of her mother's wedding ring, which he placed upon her finger, with some feeling and beautiful words, peculiarly fitted to the occasion of his daughter's departure from the paternal roof. ... The young lady who has made our Mr. Montgomery so happy, is too well known to need an extended eulogy form us, we simply add our endorsement of her amiable character, and give both herself and husband, our best heart greeting for a long life of perfect bliss, in which there shall neither come cloud, or storm, to ruffle the serenity of the atmosphere which now surrounds them.

After a pleasant half hour of conversation the whole party departed for the Christmas Eve Ball at Drovers Cottage. (17)

The year 1874 would be remembered as a year of change in Kansas. Indians were rarely seen. The buffalo were disappearing. In spite of the grasshoppers and drought, farmers were turning the prairie upside down, forcing cattlemen to shift operations further west. Ellsworth was caught in the inevitable destiny of transformation from a wild-and-woolly cattle town to a true community of enduring principles.

Chapter Eleven

THE END OF AN ERA

The new year of 1875 brought expectations of a settled Ellsworth, free of the wild Texas cowboy. Farm interests were gathering support for the new improved Herd Law that had been discussed at the end of the 1874 season. The Grange movement was sweeping over not only Ellsworth County, but the entire settled portion of the state. Grangers proposed to establish a quarantine that would include an inlet to the Wichita market. Their proposal excluded both Ellsworth and Great Bend from access to the cattle trail. The bill mysteriously disappeared from the docket clerk's desk at the statehouse in Topeka, narrowly averting a closing of the Ellsworth Cattle Trail.

Ellsworth's businessmen were caught between the profitable environment of cattle town economics and the advancement of civilization with its more reserved but stable economy. Settlement in Ellsworth County had not grown to a degree that would support the large business district that had developed in the city. Merchants needed the cattle trade to survive while the settlers needed the same open range that provided grazing for the Texas herds.

As the discussion threatened to return to the atmosphere of '73, namely severe division between urban and rural elements, Mother Nature provided a distraction. The cold was the most bitter in memory. Temperatures dropped to twenty degrees below zero.

The last remnant of the Red River War against Indians who refused the reservation system was drawing to a close on the Staked Plains (primarily the panhandle) of Texas. Reports filtered in from the camps of badly frozen people, many suffering from swollen limbs. The Indians would later say that they had never seen a summer as hot as 1874 nor a winter as cold as 1874-75.

A severe blizzard struck the plains January 7, 1875. Four buffalo hunters, later identified as S. S. Vansickle, Joe Bernard, George Pierson, and John Born were caught in the open. John Born is believed to have been the brother of horse thief Dutch Henry Born.

The men camped "about sixty miles west of south from Dodge City," between Crooked Creek and the dry Cimarron. As they went into camp the wind was from the south and the men quite naturally made their beds on the north side of the wagon. During the night a terrible storm commenced blowing fiercely from the

170

south. It suddenly stopped, followed by an "ominous calm." Within a few short minutes an intense gale swept from the north, accompanied by heavy snow fall. The men pulled their coverings over their heads and lay still as the snow drifted over them. "The snow was driven with such force and the cold so intense that the snowdrift forming over them was at once frozen almost hard as ice."

The men could communicate with each other but the snowpack prevented them from reaching one another. They couldn't even turn over. They were trapped throughout the next day, unable to dig out of the ice-frozen snowbank. One man died "sometime during the long night that followed."

Just before daylight January 9th, Vansickle found that he could barely move in the direction of his head and began to dig a little at a time to free himself.

> His case was a desperate one. His strength failing from exposure and hunger, there was good reason to fear that his prison would in short time become his tomb, but thoughts of home and loved ones lent him strength, and, with one last desperate effort, he succeeded in breaking the shell that held him a prisoner, and emerged from his living grave.

Whether his companions had already expired was not reported. His horses had miraculously survived while picketed nearby. Vansickle cut one horse loose and rode it twenty-five miles to a secure camp. Parties were sent to the camp site and reportedly found two of the men frozen to death but did not located the third man.

Dutch Henry Born told his family that his brother had frozen to death in a blizzard on the plains, but had never given the details. Vansickle's hands and feet were badly frozen but according to the *Reporter* "what will be the result so far ... cannot be certainly known."

Three Ellsworth County men were also hunting buffalo when the storm struck. The paper reported on April 1st "For several weeks the friends of Levi Johnson, his younger brother and James Hammons, have been very anxious to obtain some information respecting them, as report brought the information that just before the terrible snow storm of the 8th of January last, they were known to have been out upon the prairie buffalo range thirty or forty miles from any timber."

J. Young, a buffalo hunter from Ness City sent word of their fate. He and three others traveled west of Ness for three days, arriving at a place he called "sand creek." Having been to the camp of some Ellsworth men in December, the men thought they would pass by their camp again.

Upon their arrival they discovered the "dugout" to be full of snow. Not having tools to dig, the men returned to their own camp to retrieve a spade. They returned to the dugout the next day.

> We removed the snow, and rolled back the robes. I beheld the saddest sight I ever saw, three men side by side frozen to death. The last act of one man was to try to kindle a fire, there was the matches and the shavings laying by his head, but the fire did not kindle ... There was a three banded needle gun in the camp. We dug a grave near by and placed the bodies in it, just as they died, and buried them the best we could under the circumstances.

Perhaps the dead of winter brings mortal men to think more closely of their final end. Whatever the motivation, Major Inman felt compelled to investigate Ellsworth's burying grounds east of the city.

On a bright day last week, we walked out to the 'city of our dead,' way off on the hills. A greater disgrace never existed in a community that makes any pretentions to civilization and refinement. Not a fence or a tree, not even a ditch, to mark the boundary within which those who die among us are supposed to be quietly sleeping. The Indian, whom we on the frontier, hold up to the world as the quintessence of all that is diabolical and savage, would blush for his race, if it paid no greater respect to their dead than we of Ellsworth, who arrogate to ourselves the culture and intelligence of the nineteenth century.

The Ellsworth City Council evidently took Major Inman's words to heart, for on February 17, 1875, Ordinance Number 10 was adopted. Ten acres of land was purchased from S. Atwood and M. Atwood, his wife, for one hundred dollars. One acre was fenced and laid out into lots with the balance leased for farming to Arthur Larkin. (1)

Concern for the advancement of the community extended to the education of the public as to proper etiquette toward pedestrians.

People in wagons should remember that street crossings are for pedestrians. Some people occasionally stop with their wagons on the walk, and indulge in a chat with somebody they haven't seen for a day or two, and the pedestrian can take his choice between crawling under the wagon, climbing over or walking around it, if he has time and the mud is not too deep." (2)

Out in the rural sections of Ellsworth County protectionists were circulating petitions for the establishment of the amended Herd Law. Ellsworth County Commissioners, knowing that any attempt to restrict Texas cattle in the county would prove devastating to business, put off considering the petitions when they were first received on March 10th. However, on March 23, 1875, the commissioners reluctantly mandated the new Herd Law effective May 1, 1875.

Feeling a new political strength, the farmers in the Wilson area called for a removal of the quarantine line west of Ellsworth County. Meeting with counterparts from Russell County a "Farmers Protective Union" was formed "to enforce the laws, and protect ourselves against encroachments of herds of stock of every kind." (3)

An unfortunate distraction during the maneuvering between protectionist farmers and businessmen who needed the Texas trade occurred just over the Ellsworth County line in Lincoln County. John Lyden had not been seen for some time by his neighbors which raised suspicion that he may well have come to an untimely end.

Lyden had been a Forsyth Scout during the Indian War in 1868. He continued scouting for the army through Sheridan's Winter Campaign and was discharged in March of 1869. He was known to be "a fine revolver shot with either hand."

Nothing is known of the course of events that led to Lyden's death, except that he owned a herd of cattle that were being grazed in Lincoln County. A young cowboy by the last name of Eaton was suspected of killing Lyden, whose body was found at the bottom of a well.

> A few days after the body was found, young Eaton, of this place (Ellsworth), was suspected, and by some friend he was so informed; he then secured a fine race horse, belonging to Lydon, and skipped the country. The horse was a fine fleet animal and was marked with the letter "P" on the left shoulder ... Some think he made direct for Indian territory, and others that he has gone to Colorado. His mother thinks him guilty." (4)

Economics also played an enormous role in the development of the cattle trade along the original Kansas Pacific Railroad route from Kansas City to Denver. In April of 1875 the financially strapped Kansas Pacific was struggling. The line had barely survived the financial panic of 1873 when long-term bonds were issued in 1874. The deep financial depression had not healed, leaving many businesses, including the Kansas Pacific, overcapitalized and debt-ridden. Financier Jay Gould of the Union Pacific Railroad recognized opportunity, offering to merge the Kansas Pacific with the Denver Pacific and the Colorado Central into one line under Union Pacific management. The Colorado Central balked on the deal, leaving the Kansas Pacific struggling to stay in business.

Ellsworth was the main shipping point for the KP from 1872 through 1874. Increased settlement around Wilson to the west and south toward Ellinwood had all but closed the cattle trail. The only open crossing on the Arkansas River was at Fort Zarah where Titus Buckbee of Ellsworth owned land. Buckbee and his brother-in-law, Ellsworth businessman Perry Hodgden took over management of the Kansas Pacific Stock Yards in Ellsworth.

The Kansas Pacific Railway appointed a Texan, Captain M. B. Loyd as Special Stock Agent with headquarters in Fort Worth, Texas. The K. P. publicized Ellsworth as "the best grazing district in Kansas," with the advantage of being "near the great corn producing valleys of the Kansas, Saline, Solomon and Republican rivers and their tributaries and with easy access to buyers from Nebraska, Colorado, Wyoming and the North West," adding that "The packing houses at Kansas City prefer and pay more for cattle grazed in the vicinity of Ellsworth than for those from other portions of Kansas."

The Ellsworth City Council made a special provision to allow highly respected City Marshal Charley Brown to work as Ellsworth's full-time trail representative to the incoming Texas herds without loss of pay. The appointment speaks volumes as to Marshal Brown's character. No city marshal in any cattle town in the west rose to the level of respect and admiration from both the cattlemen and city officials than did J. Charles "Charley" Brown.

Considering the amount of effort that was going into attracting the 1875 drive, there could be little doubt that Ellsworth was going to have its work cut out for it regardless. Many drovers were loyal to the Kansas Pacific and the market at Ellsworth, but the new Herd Law made marketing cattle in Ellsworth much more difficult than at other shipping points.

That didn't stop Major Inman from noticing "The prairies were never more beautiful than now; acres of delicately tinted anemones, interspersed with the modest violet deck this whole country round. Other flowers without a name, but whose exquisite tracery would grace an Empress' boudoir, are as common as the blades of emerald grass, which carpet the miles of earth that stretch out before you."

The economic reality of the times was reflected in the appearance and operation of the Drovers Cottage. The hotel had been a central gathering place for drovers and cattle buyers since its opening in 1872. James W. and Louisa Gore were well respected among the townsfolk and Texans alike. They initially established themselves in Abilene in 1868. Joseph McCoy described Mrs. Gore in the most complimentary terms.

Mrs. Lou Gore took good care of her "Texas boys," bringing universal devotion from one and all in cattle country. Illustrated by Professor Henry Worrall - Historic Sketches of the Cattle Trade by Joseph McCoy.

In a brief time it was apparent that in the person of the new landlady of the cottage the drovers had a true sympathizing friend, and in their sickness a true guardian and nurse, one whose kind motherly heart was ever ready to provide for their every proper want -- be they hungry, tired, thirsty or sick, it mattered not; she was the Florence Nightingale to relieve them. From her earliest memory her home has been in a hotel, her father being to this day the proprietor of a large one at Niagara Falls, at which drovers en route to New York or Boston, going via the Falls, delight to stop. Many a sick and wearied drover has she nursed and tenderly cared for until health was restored; or in the event death soothed their dying moments with all the kind offices that a true sister only so well understands how to perform. Many western drovers, rough, uncouth men, such as nature and the wild frontier produces, will ever hear the name of Mrs. Lou. Gore mentioned only with emotions of kindest respect and tenderest memory, and feelings near akin to the holy passion that binds earth to Heaven.

To many who knew them, the Gores were the epitome of honor and reliability. Few would have imagined the lengths that James Gore would go to recover his former state of affluence. Diminished business forced the closing of Drovers Cottage in the fall of 1874. The Gores returned to Abilene where they resumed operation of the original Drovers Cottage, now known as the Cottage House. Ellsworth's Drovers Cottage stood neglected and unoccupied.

During the night of Thursday, April 29, 1875, William Moffat, a watchman at Drovers Cottage saw a dim light issuing from the window of a third story room.

He proceeded with a friend to make an investigation, and upon bursting open the door of the room from whence the light appeared, discovered that a most ingenious plan had been laid to destroy the premises. The room in question was used as a store room for mattrasses, and had but one window, which was shut and the blinds closed. This room had a recess in it, and a hole was cut through the partition in this recess, opening into the next room, and a hole also cut in the roof over the recess. The window in the next room was open, evidently intended (with the holes cut in the partition and in the roof) to cause a draft and insure perfect combustion.

In the recess referred to, eighteen or twenty husk mattrasses were piled, and another placed at the foot of the pile was cut open, exposing the husks, which had been liberally sprinkled with kerosene oil, and in the midst of this a lamp globe with a railroad candle in it had been fixed, with a well saturated wick leading from the bottom of the candle into the husks that had been gathered up around it. The whole thing was dexterously arranged and would have fulfilled its mission most completely but for the vigilance of Moffat ...

Suspicion immediately fell upon Jim Gore who was known to have been in town. He left Ellsworth aboard a train the same evening that the attempted arson was discovered. Upon his return the following day Gore was arrested and placed in jail.

No one was particularly happy to see Jim Gore in jail. His past associations had always been regarded favorably by one and all, and although he had treacherously put the entire business district south of the tracks in jeopardy, he was allowed to leave town without prosecution.

Upon reflection of the recent turn of events, investigators recalled a similar event in 1874. At that time the fire "was speedily checked by the timely use of a fire extinguisher." Gore collected a small claim from his fire insurance. No one suspected arson and perhaps would not have connected that event to Gore, except that on this most recent attempt to burn the hotel the fire extinguisher was rendered useless "by a large hole made in the bottom." (5)

Every spring brought excitement to the cattle towns. Ellsworth businessmen were dangling on every particle of information that brought word of the coming cattle drive. Drovers were reported to be on the trail and by May some were crossing into Kansas. The May 20, 1875, Ellsworth *Reporter* carried a letter from Marshal Charley Brown describing the herds that he had met.

Mr. J. C. Brown who went down to pilot the advance herds of Texas cattle to their great feeding grounds in the vicinity of Ellsworth writes from Ellinwood on date of the 16th inst. 'That he should leave on the morning of the 17th to conduct the droves over the new trail which has been marked out from the crossing of the "Rattlesnake" to Ellsworth via Fort Zarah and the head of Cow Creek.' Mr. Brown desires in his purpose 'to bring them through, and settle them on the grazing grounds in this vicinity without infringing on the rights of any settler, or driving the cattle over any man's land without permission. He does not propose to go near the thickly settled part of the county near Wilson, and wants us to assure the farmers in those localities that their ground shall not be trampled upon by any of the "Long Horns."' - Mr. Brown seems to have taken special pains in these particulars, and we congratulate him upon his well directed efforts to prevent any conflict between legitimate stock driving and agriculture - in fact there is no necessity for any - the county is large enough, there is no need of treading on each other toes. Mr. Brown states further that he finds the prospect of a large trade much better than he anticipated and if Ellsworth does not get her fair proportion it will be her own fault for not making more strenuous efforts. Great Bend is holding much stronger inducements (he states) than Ellsworth, though Great Bend labors under disadvantages from which Ellsworth is free. Great Bend feeding grounds are in the low bottoms of the Arkansas, and in this damp season, more than ever before, the mosquitoes and gnats will worry the herds beyond endurance. The fact is an important one to drovers and in this particular Ellsworth is placed far ahead of Great Bend. No matter how much Great Bend may attempt to deny this, the people know this to be true. Mr. Brown reiterates the statement that with proper efforts, Ellsworth can secure eighty per cent of the trade. Mr. Brown expects to locate 10,000 head (as a starter) near Ellsworth at once.

A week later, Marshal Brown followed with the following remarks.

Ellsworth will get nearly all the cattle not driven directly out of the state to Western and Northern markets. – Last Saturday was quite lively at Great Bend, fourteen herders got on an old fashioned tear, all wild and mounted, but it lasted only one day and peace was restored. Most of those who indulged in this spree have gone home to Texas, having used up all of their loose change either at the saloons or at the Police Court, where they received a lesson that should last them for years. Within a week Ellsworth will be alive with her old cattle friends, who think she has better men to deal with than any other cattle shipping point. The cattle are coming through without any difficulty, there is plenty of room, and they are looking finely and will rapidly improve on the unusually fine grass in Ellsworth county.

The register at the Grand Central Hotel seemed to bear out Marshal Brown's claim that Ellsworth would have a successful 1875 cattle season. Big Jim Ellison, William Butler, John Dewees, Captain Millett and Major Mabry who annually controlled a large portion of the cattle driven to Kansas were all on hand. In addition to influential Texas drovers, several important cattle buyers were also staying at the Grand Central. The May 27, 1875, Ellsworth *Reporter* noted, "Several herds of cattle have changed hands this week." (6)

If ever a spring could inspire confidence in the future, the spring of 1875 was the one. Major Inman reflected the opinion of the majority in the *Reporter* with a piece entitled "June."

We have crossed the margin of sweet leafy June – beautiful gateway of the summer. Month of long hours, and balmy nights. 'Then, if ever, come perfect days,' says the poet. The grain turns into gold, and the harvest is assured – if the grasshoppers will only keep their 'passover' as religiously for the next months as they have in the last.

George Green of Lincoln Center echoed Inman's sentiments, reporting that crops in Lincoln County were all that could be desired and, "we have no grasshoppers."

A new sport was taking the entire country by storm. The National Association of Professional Base Ball Players was formed in 1871. By 1875 baseball was recognized as the "National Game." Ellsworth formed a team which quite naturally was named the "Border Ruffians." The first game was against the Smoky Valley Club of Salina on May 28, 1875.

An intense interest has manifested itself in this coming friendly contest of science and expertness, and we predict such an influx of strangers to witness the game as Ellsworth has never seen. – A hop will end the festivities in honor of the Salina club who have so cheerfully accepted the Border Ruffian's proviso to play them on their grounds in this city.

177

Smoky Valley won the game 31 to 29. Major Inman announced, "We have never witnessed a game where more perfect unanimity of feeling prevailed, or where more perfect justice was shown by an umpire." The game was distinguished by one particular incident that warranted a separate report elsewhere in the *Reporter*.

"Judgment on that ball" yelled the "center fielder," in the game at the city park last Friday, as "a daisy cutter" fresh from the bat of one of the Salina nine took the head neatly off of Dr. Minnick's favorite rooster, who was quietly discussing a few native grasshoppers close to the garden fence. – "Fowl" replied the umpire as he gently turned his umbrella in the direction of the setting sun.

A return match in Salina on June 11, beheld "An immense concourse of spectators assembled to witness the match; business was suspended, court adjourned and the farmers of the surrounding country let the weeds grow one day, and bundled their whole families into the wagon for a holiday. Probably central Kansas never experienced such a gala day since the time the Indians used to celebrate their great feasts, under the giant cottonwoods on the Saline and Smoky, a hundred years ago."

The Border Ruffians won that match 33 to 22 which encouraged them to the degree that they felt certain, perhaps tongue-in-cheek, that another win against Salina would place them in a caliber equal to the task of playing a game against the renowned Chicago White Stockings.

The baseball craze quickly spread to the youth, generating two Ellsworth teams, The Stars of the West and the White Stockings. (7)

However much Ellsworth wanted to immerse itself in the pleasantry of the national pastime, tragedy was never far away. Word of the death of a former Ellsworth man in Trinidad, Colorado, touched the Ellsworth business community. Saloonkeeper Joseph Brennan had been in Ellsworth since the earliest days of '67 when the town was on the river bank. He and his brother Myles had had their share of excitement. They were accused of stealing seventy-one head of mules in 1869. The outcome of that dispute was not recorded. According to the report from Trinidad, Myles was building a house on disputed property. Morris James walked to within twenty-five yards of Myles Brennan with shotgun in hand. While Brennan was sawing a piece of lumber James fired both barrels loaded with "buck, and slugs" at Brennan. Doctors amputated Brennan's hip joint. Brennan died following he amputation. (8)

No matter the tragedy the business of Ellsworth made no allowances for blood, sweat and tears. Expectations waited for no man. Writing for the Kansas City *Price Current and Live Stock Reporter*, L. A. Allen spoke in praise of the potential for marketing cattle at Ellsworth. "Several large herds of cattle have changed hands at this place lately, and the fortunate sellers are returning to Texas well satisfied … Everything looks prosperous about Ellsworth. Some of the settlers think that western Kansas is the garden spot of the world."

In contrast, a letter to the *Reporter* entitled "From Plum Creek" reflected the opinion of many settlers west of Ellsworth. The letter written by a man identifying himself as Duncan McGregor was critical of Marshal Brown and his observation of "the good friendship existing between them (drovers) and the settlers. Mr. Brown says he will settle all disputes; does he say he will pay the bills for all damages? Who is this Mr. Brown, Mr. Editor?"

Mr. McGregor continued, suggesting that Marshal Brown had a financial interest in the cattle and that Mr. Brown should come out among the settlers and have a friendly talk if he was interested in learning something to his advantage.

McGregor complained that Texas cattle were allowed to roam where they please "as a herder told me the other day with revolver in hand ... Does Ellsworth allow this while a farmer has to picket out the little stock he may possess?" McGregor concluded with a request for the editor to publish the Herd Law in the next issue.

Ellsworth *Reporter* editor Major Inman replied in support of Marshal Brown, saying that he represented the city of Ellsworth and that Marshal Brown had heeded Mr. McGregor's letter, traveling to Plum Creek only to find no one in the vicinity by the name of Duncan McGregor. Inman added "We have already published the law three times in the *Reporter*; and to accommodate one man by publishing it again, we think would be too much of an affliction."

While an occasional drover may have resorted to intimidation of an unfriendly farmer most were just trying to do a job. One young cowboy who was with a herd north of Ellsworth the summer of 1875 nearly didn't live to tell his story. James Cook and another young man whom Cook never names were with a bunch of big Texas steers, allowing them to graze and fatten before being shipped to Kansas City.

> We were holding these cattle a few miles north of Ellsworth, Kansas. A few hundred yards from the spot where we bedded them down for the night there was a small stream of water which meandered through a deeply cut channel. Gullies cut into both sides of this channel-bed through a little high uplift of country.

On the particular evening in question the boys had taken turns eating supper and changing horses as they could see a bad storm was approaching.

> Hastily snatching a bite of food and preparing himself for a hailstorm, my companion rode back where I was trying to hold the cattle on the bed-ground. They were trying to drift with the storm, but did not appear to be frightened or excited. We could hear the roar of the approaching storm.

Cook returned to camp for an extra blanket to wear over his head and shoulders for protection from the coming hailstorm. As he was returning to the herd "A terrific clap of thunder, which fairly jarred the earth," set the herd into a mad stampede.

> It had now become so dark that it was impossible for me to see the cattle except during the flashes of lightning which came with blinding effect every few seconds. I rode at the top speed of my horse in order to reach the lead cattle and help my pard swing them. Between the flashes of lightning the darkness was so intense that I could not even see the horse I was riding.

The cattle ran in the direction of the rough ground and the creek channel. They happened to head into a sharp bend of the creek, where the cut banks were very high and perpendicular. A sudden flash of lightning lit the surroundings just in time to save my life and picture a scene I can never forget. My companion and his horse seemed poised in mid-air for a moment, far out over the edge of the high bank of the creek! Several head of the lead cattle were following him to what was undoubtedly certain death. My horse needed no tug at the reins to stop his headlong rush: he braced his forefeet into the earth suddenly and firmly enough to bring him to a sudden halt, not more than five or six feet from the edge of the bluff ... how it happened that the cattle following in my rear did not crash against my horse and send us both over the bank, I shall never know. An instant of blinding light, and then intense and inky darkness reigned again.

In the black darkness Cook was unable to find his companion. He turned and rode to Ellsworth for help. H. D. Stebbins, appointed following Chauncey Whitney's death was the Ellsworth County Sheriff. At daylight Cook led Sheriff Stebbins and Coroner Fox to the scene. They found the young man crushed beneath the body of his horse. A dozen or more cattle lay dead along the creek. "His body was taken to Ellsworth and there buried by the authorities – for nobody knew where he was from." (9)

By late July it was evident that even though some cattlemen had successfully marketed at Ellsworth, few cattle would be driven through the settlements to reach the stockyards. The inevitable march of civilization reduced Ellsworth's cattle business to a trickle. The combination of the settler's natural aversion to free grazing, cattlemen, and the threat of the spread of Texas Cattle Fever to domestic cattle brought an end to the Ellsworth market, just as it had done to Abilene and Newton. The Ellsworth *Reporter* conceded, "... the days of the Texas cattle trade is numbered among the things that were."

Also numbered among the things that were was the need for the kind of lawman that could look a badman in the eye and back him down in any situation. On July 20, 1875, Ellsworth City Marshal J. Charles "Charley" Brown "... resigned his position to fill one of like character on the frontier." Brown had performed admirably, working a near miracle by holding Ellsworth's violence to a minimum, all the while gaining the respect of both the townspeople and the cattlemen. The Ellsworth City Council published a resolution in support of Marshal Brown in the Ellsworth *Reporter*, July 22, 1875. The document acknowledged the marshal's resignation and praised his performance over the past two years saying "Mr. J. C. Brown has for the past two years performed his duty to the entire satisfaction of our citizens ... we cheerfully recommend him as an officer who is fearless, prompt, honest, and always on hand to attend to his duty and equal to any emergency." With that, Charley Brown took his leave and vanished from history. (10)

Interests began to turn from cattle to grain production. The Ellsworth *Reporter* began to publish articles featuring the farmers and stockmen of Ellsworth County. D. W. Powers and Company, famous for their cattle enterprises, announced that

MIDNIGHT STORM AND STAMPEDE.

"It had now become so dark that it was impossible for me to see the cattle except during the flashes of lightning which came with blinding effect every few seconds." - James Cook.
Illustrated by Professor Henry Worrall - Historic Sketches of the Cattle Trade by Joseph McCoy.

they were planning to build a grain elevator "to store grain, of which they intend to purchase largely, and make this important trade an adjunct to their already varied and increasing business."

In an article entitled "The Crops of Ellsworth County," The county's agricultural promoters reportedly gathered specimens of wheat, rye, oats, barley, millet and corn to be exhibited at the Kansas City Exhibition in September.

In contrast to Jim Gore, who tried to alleviate his reduced patronage at Drovers Cottage by attempting to burn the place down, Joseph Anderson creatively adapted one of the oldest Ellsworth Hotels into a grain warehouse. The *Reporter* observed "The old Marshal House is rapidly being pulled to pieces, and we shall soon be able to record it in position on a firm foundation along side the track, and rehabilitated as a substantial grain warehouse."

F. P. Conway, "an old citizen in this portion of Kansas" applauded the move with his letter, "The Grain Warehouse Vs. Drovers Cottage" saying "how have the mighty fallen," referring to Jim Gore as "the lion of the day." Conway scorned all that Gore and his hotel represented.

… The Cottage stands to-day like a body without a soul, stripped of all its furniture and appointments, and a mere watchman left to look after the once admired and renowned (?) hotel. Its flattered and honored landlord, ex-councilman, ex-mayor, &c., gone, under circumstances which reflected but little credit upon that worthy gentleman.

Weeds grow in the streets where Texas cattle once pawed the earth. "... the days of the Texas cattle trade is numbered among the things that were."
Courtesy Ellsworth County Historical Society.

Conway continued to document the restless days in which Drovers Cottage reigned supreme.

> The "Dance House," the "Gambling Tables," the "Saloons," and "Houses of Prostitution," were in their glory. But "Man can tether time nor tide," the day has come "Long Horns" must forswear their claims and give place to far more precious stock and avocations ... The most sanguine expectations agriculturally have been exceeded. In place of the Drovers Cottage and its uproarious inmates, we have the quiet unpretending Grain Warehouse ...

Speaking of Joseph Anderson, Conway pictured a man, "laboring earnestly to promote the solid interests of the county, not merely for four months in the year, but for twelve, and for every year. While the Texas cattle trade drove farmers from the county, and threw the burden of taxation upon the city, the Grain Warehouse will be the medium indirectly, if not directly, of bringing hundreds of farmers to the county, and thus equalize the taxes between town and country ... I for one, think that an enterprise which will surely bring wealth to the county, and prosperity to our merchants, and mechanics, should at least receive the thanks of the city."

One by one the symbols of the Texas cattle trade began to disappear from Ellsworth. In early August raucous Nauchville turned quiet and her festive lights grew dim. "Most of the gilt edged women of the town have gone, and taken their infatuated, peripatetic and worthless paramours with them, there are few more of the same sort left hanging around town, and we hope soon to record their departure too, then

Ellsworth will have well gotten rid of an element which has been the fertile cause of keeping more good people away, than would have ever been compensated by a population of ten thousand such as have left us."

Times were certainly changing on the streets of Ellsworth. The Mayor's office issued a notice August 23, 1875, "From to-day all stores, saloons, and places of business, will be kept closed on Sunday. The trading public will take notice, and govern themselves accordingly."

Perhaps most telling among the exodus of businessmen was the closing of Mayer Goldsoll's Old Reliable House. The loss of one of the most vigorous commercial houses in Ellsworth signaled the end of the dynamic frontier element that had heightened commerce to a degree seldom seen elsewhere in Kansas.

Goldsoll announced in the August 19, 1875, issue of the *Reporter* that his goods, including wagons, groceries of all kinds, boots and shoes, clothing, hats, caps, etc., were on sale at greatly reduced prices. The *Reporter* eulogized "M. Goldsoll was one of the earliest merchants of Ellsworth and did an immense business in the days of the Texas cattle trade. Besides the house here, Mr. Goldsoll had branch establishments at Russell, Denison and Great Bend. These three are continued and the Ellsworth business removed to Texarkana in Texas. Mr. Goldsoll was always an earnest supporter and friend of the *Reporter*, and we shall miss his kind words and liberality more than others perhaps. We wish him all the success possible, and shall always remember him with the kindest of feelings."

John Mueller was not far behind Goldsoll. Mueller's store, with the sign of the big red boot, was a landmark along the false fronted buildings of South Main. Mueller resigned his position on the city council, announcing his intentions to go to the "new town, near the Military Post, in the Pan Handle of Texas." On further inspection he must have changed his mind for he opened a new boot and shoe store in Dodge City not long after leaving Ellsworth. "Mr. Mueller was one of our most enterprising citizens, liberal, straightforward, and a constant patron of the *Reporter*." (11)

The peace and quiet on the streets of Ellsworth was shattered a little after midnight November 12, 1875, when the cry of "Fire!" swept through Ellsworth. Before a defense could be mounted, flames were bursting through the roof and sides of C. H. Foster's carriage painting business near the corner of South Main and G Street (Kansas Avenue). The combustible nature of the painting business "rendered it impossible to suppress or confine the fire to its place of beginning, and in a few moments it had enveloped the adjoining buildings, which also constructed, of wood, it licked up like so much straw, and was rapidly threatening the destruction of the whole town."

O. W. Whaley wrote, "I have been at a number of large fires, but I never saw people turn out so quickly, or work with such perfect good order. I was surprised at the number of men. I did not think there were more than half so many in the place. I noticed several men from Beloit hard at work carrying out goods … I must say for Leo. Herzig, that I think he can throw water higher with a bucket than any other man I ever saw try."

According to the *Reporter* there were "immediately a hundred willing hands with twice as many buckets who were throwing water over the large warehouse (The Grain Warehouse) on the corner of F and Main …" While merchandise was being carried to safety, others fought to contain the fire to just one block. Several men united to stop the fire from crossing east of F Street (South Douglas Avenue). The entire block was consumed, destroying approximately twenty-two to twenty five buildings.

Sparks and cinders blown across the river ignited the prairie, sending a massive wall of fire over farms and ranches The prairie fire roared all the way to the Little Arkansas River some eighteen to twenty miles south of Ellsworth.

Major Inman was quick to praise the pluck of Ellsworth's businessmen who vowed to rebuild with substantial stone stores as soon as spring was upon them. "Such men will win in the end, and their field of operations will grow larger every year." With that, Inman posed the question as to the wisdom of rebuilding on the south side of the railroad. "The idea in our opinion, of making a business center on both sides of the railroad should be abandoned; our merchants should concentrate on one or both of the streets north of the track, leaving one side of the railroad avenue only for warehouses and grain elevators." Inman suggested that perhaps the burnt out block could become a beautiful park leading to the river. "We earnestly hope our citizens will give these ideas serious thought, and turn the town in the direction nature emphatically demands it should go." (12)

The fire was the final death blow to frontier Ellsworth. Out of the ashes a new agriculturally based society laid a fresh foundation for a future of civility and opportunity. But the Wild West was only a breath away. On the night of December 2, 1875, two horses were stolen from a Mr. Williams four miles south of Brookville. After two days of tracking, Williams arrived at H. T. Anderson's, southeast of Ellsworth (the mouth of Horsethief Canyon at Kanopolis Lake). He and Anderson tracked the thieves into Barton County and captured two men with seven head of horses. As they were returning the outlaws attempted an escape. One man was killed, the other escaped and was never recaptured.

Ellsworth suffered, celebrated, and overcame adversity in a way that no other town would ever know. Ironically, city fathers looked beyond the bleak winter to the green grass of spring for a fresh start. In place of the wild Texas steer, the new wealth would be measured by the influx of families to the once open prairie. (13)

Ellsworth may have declared itself squarely civilized and prepared to meet the future with a gracious consciousness, but the violent frontier was never far away and was apparently not about to depart with comparable courtesy.

Chapter Twelve

LEAVES OF PROMISE

As a desperate seed, Ellsworth gnarled its way through life, growing through both anticipation and disappointment. In eight short, volatile years Ellsworth developed from a ravenous denizen demanding "a man for breakfast" to a resilient sapling, more intent on the game of base ball than on its own security. Each year uncertain obstacles and fervent support were met with courage and determination as leaves of promise carried forth the vision.

Immigration filled the vacuum left by the Texas cattlemen who abandoned Ellsworth County for less populated sections of western Kansas. Farms and ranches were the hallmark of a modern agrarian society advanced as the redeemer of civilization. Harvest fairs and stock shows took the place of gambling dens and dance halls. The frontier was so far removed from Ellsworth's presence that Ellsworth *Reporter* editor Major Henry Inman assumed the additional role of Ellsworth County's first historian. Several of the 1876 *Reporter* issues were dedicated to the chronology and significance of the cultivation of a modern society on the wild plains of Kansas.

There would be continued episodes to serve as reminders of Ellsworth's violent origin. 1876 brought news of the deaths of Wild Bill Hickok and General George Armstrong Custer. Both men had forged legendary reputations in the environs of the enduring Smoky Hills.

One more fire in March of 1877 destroyed the remnants of South Main between today's Douglas Avenue and Lincoln Avenue. The fire erased all evidence of the bawdy lifestyle that had once classed Ellsworth among the wildest of western towns.

Sheriff Whitney's killer was captured and returned to Ellsworth for trial. Fearing he might escape, or worse, hung by vigilantes, Billy Thompson was transferred to Leavenworth for safe keeping.

Thompson's trial commenced September 5, 1877, requiring his return to the Ellsworth County Jail where "The good ladies of the town forgot he was a bad man and showered him with bouquets of choice flowers and fed him the delicacies of the season."

The trial lasted nine days and to the surprise of many of Ellsworth's citizens the clerk read the words "not guilty," upholding the position that the shooting was accidental. (1)

Perhaps it was her association with Wild Bill Hickok. Perhaps it was the mystery which surrounded her. Whatever the reason, Indian Annie was one of those individuals

Anna Wilson, popularly known as Indian Annie, and her daughter Birdie Daisy. Indian Annie was well known to Ellsworth residents as Wild Bill Hickok's wife, who was faithlessly abandoned in 1871.
Courtesy Ellsworth County Historical Society.

that left an impression on almost everyone who met or even heard of her.

When news of Hickok's death reached Ellsworth Indian Annie was on her knees scrubbing floors in Larkin's Grand Central Hotel. According to Arthur Larkin's son, Charles, she paused for only a moment to look up and declare "I'm damned glad of it," before returning to her scrubbing.

A *Reporter* for the Leavenworth *Daily Times* left a fortunate account of a youngster in Ellsworth who has often been overlooked in the chronicles of the Old West. The boy was the son of Anna Wilson, Wild Bill's companion for many years until he abandoned her in Abilene in 1871. Indian Annie returned to Ellsworth to eek out a living, give birth to Hickok's son, Willie, and raise him as best she could. The October 21, 1877, edition of the *Daily Times* reported, "Young Wild Bill, now a lad of nine or ten years of age, is exactly like his father, built upon the same architectural plan, and is possessed of the same spirit. It takes a tough lad to get away with him, and he 'runs the ranch' usually wherever he goes ... Mrs. Wilson, or Mrs. Wild Bill, or Mrs. Hickok, or whichever-name-you-choose-to-call-her, is an Indian of low stature, not bad looking."

Historians have supposed that Anna Wilson had taken up with a man by the name of Wilson after Hickok abandoned her in 1871, but she was using the name "Wilson" in 1870 when she was with Hickok. A daughter, Birdie Daisey was born to Anna Wilson April 17, 1878. When Birdie was three years of age, circa 1881, Willie died of a childhood disease and was buried on the hill east of Ellsworth in a pauper's grave.

Anna was not long in following her son to the old burying place on the hill. She suffered from consumption and died at the County Poor Farm. The Ellsworth *Democrat* carried her obituary.

Mrs. Wilson, well-known to our citizens as the "little Indian woman", and wife of Wild Bill, died last Tuesday morning (November 10, 1885) at 5 o'clock. She leaves a little girl about seven years of age, who will be provided for by Mr. Thompson, of Mulberry Creek. (2)

A chronicle of the participants in Ellsworth's days of discord could more than likely fill another book. One Nauchville girl, Mollie Brennan, turned up in a buffalo camp on Sweetwater Creek in the Texas panhandle. She was in conversation with a young buffalo hunter by the name of Bat Masterson when a jealous lover opened fire. Bat was hit in the pelvis as Mollie fell to the floor with a mortal wound. While lying next to Mollie, their blood mingling on the floor, Bat fired, killing the attacker. (3)

Another Nauchville girl, Alice Chambers moved on to Dodge City. She was well-known for keeping a squirrel as a pet. Squirrel Tooth Alice was one of Dodge City's favorite girls. Alice and a gambler by the name of Charlie Ronan were known to be lovers. Owing to Alice's profession, a certain leniency toward unfamiliar affections was essential to a lasting relationship. Unfortunately Ronan wavered in his uncertainty to Alice's devotion. In a moment of anger Ronan pistol-whipped Alice unmercifully. She never recovered. Alice Chambers was buried on Boot Hill May 5, 1878, the very last person to be laid to rest there. (4)

The most famous Nauchville woman was Lizzie Palmer. Her dance hall, The

Nauch, had given rise to the identity of the whole district. Lizzy's end was recorded by Paul Wellman in *The Trampling Herd*. Quoting a Mrs. Annie Anderson who had once been a dance hall girl in Ellsworth, Newton and Dodge City, Wellman told of a classic cat fight between Lizzie and another girl. There was scratching and hair pulling, with Lizzie receiving a scalp wound which became infected. She died from blood poisoning. The cowboys hired a preacher to perform a proper funeral and buried her on Boot Hill. (5)

Rowdy Joe and Rowdy Kate found trouble just about everywhere they went. Joe killed a man in Newton in '72 and another in the brothel district of Wichita in '73. They lit out to Texas and finally separated. Joe was killed in a saloon fight in Denver in 1899. Rowdy Kate's end is unknown. (6)

A train robbery at Kinsley eventually brought several gang members to Ellsworth County in the fall of 1878. Mike Roark, Dan Dement, Ed Brooks and a man known only as Tillman were hiding out at Titus Buckbee's place on Thompson Creek, approximately seven miles southeast of Ellsworth. Buckbee's ranch utilized a natural box canyon for protection. The house and barn were situated at the mouth of the canyon.

Apparently Dan Dement had shown too much affection for the wife of saloon man, William Kersey at Brookville. On Kersey's information, local law enforcement learned that the men were bold and daring train robbers.

During the night of October 18, 1878, County Sheriffs from Ellsworth, Saline and Ellis Counties led a posse toward Buckbee's ranch southwest of the Smoky Hill River. The ranch was quietly surrounded as lawmen waited until morning for their prey to waken. One by one the outlaws were taken as they sleepily stepped into the barn to tend to their horses. Several of the men were alerted and ran for the brush. Tillman, Brooks, and Dement escaped.

Dement made it back to Evander Light's farm west of Salina near Bavaria, Kansas, on Monday, October 21, 1878. Unknown to Dement was the fact that Evander Light, who first met the outlaws following the Kinsley robbery, was working under cover as a special agent for the Santa Fe Railroad. Light announced "I have been looking for you for more than four months. I want you, and I want you right now. I have a warrant in my pocket for your arrest."

Dement went for his gun. A quick shot passed near Light's face. Light was able to get off a load from his shotgun just before Dement fired his second shot. Dement heaved over backward, never showing a sign of life after he went down.

While not positively identified, the Tillman involved with the gang may have been Bill Tilghman, who was familiar with Ellsworth County and was known to run with men such as Dutch Henry Born. Tilghman would go on to become one of the West's most famous lawmen. (7)

The Texans may have moved on to greener pastures in the latter half of the eighteen seventies but one Texan returned to build a prosperous ranch. Captain Eugene Millett was well known on the cattle trail. He and his brothers annually drove several herds north from Texas. The Captain had served faithfully in the Thirty-second Texas Cavalry under the flag of the Confederate States of America. When the war was over he embraced the cattle business and eventually purchased the old Powers Ranch on Bluff Creek. The ranch was named in honor of his wife

Ida. Idavale became a showplace of purebred cattle and high-bred racing horses. Arthur Larkin and Captain Millett established a lasting friendship, perhaps spending many hours reflecting upon the uncertain past they had survived.

Arthur Larkin, seated, and Captain Eugene Millet, standing.
Each man forged his own unique life with great affection for Ellsworth.
Courtesy Ellsworth County Historical Society.

Ellsworth during the later part of the nineteenth century easily brings to mind an image of the classic western town portrayed in the "B" western movies. A day on the street during those times reflected a culture of businessmen in neatly pressed suits offering hearty greetings to farmers as teams and wagons were tied to railings at busy storefronts. Ranch men may have gathered at the feed store to discuss the condition of the range while ladies stepped into shops to make selections for the home. The bar certainly was not a thing of the past, although its celebrations were noticeably subdued.

In that atmosphere the waning months of 1881 brought back a sharp memories of an Ellsworth most residents of Ellsworth County wanted to forget. The January 4, 1882, edition of the Ellsworth *Reporter* shockingly printed the story, "MURDERED AND BURNED, Ellsworth In A State Of Excitement." The town was startled at the report that a farmer in the southeast part of the county had been found burned to death in his shanty on December 28, 1881. The shock of Phillip Agley's death was even more pronounced when his nephew, W. E. Graham was arrested after "spending considerable money since ..." Graham confessed to the murder saying, "he had struck his uncle over the head with a boot tree, and then set fire to the shanty, and succeeded in burning that portion of the head upon which the blow was dealt, so it was impossible to discover how he had murdered him. The amount taken from his uncle was about $135."

The murder offered up hollow images of the blood and thunder days that Ellsworth had thought it had left behind. The frontier appeared to be backing its way into Ellsworth. Only three months earlier, in late September, 1881, Louis A. Rose murdered Andrew Ware and his son and then buried them in his potato patch. One month later Rose was captured by officers in Oxford, Kansas, and returned to Ellsworth.

Philip Agley's murder was more than the community could stand. A gang of vigilantes formed on Monday, January 2, 1882, and as word spread the crowd grew.

> A party of two or three hundred men, supposed to have come from all parts of the county, assembled at the court house, and at a given signal by some one, a rush was made for the jail, the outer door was bursted open, the sheriff and his guards over powered and taken into custody by some of the party ...

Graham was hauled from his cell on that cold January night and taken to the first telegraph pole outside the jail. The vigilance committee entertained the prisoner with a quick trial which found him guilty. Just as in its turbulent years, Judge Lynch dealt exacting justice. Graham was soon hanging from the telephone pole, "... until he, W. E. Graham, was dead! dead! dead!!"

While Graham was still dangling from the pole in front of the jail the vigilantes returned to the cells, seeking to deliver the same fate to Louis Rose. The crowd was disappointed to find an empty cell. Officers had slipped Rose out the back while the vigilantes were occupied with Graham. (8)

North Main in the latter part of the Nineteenth Century, looking east from Douglas Avneue. Courtesy Ellsworth County Historical Society.

Louis Rose escaped the Ellsworth vigilantes but on Thursday afternoon, March 9, 1882, his blood surely ran cold when at the conclusion of his trial the foreman of the jury announced, "We the jury, find the defendant, Louis A. Rose, guilty of murder in the first degree."

A motion for a new trial was overruled. Judge J. H. Prescott addressed the prisoner,

> So heinous is this offense that the law has foreordained with certainty what its orders shall be, and I, and all must humbly bow to its decree. Such is my duty ... that judgment of the law which I must now pronounce, is that you be taken from the jail of this county, and by the sheriff of this county conveyed to the State penitentiary, delivered to its authorities, confined at hard labor, and there upon such day as the governor of this state shall appoint, be hanged by the neck until you are dead.

Two separate murders; one avenged by mob rule, the other decided by the rule of law, contrasted the violent culture of the past against the orderly culture Ellsworth tenaciously strived to achieve. (9)

The ghosts of Ellsworth's violent past seemed to be awakening in 1882. Under-Sheriff C. F. Clark received a telegram on Sunday, April 2, 1882, advising him to be on the look-out for deserters from Fort Hays. That evening the 7 p.m. train was boarded at Ellsworth by Clark and Deputy Charley Bell. Two of the deserters were identified and taken into custody. As the officers and their prisoners stepped from the train one of the deserters broke away. Ignoring Under-Sheriff Clark's warning to "halt" proved to be unfortunate for the fleeing deserter. Shots were fired.

191

The first striking him in the left shoulder and the others missing him. The wound did not stop his onward course, and as he passed up the avenue J. S. Barnum fired two shots striking in the same place that Clark's two last shots did. By this time the "discouraged" soldier concluded that he would rather live than die, and stopped running. (10)

From time to time Ellsworth would revisit the past, however seriously its citizens desired to forget. There were always those who chose to remember. One of the legends of Ellsworth is that of a young woman known as Prairie Rose. She was supposed to have been one of the "darlings of Ellsworth's dance halls" who made her living in the wild atmosphere at the end of the cattle trail. She was supposed to have taken a fifty dollar bet requiring her to walk unclothed down Ellsworth's main street. The next morning at five o'clock the Wild West Lady Godiva showed up with "a six-gun in each hand threatening to shoot out any eye that showed." The legend closes with no one having the nerve to look and no shots being fired.

The story of Prairie Rose has been repeated in perhaps dozens of Old West stories, but it is only partially true. Prairie Rose was not one of the fancy ladies at the "end of the trail" in Ellsworth. She was actually a wild teenage girl of the late 1890's. The story became so distorted that it is impossible to know the actual sequence of events.

It appears that a certain group of Ellsworth's young folks were drinking and carousing in a way that their parents would not have approved. Some of the young men were from local cattle ranches and lived the cowboy lifestyle. The young women drawn to these dashing cowboys were themselves daring and out of control.

Perhaps reflecting upon Ellsworth's wild and woolly past, the proposition of walking down the street naked was posed. It may well have been that more than one person shed their clothes, for a John Doe was arrested August 20, 1897, after he "appeared in the streets of the city of Ellsworth in a nude condition and intentionally exposed his person." Be that as it may, the young lady that shed her clothes grew to legendary proportions as the story was told and retold. Years later historians picked up the story and attributed it to the wrong decade. Prairie Rose, who may have yearned for those days of yesteryear, quite unintentionally became an icon for those very days, a legend out of her time. (11)

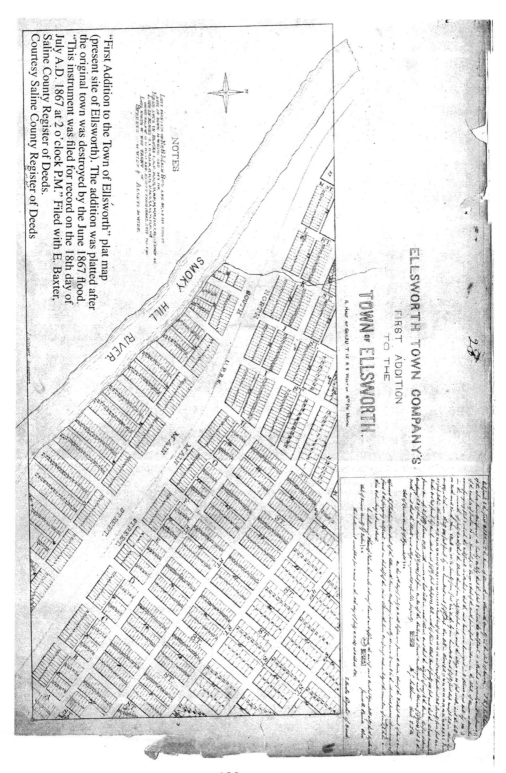

ELLSWORTH TOWN COMPANY'S

FIRST ADDITION

TO THE

TOWN OF ELLSWORTH.

R. MAP OF GRAND T. 15 R 8 WEST OF 6TH PR. MERID.

NOTES

"First Addition to the Town of Ellsworth" plat map (present site of Ellsworth). The addition was platted after the original town was destroyed by the June 1867 flood. "This instrument was filed for record on the 18th day of July A.D. 1867 at 2 o'clock P.M." Filed with E. Baxter, Saline County Register of Deeds.

Courtesy Saline County Register of Deeds

193

Crossing The Smoky Hill River at Ellsworth
Alexander Garner Photograph – Author's Collection

EPILOGUE

"... There is a "seed" time as well as a harvest
... without seed there can be no harvest."

-Major Henry Inman

The story of Ellsworth's founding and violent years of struggle is one that sets the town apart from most any town the United States has ever produced. Ellsworth was indeed a desperate seed struggling for life in a forbiddingly harsh soil.

The town eventually reinvented itself, moving its business district away from the plaza to form a stable business district central to the needs of its citizens. South of the tracks, one hotel continued along Douglas Avenue with a conveniently located livery nearby. Homes were built and the echo of the bawdy dance was forgotten.

"... There is a "seed" time as well as a harvest ... without seed there can be no harvest." Quietly, a seed found refuge in that unforgiving soil. The seed somehow sprung to life near the tracks that had brought so much excitement to this place on the banks of the Smoky. Miraculously, the sprout became a sapling and was perhaps ignored through its ungainly first years of life. When it first drew attention none can say. But as the years swept by the desperate seed that had sought refuge in this historic place became a majestic cottonwood tree.

There is no other place on earth like Ellsworth, Kansas. There never will be. One tree bears witness that from a desperate struggle a treasure can flourish while beneath its branches a heritage is remembered. God bless the desperate seed.

195

NOTES

CHAPTER ONE

(1) Wayne C. Lee, Howard C. Raynesford, *Trails of the Smoky Hill,* The Caxton Printers LTD, Caxton, Idaho, 1980, p. 152-153.
(2) Charles J. Lyon, *The Compendias History of Ellsworth County, Kansas, From Its Settlement to the Present Time,* Reporter Press, 1879, Reprint of First Edition, Prepared by Patricia Svaty, Ellsworth, Kansas, 1998. p. 25.
(3) Lee, p. 154
(4) John F. Choitz, *A History of Ellsworth County, 1854-1885.* Master's Thesis, Fort Hays State College, Hays, Kansas, 1942, Republished by Alfred H. Choitz, South Bend, Indiana, 1999, p. 7.; George Jelinek, *The Ellsworth Story, 90 Years of Ellsworth and Ellsworth County History,* The *Messenger Press,* Ellsworth, Kansas. p. 11; Alfred Thayer Andreas, [With William G. Cutler], *History of the State of Kansas,* 1883. Chicago, A.T. Andreas. p. 1274; Marsha King, *Results of Archaeological Investigations at Fort Harker, 14EW310, Ellsworth, County, Kansas,* Contract Archaeology Publication No. 17, Kansas State Historical Society, 1997. p. 85
(5) Choitz, p. 10, Andreas, p. 1276
(6) Robert K. Dykstra, *The Cattle Towns,* University of Nebraska Press, 1983, p. 18-19
(7) Lee, p. 94-95; King, 94-95; Oliver Knight, *Following The Indian Wars,* University of Oklahoma Press, 1993, p. 57-62
(8) L. O. Wight, Draftsman, *Plat of Ellsworth, Kansas,* Book A, Plat Books, Saline County Register of Deeds, May 4, 1867,
Andreas, p. 1276
Dykstra, p. 34-35
(9) Lee, 96-102, King, 95-96
(10) Lee, p. 158, Choitz, p. 11, Jelinek, p. 1, Dykstra, p. 33, Andreas, p. 1276, Wight, *Plat of Ellsworth Kansas*
(11) Fanny Kelly, *Narrative of my Captivity Among the Sioux Indians,* R.R. Donnelley & Sons, Co. 1891, p. 233-234
(12) Lyon, p. 25
(13) Choitz, 11-12, Dykstra, 33
(14) Junction City *Union,* July 6, 1867
(15) Kelly, p. 234
(16) Lee, p. 159-160
(17) George Augustus Armes, *Ups and Downs of an Army Officer,* Self Published, 1900, p. 232-233
(18) Lee, p. 160, King, p. 97-99, Andreas, p. 1276, Dykstra, p. 34, Choitz, p. 17-18
(19) Andreas, p. 1276-1277; Lee, p. 160
(20) Lee, p. 115-116
(21) Kelly, p. 234-235

(22) Alice Blackwood Baldwin and Eleanor R. Carriker, *An Army Wife on the Frontier*, Tanner Trust Fund, 1975, p. 42-43

(23) Dykstra, p.19

(24) Miguel Antonio Otero, *My Life on the Frontier*, 1864-1882, The Press of the Pioneers, Inc., 1935, p. 8-10

(25) Henry M. Stanley, *My Early Travels and Adventures in America and Asia*, Charles Scribner's Sons, 1895, p. 96-97; Joseph G. Rosa, *They Called Him Wild Bill*, University of Oklahoma Press, Second Edition, 1974, p. 115

(26) Nyle H. Miller and Joseph W. Snell, *Why The West Was Wild*, University of Oklahoma Press, 2003, p. 186-187, Rosa, Joseph G. and Waldo E. Koop, *Rowdy Joe Lowe, Gambler with a Gun*, University of Oklahoma Press, 1989, p. 16, Choitz, p. 18; Rosa, *They Called Him Wild Bill*, p. 116

(27) Andreas, p. 1277, Rosa & Koop, p. 17-18

(28) Miller & Snell, p. 630

(29) Elizabeth Bacon Custer, *Tenting on the Plains or General Custer in Kansas and Texas*, University of Oklahoma Press, 1994, 395-397

(30) Joe E. Milner and Earle R. Forrest, *California Joe, Noted Scout and Indian Fighter*, University of Nebraska Press, 1987, p. 155-158

(31) Leavenworth *Daily Bulletin*, February 13, 1867

(32) John Hanson Beedle, *Western Wilds and The Men Who Redeem Them*, Jones Brothers Publishers, 1877, p. 213

(33) Orvel A. Criqi, *Fifty Fearless Men*, Walsworth Publishing Company, Marcelene, MD, 1997, P. 74, Dykstra, p. 35-36

(34) Lee, p. 118

(35) Blaine Burkey, *Wild Bill Hickok, The Law in Hays City*, Third Edition, Slightly Revised, Ellis County Historical Society, 1996, p. 11; Rosa, *They Called Him Wild Bill*, p. 146

(36) Wilson, p. 15

CHAPTER TWO

(1) James Hollister Ovando, *The Mines of Colorado*, Samuel Bowles & Co., 1867, Advertisement.

(2) Jelinek, p. 19-20; The Hays City *Railway Advance*, January 16, 1868

(3) William A. Sternberg, Chased By Indians, William Sternberg Collection, Ellsworth County Historical Society

(4) Rosa & Koop, p 18

(5) Leavenworth *Daily Conservative*, March 17, 1868; Joeseph G. Rosa, *They Called Him Wild Bill*, University of Oklahoma Press, Norman, Oklahoma, 1974, p. 119

(6) Biennial Report, Kansas State Historical Society, 1881, p. 1676

(7) Jelinek, p. 18-19; W. F. Thompson, *Peter Robidoux: A Real Kansas Pioneer*, Collections of the Kansas State Historical Society, Vol. XVII (1926-1928) p. 285-286

(8) Choitz, p. 21-22

(9) Lee, p. 172-173

(10) Jerome A. Greene, *Washita: The U. S. Army and the Southern Cheyennes*, 1867-1869. University of Oklahoma Press, 2004, p. 47

(11) Ellsworth Messenger, July 15, 1948, *Stampeded Buffalo Through Town*

(12) C. Bernhardt, *Indian Raids*, The Lincoln Sentinal Print, 1910, p. 42-43; Elizabeth N. Barr, *A Souvenir History of Lincoln County, Kansas*, 1908, Reproduction by the Centennial History Book Committee, p. 30-32; Lee, p. 121-123

(13) Criqui, p. 245

(14) Adolph Roenigk, *Pioneer History of Kansas*, 1933, Reprinted by the Lincoln
County Historical Society, 1973, p. 166

(15) Robert Collins, *Kansas Pacific, An Illustrated History*, Service Press, 1998, p. 23; Lee, 173

(16) Criqui, p. xv-xxii; Lee 123-132

(17) Nellie Seaver, Undated letter to her daughter, Mary Elizabeth (Whitney) Sutton,
Kansas State Historical Society; Whitney, Chauncey B., *Diary of Chauncey
B. Whitney*, Kansas Historical Collections, Vol. 12 p. 296-299; Miller & Snell,
p. 629-630

(18) Blaine Burkey, *Custer Come At Once!*, Society of Friends of Historic Fort Hays,
1991, p. 41-42

(19) Lee, p. 122

(20) De B. Randolph Keim, *Sheridan's Troopers on the Borders,* University of Nebraska
Press, 1985, Reprint of the 1885 edition, p. 14-15

(21) Choitz, p. 18, Jelinek, p. 16-17

(22) Samuel Johnson Crawford, *Kansas In The Sixties*, A.C. McClury and Co., 1911,
p. 321-335; Hutton, Paul Andrew, *Phil Sheridan and His Army*,
University of Nebraska Press, 1985, p. 64-65; Armes, p. 274; Greene, p. 87-88

(23) Walter Barlow Stevens, *Centennial History of Missouri*, S. J. Clark Publishing Company,
1921, p. 810; Talcott, Mary Kingsbury, editor, *The Genealogy And Decendants
Of Henry Kingsbury Of Ipswich And Haverhill, Mass, from collections made
by Frederick John Kingsbury*, Hartford Press: The Case, Lockwood & Brainard
Company, 1905, p. 155; Choitz, p. 19

(24) H. Putnam, *A Trip to the End of the Union Pacific in 1868*, Kansas Historical Quarterly,
Vol. 13 No 3, p. 197-198

(25) Walt Whitman, edited by Arthur Stedman, *Selected Poems*, D. McKay, 1892, p. 162

CHAPTER THREE

(1) Nellie Seaver, Undated letter to her daughter, Mary Elizabeth (Whitney) Sutton,
Kansas State Historical Society;

(2) Theodore Davis, *The Buffalo Range*, Harper's New Monthly Magazine, January, 1869

(3) Rosa & Koop, p. 23; Crawford, p. 323-324; Paul Andrew Hutton, *Phil Sheridan and
His Army*, University of Nebraska Press, 1985, p. 64-65; Armes, p. 274; Greene,
p. 87-88

(4) Miller & Snell, p.630-631; Choitz, p. 19

(5) Frank Wilson Blackmar, Editor, Kansas: *A Cyclopedia of State History, Embracing
Events, Institutions, Industries, Counties, Cities, Towns, Prominent Persons, Etc.
Vol. 1,* Standard Publishing Company, Chicago, IL, p. 818

(6) Lee, p. 174; Collins, 25

(7) Jim Gray, *Ellsworth Kansas 1869*, Kansas Cowboy, Vol. 3 No. 2, January 1999
Ellsworth, Kansas, p. 10; Rosa, *They Called Him Wild Bill*, p. 100-101; Stanley, p. 8

(8) General George Armstrong Custer, *My Life On The Plains or Personal Experiences
with Indians*, University of Oklahoma Press, 371-375; Burkey, p. 35-47; James
A. Hadley, *The 19ᵗʰ Kansas Cavalry and the Conquest of the Plains Indians*,
Collections of the Kansas State Historical Society 10 (1907-1908), p. 428-456

(9) General Nelson A. Miles, *Personal Recollections and Observations of General Nelson A. Miles, Embracing a Brief View of the Civil War: Or, From New England to the Golden Gate, and the Story of His Indian Campaigns, with Comments on the Exploration, Development and Progress of Our Great Western Empire,* The Werner Company, 1896, p. 151-152

(10) Gray, *Ellsworth Kansas, In 1869,* Kansas Cowboy, Vol 5, No. 3, March 2001, Ellsworth, Kansas, p. 7, 14. 16; State of Kansas Vs Joseph Brennan, Ellsworth County Court Records

(11) Blackmar, p. 818

(12) Lee, p. 174-175

(13) Floyd B. Streeter, *Ellsworth as a Texas Cattle Market,* The Kansas Historical Quarterly, November 1935, Vol. 4, No. 4, p. 388-389; Robert R. Dykstra, *Ellsworth, 1869-1875, The Rise and Fall of a Kansas Cowtown,* Kansas Historical Quarterly, Summer 1961, Vol 27, No. 2, 167-168, Miller & Snell, p. 18-19

(14) Rosa, p. 102-102

(15) Joseph G. McCoy, *Historic Sketches of the Cattle Trade of the West and Southwest,* Ramsey, Millett & Hudson, Kansas City, Missouri, 1874, p. 190-191; Dykstra, *Cattle Towns,* p. 37

(16) Jim Gray, *Kansas In 1869,* Kansas Cowboy, Vol 10 No. 3, March-April 2006, Ellsworth, Kansas, p. 15-16, Roenegk, p.170-176

(17) Leavenworth *Times and Conservative,* June 5, 1869

(18) Elijah W. Halford, "Prairie Landscape," Indianapolis (Indiana) *Journal,* July 15, 1869

(19) Andreas, p. 1280; Dykstra, *Ellsworth 1869-1875,* p. 166, Gray, *Powers Ranch,* Kansas Cowboy, Vol 6 No.3, March 2002, p. 6

(20) Cyrus Townsend Brady, *Indian Fights and Fighters,* University of Nebraska Press, Lincoln, Nebraska, 1971, p, 173-179.

(21) Ellsworth County Historical Society, Ellsworth Vigilante Committee Document, 1869

(22) Criqui, p. 251

(23) Rosa & Koop, p. 23

(24) McCoy, p. 57

(25) Dykstra, *The Cattle Towns,* p. 36

(26) Annual Report, Western Union Telegraph Company, 1869, p. 12

(27) Rosa and Koop, p. 22-23; Dykstra, *Ellsworth, 1869-1875,* p. 168; Armes, p. 301

(28) Robert E. Yarmer, *Evander Light,* Unpublished Manuscript, Ellinwood, Kansas; Gray, *Fraud On The Wild Frontier Or Evander Light & the Indians,* Kansas Cowboy, Vol. 8 No. 3, March-April, 2004

(29) Rosa, *They Called Him Wild Bill,* p. 139-141

(30) Rosa, *They Called Him Wild Bill,* p. 147-148

(31) James David Drees, "The Army and the Horse Thieves", *Kansas History, A Journal of the Central Plains,* Vol. 11 No 1, Spring 1998, p. 40; Gray, "Kansas In 1869", p. 17

(32) Miller & Snell, p. 63

(33) Junction City *Weekly Union,* September 25, 1869

CHAPTER FOUR

(1) Junction City *Union,* January 15, 1870; Gray, "The Life & Times of Jim Curry, The Devil's Own Desperado," *Kansas Cowboy,* Vol. 10 No. 1, November-December 2005, p. 23

(2) Ellsworth City Police Book; Inhabitants of Ellsworth, County of Ellsworth, State of Kansas, 1870 Census; Rosa & Koop, p. 23 – 24.

(3) Dykstra, *The Cattle Towns*, p. 47

(4) *New Harpers Monthly Magazine*, "Editor's Historical Record," Vol. 40 No. 240, May 1870, p. 937

(5) National *Police Gazette*, February 22, 1879; Correspondence with Mr. Lewis Wagner, Tucson, Arizona, 2003

(6) Minutes of the Ellsworth Board of Trustees; Ellsworth Village Odinances, 1870; Inhabitants of Ellsworth, County of Ellsworth, State of Kansas, 1870 Census; Rosa, Rowdy Joe Lowe, p. 24 – 25.; General Laws of the State of Kansas Passed At The Tenth Session of the Legislature, Commenced At The State Capital, On Tuesday, January 11, 1870, Topeka, Kansas, Published by State Printing House, 1870, P. 277-284

(7) Wayne Gard, *The Chisholm Trail*, University of Oklahoma Press, Norman, Oklahoma, 1954, p. 142; Glenn Danford Bradley, *The Story of the Santa Fe*, The Gorham Press, Boston, 1920, p. 83

(8) Miller & Snell, p. 577

(9) Rosa, *They Called Him Wild Bill*, p. 156-160; Drees, James D., *Bloody Prairie II*, Hays Daily News, 1997, p. 27-28; Burkey, Blaine, *Wild Bill Hickok, The Law In Hays City*, p. 19-21

(10) Wilson, p. 14

(11) Drees, "The Army and the Horse Thieves", p 35-53; James D. Drees, "Outlaws, Lawmen & Lawyers", *At Home In Ellis County, 1867-1992*, Hays Kansas, Ellis County Historical Society, 1991; Gaylynn Childs, *Museum Musings*, "Frontier Justice Possibly Saw Innocent Men Killed, Lynched", Junction City *Union*, August 19, 2007; J. Mark Alley, *The Violent Years, The Founding of a Kansas Town*, Multi Business Press, Hillsboro, Kansas, p. 29-54; Gray, "The Life of Jack Bridges Frontier Lawman," *Kansas Cowboy*, Vol. 8 No. 2, January-February 2004, p. 4

(12) Dana, Charles Anderson, Compiled by Thomas Jefferson Conant, Blandina Conant, *The American Cyclopaedia: A Popular Dictionary of General Knowledge*, Appleton, 1874, p. 549; Blackmar, p. 580

(13) Hutchinson, Clinton Carter, *Resources of Kansas: Fifteen Years Experience*, Published by The author, 1871, p. 102-105

(14) McCoy, p. 225

CHAPTER FIVE

(1) Dykstra, *The Cattle Towns*, p. 91-92; Ellsworth *Reporter*, December 26, 1871

(2) Hutchinson, p. 105-106

(3) Beccy Tanner, *Bear Grease, Builders and Bandits, The Men and Women of Wichita's Past*, Mennonite Press, Inc., Newton, Kansas, 1991, p. 43-44; Drees, "The Army and the Horse Thieves", p 35-53; James D. Drees, "Outlaws, Lawmen & Lawyers."; Gaylynn Childs, Junction City *Union*, August 19, 2007; J. Mark Alley, p. 29-54; Gray, "The Life of Jack Bridges Frontier Lawman," p. 4

(4) Rosa, Rowdy Joe Lowe, p. 25-26

(5) Rosa, *They Called Him Wild Bill*, p.180

(6) Edward J. Dodge, 1912 Biographical History of Barton County, Kansas

(7) Wayne R. Kime, *Colonel Richard Irving Dodge: The Life And Times of a Career Army Officer*, University of Oklahoma Press, Norman, Oklahoma, 2006
(8) Gard, p.158-159
(9) J. Marvin Hunter, *The Trail Drivers of Texas*, "Ate Terrapin And Dog Meat, And Was Glad To Get It," University of Texas Press, Austin, Texas, 1996, p. 625
(10) J. Marvin Hunter, *The Trail Drivers of Texas*, "Reflections Of The Trail," University of Texas Press, Austin, Texas, 1996, p. 430-431
(11) J. Marvin Hunter, *The Trail Drivers of Texas*, "A Long Hard Trip," University of Texas Press, Austin, Texas, 1996, p. 807-809
(12) Dykstra, *The Cattle Towns*, 160- 161
(13) John Wesley Hardin, *The Life of John Wesley Hardin, As Written By Himself*, University of Oklahoma Press, Norman, Oklahoma, 1961, p. 38
(14) Gray, *Kansas Cowboy*, "Col. James F. Ellison, A Genuine, Good Cattleman," Vol. 4 No. 6, September 2000, p. 4
(15) Charles Gross to J. B. Edwards, August 23, 1922; June 15, 1925, J. B. Edwards Collection, Kansas State Historical Society, Topeka, Kansas; James D. Drees, *Bloody Prairie*, Vol. 2, Hays Daily News, Hays, Kansas, 1997, p. 28; Gray, *Kansas Cowboy*, "In The Shadow of Wild Bill ... Retracing The Steps of Indian Annie" Vol. 5 No. 6, September 2001, p. 6
(16) Rosa, *Rowdy Joe Lowe*, p. 31-34
(17) Rosa, *Rowdy Joe Lowe*, p. 31
(18) Dykstra, *Ellsworth, 1869-1875*, p. 168
(19) Dykstra, *The Cattle Towns*, p. 38; Gard, p. 160
(20) Seaver, Nellie, Letter to her daughter Elizabeth Sutton, Kansas State Historical Society
(21) Wilson, Francis L., *A History of Ellsworth County Kansas*, Ellsworth County Historical Society, p. 16; Andreas, p. 1279; Miller & Snell, p. 632
(22) Rosa & Koop, p. 35
(23) Miller & Snell, p. 201
(24) Emmett, Chris, *Shanghai Pierce, A Fair Likeness*, University of Oklahoma Press, 1953, p. 72-73
(25) Rosa & Koop, p. 31
(26) Emmett, p. p.73
(27) Ellsworth County Commission Record Book
(28) Ellsworth *Reporter*, December 8, 1921, Vol. 51, No. 1
(29) Ellsworth *Reporter*, December 26, 1871, Vol. 1, No. 4

CHAPTER SIX

(1) Ellsworth *Reporter*, January 11, 1872
(2) Ellsworth *Reporter*, January 25, 1872; Wikipedia, *Grand Duke Alexei Alexandrovich of Russia*
(3) Dykstra, *The Cattle Towns*, p. 304
(4) Miller & Snell, p. 107-108; Ellsworth *Reporter*, February 29, 1872
(5) Dykstra, *Ellsworth, 1869- 1875*, p. 171
(6) Ellsworth *Reporter*, February 22, 1872; Wikipedia, *Nauch*; (6) Ellsworth *Reporter*, February 29, 1872; March 7, 1872
(7) Ellsworth *Reporter*, February 29, 1872; March 7, 1872; March 14, 1872
(8) Ellsworth *Reporter*, March 28, 1872; Ellsworth County Police Record Book, Ellsworth County Historical Society

(9) Records of the Ellsworth City Council, Ellsworth County Historical Society; Ellsworth *Reporter*, March 28; May 16, 1872

(10) Ellsworth County *Reporter*, March 14, 1872

(11) J. Marvin Hunter, *The Trail Drivers of Texas*, "Hardships Of A Cowboy's Life In the Early Days In Texas" University of Texas Press, Austin, Texas, 1996, p. 760

(12) Ellsworth *Reporter*, March 21, 1872

(13) Miller & Snell, p. 122

(14) Ellsworth *Reporter*, April 4, 1872

(15) Ellsworth *Reporter*, April 11, 1872

(16) Ellsworth *Reporter*, April 18, 1872

(17) Ellsworth *Reporter*, April 25, 1872

(18) Robert Yarmer, *Zack Light*, Unpublished, Ellinwood, Kansas, p. 3-5

(19) Ellsworth *Reporter*, February 22; May 2, June 31, 1872

(20) Plat of Out Lots, Ellsworth County Register of Deeds; Miller & Snell, p. 122-123; Ellsworth City Council Records; Ellsworth *Reporter*, May 9, 1872

(21) Dykstra, *The Cattle Towns*, p. 55

(22) Ellsworth *Reporter*, May 23; June 6, 1872; McCoy, p. 120-121

(23) J. Marvin Hunter, *The Trail Drivers of Texas*, "Cowboy From The Plains Of Nebraska" University of Texas Press, Austin, Texas, 1996, p. 549-551

(24) Ellsworth *Reporter*, June 6; June 13, 1872

(25) Gray, *Kansas Cowboy*, "Kansas In 1872," Vol. 10 No 6, September-October 2006, Ellsworth, Kansas, p. 16

(26) G. N. Moses, "The Return of a Western Sheriff." The Great Bend *Tribune* (Weekly), Vol. 33, No. 23, Page 1, Friday, January 15, 1909.

(27) Seaver, Nellie, Letter to her daughter Elizabeth Sutton, Kansas State Historical Society; Sutton family records; Criqui, p. 254

(28) Records of the Ellsworth City Council

(29) Harry E. Chrisman, *The Ladder of Rivers, The Story of (I. P. Print) Olive*, Revised Edition, p. 118-122; Gray, *Kansas Cowboy*, "A Father's Legacy Or Why Jim Kenedy Was So Treacherous" Vol. 6 No 1, November 2001, Ellsworth, Kansas, p. 14; Ellsworth *Reporter*, August 1, 1872

(30) Ellsworth *Reporter*, July 25, 1872

CHAPTER SEVEN

(1) Tilghman, Zoe A., *Marshal of the Last Frontier, Life and Services of William Matthew (Bill) Tilghman*, The Arthur A. Clark Company, Glendale, California, 1964, p. 71-75; Don Carlos Seitz, *From Kaw Teepee to Capitol, The Life Story of Charles Curtis, Indian, Who Has Risen to High Estate*, Frederick A. Stokes Co., New York, 1928, p. 81-81.

(2) Ellsworth *Reporter*, July 25, 1872

(3) Ellsworth *Reporter*, July 11, August 8, 1872

(4) Ellsworth *Reporter*, June 27, 1872; August 1, 1872

(5) Ellsworth City Council Records; Miller & Snell, p 218

(6) Dykstra, *The Cattle Towns*, p. 225-228; Ellsworth *Reporter*, August 1; August 15; August 29, 1872

(7) Abilene *Chronicle*, October 21, 1872, Ellsworth *Reporter*, June 27; August 15, 1872; Wayne Gard, *The Chisholm Trail*, University of Oklahoma Press, Norman, Oklahoma, 1954, p. 48

(8) James D. Drees, *Outlaws, Lawmen & Lawyers*

(9) Dykstra, *Ellsworth 1869-1875*, p. 176-179; Diary of Abraham Essick

(10) Ellsworth *Reporter*, October 3, 1872

(11) McCoy, p. 139-141; Miller & Snell, p. 218

(12) Ellsworth *Reporter*, October 17, 1872

(13) Dykstra, *The Cattle Towns*, p. 188-189 ; Ellsworth *Reporter*, November 7,
February 2, 1872

(14) Ellsworth *Reporter*, November 14, 1872; George Doud Freeman, *Midnight
and Noonday*, G.D. Freeman, 1892, p. 100-117

(15) Ellsworth *Reporter*, November 21; December 5, 1872

(16) Ellsworth *Reporter*, December 26, 1872

(17) Dykstra, *The Cattle Towns*, p. 161

CHAPTER EIGHT

(1) Ellsworth *Reporter*, January 9, 1873; Ellsworth *Reporter*, January 16, 1873

(2) Ellsworth *Reporter*, January 23, 1873, (The location of the cemetery is believed to be on
the grounds of the St. Francis Boys Home. This cemetery predates the Poor
Farm Cemetery and probably was west of that location.)

(3) Ellsworth *Reporter*, February 6, 1873

(4) Ellsworth *Reporter*, March 13, 1873; March 20, 1873; March 27, 1873; April 24, 1873;
May 1, 1873.

(5) Ellsworth *Reporter*, April 17, 1873; Joseph McCoy. *Historic Sketches*, p. 36

(6) Ellsworth *Reporter*, May 1, 1873; May 29, 1873; Floyd Benjamin Streeter, *Longhorns,
Shorthorns, The Life and Times of Captain Eugene Bartlett Millett, A
Cattleman of the Old West*, Ellsworth County Historical Society,
Ellsworth, Kansas

(7) Gray, *Kansas Cowboy*, "Col. James F. Ellison, A Genuine, Good Cattleman," Vol. 4
No. 6, September 2000, p. 4

(8) Ellsworth *Reporter*, (various issues throughout 1873); City of Ellsworth Tax Rolls,
Ellsworth County Clerk's Office; Choitz, p. 37-39; Streeter, *Prairie Trails
and Cowtowns*, p. 94-95

(9) Ellsworth *Reporter*, May 15, 1873

(10) Ellsworth *Reporter*, May 29, 1873; Ellsworth *Reporter*, June 6, 1873; Ellsworth
Reporter, June 12, 1873

(11) Floyd Benjamin Streeter, *Ben Thompson, Man With A Gun*, Frederick Fell, Inc.
Publishers, New York, 1957, p. 93; Ellsworth *Reporter*, June 12, 1873;
Kansas Cowboy, "Josiah Clarborne Traylor", July 1998, p. 5; Bruce Cody
Gray, Jr., Gray family story from his father B. C. Gray, Sr.

(12) Ellsworth *Reporter*, June 26, 1873; Dyskstra, p. 137.

(13) Ellsworth *Reporter*, July 3, 1873

(14) Ellsworth *Reporter*, July 10, 1873

CHAPTER NINE

(1) J. Marvin Hunter, *Trail Drivers of Texas*, Richard (Dick) Withers, "The
Experiences of an Old Trail Driver", University of Texas Press, Austin,
Texas, 1996, p. 210-311; Ibid, "Dodging Indians Near Packsaddle Mountain", p. 33

(2) Ira E. Lloyd, *Exciting Early Day History of Ellsworth*, Diary of Late Ira E. Lloyd Relates In Detail Early Day Lawless Cowtown, Ellsworth County Historical Society. (Lloyd's recollections of names and events are not entirely accurate but his account does substantiate certain events during 1873 and can be used to clarify documented incidents.)

(3) Ellsworth *Reporter*, July 17, 1873

(4) Miller & Snell, *Why The West Was Wild*, p. 507

(5) Robert E Yarmer, Madge B Yarmer, Unpublished Monograph of the Light Family, "Evander Light", p. 11, 12; Ellsworth *Reporter*, July 31, 1873; Ellsworth *Reporter*, August 7, 1873; Topeka *Commonwealth*, August 12, 1873. (The Episcopal Church was on the N. E. corner of North Douglas & 1st Street. The cemetery was east of the church. Whitney's home was east of the cemetery on the southeast corner of the same block.)

(6) Ellsworth *Reporter*, July 31, 1873; August 14, 1873.

(7) Ira E. Lloyd.

(8) Ellsworth *Reporter*, July 10, 1873; August 14, 1873.

(9) Record of the Ellsworth Municipal Court, August 15, 1873.

(10) Lloyd; Robert K. DeArment, *Knights of the Green Cloth*, University of Oklahoma Press, Norman, Oklahoma, p. 68-76, 346.

(11) Thomas C. Bicknell, "Whatever Became Of Texas Billy Thompson?", *Kansas Cowboy*, January 2001, (Mar 2001); Floyd Benjamin Streeter, *Ben Thompson, Man With A Gun*, Frederick Fell, Inc., New York, 1957, p. 90 – 103; Winfield *Weekly Courier*, September 11, 1873.

(12) Choitz, p. 45, 46; Ellsworth *Reporter*, January 8, 1880.

(13) Streeter, Miller & Snell, p. 635-639; Ellsworth County Commissioners Record Book, August 15, 1873; Ellsworth *Reporter*, August 21, 1873; Nellie Seaver, Letter to Bess Sutton, Kansas State Historical Society.

(14) Kansas Cowboy, *George W. Littlefield, Cowboy Entrepreneur*, May 2001, p. 8; J. Evetts Haley, *George W. Littlefield, Texan*, University of Oklahoma Press, Norman, Oklahoma, 1972, p. 63, 64.

(15) Miller & Snell, p. 84, 507 – 508; Ellsworth *Reporter*, September 11, 1873

(16) Ellsworth *Reporter*, September 4, 1873

(17) Nellie Seaver, Letter, February 24, 1898, Kansas State Historical Society, Topeka, Kansas

(18) Ellsworth *Reporter*, September 18, 1873; September 25, 1873

(19) Dykstra, *The Cattle Towns*, p. 77, 78

(20) Ellsworth *Reporter*, October 23, 1873

(21) Ellsworth *Reporter*, November 13, 1873

(22) Ellsworth County Coroner's Inquest, November 8, 1873, Ellsworth County Court Records; Miller & Snell, p. 84, 124, 125

(23) Dykstra, p. 170

CHAPTER TEN

(1) George Ripley, Charles Anderson Dana, Editors, *The American Cyclopaedia: A Popular Dictionary of General Knowledge*, Vol. VI, Appleton & Company, 1874, p. 549

(2) Ellsworth *Reporter*, November 27, 1873,

(3) Ellsworth *Reporter*, February 5; February 12, 1874; Dykstra, *Ellsworth, 1869-1875*, p. 185

(4) Ellsworth *Reporter*, February 4, 1874, February 26, 1874; March 5, 1874; March 12, 1874

(5) Ellsworth *Reporter*, March 19, April 23, April 30, 1874; Kansas Pacific Railway Company, *Guide Map of the Great Texas Cattle Trail from Red River Crossing to the Old Reliable Kansas Pacific Railway*, Ramsey, Millett, & Hudson, Kansas City, Missouri, 1874; Dykstra, *The Cattle Towns*, p. 170 - 171

(6) J. Marvin Hunter, *Trail Drivers of Texas*, Sol West, "Courage and Hardihood on the Old Texas Cattle Trail", University of Texas Press, Austin, Texas, 1996, p. 126-132; Ellsworth *Reporter*, May 7, 1874; Great Bend *Register*, May 30, 1874, McCoy, p. 355;

(7) Ellsworth *Reporter*, April 30, 1874; McCoy, p. 333-337

(8) Frank Collinson, *Life In the Saddle*, University of Oklahoma Press, Norman, Oklahoma, 1997, p. 31-40

(9) Ellsworth *Reporter*, January 15, 1874; June 4, 1874

(10) Ellsworth *Reporter*, June 11, 1874

(11) Ellsworth *Reporter*, June 18, 1874; Tilghman, p. 110-112, 119-120; *Kansas Cowboy*, "The Uncommon Outlaw, Dutch Henry Born", November-December 2002; Personal Interview, Mrs. Mabel L. Bennett, Pagosa Springs, Colorado, 2001; David Dary, *More True Tales of Old-Time Kansas*, "Dutch Henry, Horse Thief", University of Oklahoma Press, Norman, Oklahoma, 1987

(12) *Kansas Cowboy*, "Kansas In 1874", March-April, Vol. 11, No. 3, Ellsworth, Kansas

(13) Ellsworth *Reporter*, July 30, 1874

(14) Dykstra, *Ellsworth 1869-1875*, p. 185-186

(15) Lockhart (Texas) *Post-Register*, "John J. Myers and the Early Trails", November, 1972; Dykstra, *Ellsworth, 1869-1785*, p. 189, Ellsworth *Reporter*, December 10, 1874;

(16) General H. H. Hazen, "The Great Middle Region of the United States, and its Limited Space of Arable Land," *North American Review*, January, 1875; Ellsworth *Reporter*, December 10; December 17, 1874;

(17) Ellsworth *Reporter*, January 7, 1875

CHAPTER ELEVEN

(1) Ellsworth *Reporter*, January 7; February 4; February 18, 1875; April 1, 1875; Ellsworth City Council Meeting, February 16, 1875; Dykstra, *The Cattle Towns*, p. 321

(2) Ellsworth *Reporter*, February 18, 1875

(3) Dykstra, *The Cattle Towns*, p. 316

(4) Criqui, p. 140 – 142; Ellsworth *Reporter* March 11; March 25, 1875

(5) *Kansas Cowboy*, "Kansas In 1875", May - June, Vol. 11, No. 4, Ellsworth,
   Kansas; Ellsworth *Reporter*, May 6; May 13, 1875; Dykstra, *The Cattle Towns*,
   p. 99; McCoy, p. 120-121

(6) Ellsworth *Reporter*, April 22; May 20; May 27, 1875

(7) Ellsworth *Reporter*, May 27; June 3; June 17; July 1; July 22, 1875

(8) Ellsworth *Reporter*, June 3, 1875; Rosa and Koop, p. 22

(9) James H. Cook, *Fifty Years on the Old Frontier As Cowboy, Hunter, Guide, Scout,
   and Ranchman*, University of Oklahoma Press, Norman, Oklahoma, 1980,
   p. 91-93

(10) Ellsworth *Reporter*, June 24; July 22; August 5, 1875; Dykstra, *The Cattle Towns*,
   p. 142.

(11) Ellsworth *Reporter*, July 1; August 5; September 9; September 23;
   September 30, 1875

(12) Ellsworth *Reporter*, November 18, 1875

(13) Ellsworth *Reporter*, December 16, 1875

CHAPTER TWELVE

(1) Streeter, *Ben Thompson, Man With A Gun*, p, 112-115

(2) Leavenworth *Daily Times*, October 21, 1877; Jim Gray, *Kansas Cowboy*,
   "In the Shadow of Wild Bill ... Retracing the Steps of Indian Annie,"
   September 2001, Vol. 5 No. 6; James D. Drees, *Bloody Prairie*, Volume II,
   "Wild Bill's Woman: Anna (Indian Annie) Wilson", The Hays *Daily News*,
   Hays, Kansas, 1997, p. 20-30; Ellsworth *Democrat*, November 12, 1885

(3) Robert K. DeArment, *Bat Masterson, The Man and the Legend*, University of
   Oklahoma Press, Norman, Oklahoma, 1989, p. 62-66

(4) Jim Gray, *Kansas Cowboy*, "Kansas in 1878" November-December 2007

(5) Paul Wellman, *The Trampling Herd, The Story of the Cattle Range in
   America*, University of Nebraska Press, Lincoln, Nebraska, 1988, p. 199.

(6) Rosa & Koop, p. 151

(7) Yarmer, p. 13-18

(8) Ellsworth *Reporter*. January 4, 1882

(9) Ellsworth *Reporter*. March 16, 1882

(10) Ellsworth *Reporter*. April 6, 1882

(11) Dee Brown & Martin F. Schmitt, *Trail Driving Days, The Golden Days of the
   Old Trail Driving Cattlemen*, Charles Scribners's Sons, New York, 1952,
   p. 68-69

BIBLIOGRAPHY

Government Publications

General Laws of the State of Kansas Passed At The Tenth Session of the Legislature,
    Commenced At The State Capital, On Tuesday, January 11, 1870, Topeka, Kansas,
    Published by State Printing House, 1870.
Marsha King, *Results of Archaeological Investigations at Fort Harker, 14EW310,
    Ellsworth, County, Kansas,* Contract Archaeology Publication No. 17,
    Kansas State Historical Society, 1997.
Biennial Report, Kansas State Historical Society, 1881, p. 1676

Manuscripts

Diary, Abraham Essick
Diary, Ira E. Lloyd, *Exciting Early Day History of Ellsworth,*
    Ellsworth County Historical Society.
Letter, Nellie Seaver to Mary Elizabeth (Whitney) Sutton,
    Kansas State Historical Society.
Letter, Charles Gross to J. B. Edwards, August 23, 1922
Letter, Lewis Wagner, Tucson, Arizona, To Jim Gray, 2003
J. B. Edwards Collection, Kansas State Historical Society, June 15, 1925
William Sternberg Collection, *Chased By Indians*, Ellsworth County
    Historical Society
Robert E Yarmer, Madge B Yarmer, Unpublished Monograph of the Light Family,
    "Evander Light".

Articles

Bicknell, Thomas C., "Whatever Became Of Texas Billy Thompson?",
   Kansas Cowboy, January 2001, (Mar 2001)

Childs, Gaylynn, "Frontier Justice Possibly Saw Innocent Men Killed, Lynched",
   Museum Musings, Junction City *Union,* August 19, 2007

Davis, Theo R., "The Buffalo Range", *Harper's New Monthly Magazine*, January, 1869

Dodge, Edward J., 1912 Biographical History of Barton County, Kansas

Drees, James David, *"The Army and the Horse Thieves",* *Kansas History Magazine,*
   Spring, 1988

Drees, James D., *"Bloody Prairie",* Vol. 2, Hays *Daily News*, Hays, Kansas, 1997

Drees, James David, "Outlaws, Lawmen & Lawyers*",* From *At Home In Ellis County,*
   1867-1992, Hays Kansas, Ellis County Historical Society, 1991

Dykstra, Robert, *Ellsworth, 1869-1875, The Rise and Fall of a Kansas Cowtown*,
   Kansas Historical Quarterly, Summer 1961, Vol 27, No. 2.

Hadley, James A., *The 19ᵗʰ Kansas Cavalry and the Conquest of the Plains Indians*,
   Collections of the Kansas State Historical Society 10 (1907-1908).

Halford, Elijah W., "Prairie Landscape", Indianapolis [Indiana] *Journal*, July 15, 1869

Hazen, General H. H., "The Great Middle Region of the United States, and its Limited
   Space of Arable Land," *North American Review*, January, 1875.

Moses, G. N., "The Return of a Western Sheriff." The Great Bend *Tribune*,
   January 15, 1909.

Putnam, H., *A Trip to the End of the Union Pacific in 1868,* Kansas Historical Quarterly,
   Vol. 13, No 3.

Streeter, Floyd B., *Ellsworth as a Texas Cattle Market*, The Kansas Historical Quarterly,
   November 1935, Vol. 4, No. 4.

Thompson, *Peter Robidoux: A Real Kansas Pioneer*, Collections of the Kansas State
   Historical Society, Vol. XVII, 1926-1928.

Whitney, Chauncey B., *Diary of Chauncey B. Whitney*, Kansas Historical Collections

Wilson, Francis L., *A History of Ellsworth County Kansas,* Ellsworth County
   Historical Society

Newspapers

Kansas

Abilene *Chronicle*
Ellsworth *Democrat*
Ellsworth *Messenger*
Ellsworth *Reporter*
Ellsworth *Tri-Weekly Advertiser*
Great Bend *Register*
Hays City *Railway Advance*
Hays *Daily News*
Junction City *Weekly Union*
Kansas City *Price Current and Live Stock Reporter*
Kansas Cowboy (Ellsworth)
Kansas City *Journal*
Leavenworth *Daily Bulletin*
Leavenworth *Daily Conservative*
Leavenworth *Daily Times*
Leavenworth *Times and Conservative*
Manhattan *Nationalist*
State News (Topeka)
Topeka *Commonwealth*
Topeka *Daily Commonwealth*
Topeka *Daily Kansas State Record*
Wichita *Eagle*
Winfield *Weekly Courier*

Cheyenne Daily *Leader* (Wyoming)
Gonzales *Enquirer* (Texas)
Lockhart *Post-Register*   (Texas)
Montezuma *Republican* (Iowa)
National *Police Gazette*   (New York)
Nebraska City *Press* (Nebraska)
Harper's New Monthly Magazine (New York)
New York *Herald* (New York)
Dallas *Gazette*   (Iowa)
Western Stock *Journal*   (Texas)

Books

Alley, J. Mark, *The Violent Year, The Founding of a Kansas Town,* Hillsboro, Kansas,
    Multi Business Press, 1989.
Andreas, Alfred Thayer and William G. Cutler, *History of the State of Kansas,*
    Chicago, Illinois, 1883.
Armes, George Augustus, *Ups and Downs of an Army Officer,* Self Published, 1900.
Baldwin, Alice Blackwood, and Eleanor R. Carriker, *An Army Wife on the Frontier,*
    Tanner Trust Fund, University of Utah Library, 1975.
Barr, Elizabeth N., *A Souvenir History of Lincoln County, Kansas,* 1908, Reproduction
    by the Centennial History Book Committee
Beedle, John Hanson, *Western Wilds and The Men Who Redeem Them,* Cincinnati, Ohio,
    Jones Brothers Publishers, 1877.
Bernhardt, C., *Indian Raids,* Lincoln, Kansas, The Lincoln Sentinal Print, 1910.
Blackmar, Frank Wilson, Ed., *Kansas: A Cyclopedia of State History, Embracing Events,
    Institutions, Industries, Counties, Cities, Towns, Prominent Persons, Etc. Vol. 1,*
    Chicago, Illinois, Standard Publishing Company, 1912.
Brady, Cyrus Townsend, *Indian Fights and Fighters,* Lincoln, Nebraska,
    University of Nebraska Press, 1971.
Bradley, Glenn Danford, *The Story of the Santa Fe,* Boston, Massachusetts,
    The Gorham Press, 1920.
Brown, Dee & Martin F. Schmitt, *Trail Driving Days, The Golden Days of the Old Trail
    Driving Cattlemen,* New York, New York, Charles Scribners's Sons, 1952.
Burkey, Blaine, *Custer Come At Once!,* Society of Friends of Historic Fort Hays, 1991.
Burkey, Blaine, *Wild Bill Hickok, The Law in Hays City,* Third Edition, Slightly Revised,
    Ellis County Historical Society, 1996.
Choitz, John F., *A History of Ellsworth County, 1854-1885.* Master's Thesis,
    Fort Hays State College, Hays, Kansas, 1942, Republished by Alfred H. Choitz,
    South Bend, Indiana, 1999.
Chrisman, Harry E. Chrisman, *The Ladder of Rivers, The Story of (I. P. Print) Olive,*
    Revised Edition.
Collins, Robert, *Kansas Pacific, An Illustrated History,* Service Press, 1998.
Collinson, Frank, *Life In the Saddle,* Norman, Oklahoma,
    University of Oklahoma Press, 1997.
Cook, James H. *Fifty Years on the Old Frontier As Cowboy, Hunter, Guide, Scout,
    and Ranchman,* Norman, Oklahoma, University of Oklahoma Press, 1980.
Crawford, Samuel Johnson, *Kansas In The Sixties,* A.C. McClury and Co., 1911, p. 321-335
Criqi, Orvel A., *Fifty Fearless Men,* Marcelene, Maryland,
    Walsworth Publishing Company, 1997.
Custer, Elizabeth Bacon, *Tenting on the Plains or General Custer in Kansas and Texas,*
    Norman, Oklahoma, University of Oklahoma Press, 1994.
Custer, General George Armstrong, *My Life On The Plains or Personal Experiences
    with Indians,* Norman, Oklahoma, University of Oklahoma Press, 1977.
Dana, Charles Anderson, Compiled by Thomas Jefferson Conant, Blandina Conant,
    The American Cyclopaedia: A Popular Dictionary of General Knowledge,

212

New York, New York, D. Appleton And Company, 1874.

Dary, David, *More True Tales of Old-Time Kansas*, "Dutch Henry, Horse Thief",
  Norman, Oklahoma, University of Oklahoma Press, 1987.

DeArment, Robert K., *Bat Masterson, The Man and the* Legend, Norman, Oklahoma,
  University of Oklahoma Press, 1989.

DeArment, Robert K., *Knights of the Green Cloth*, Norman, Oklahoma,
  University of Oklahoma Press, 1982.

Dykstra, Robert K., *The Cattle Towns*, Lincoln, Nebraska,
  University of Nebraska Press, 1983.

Emmett, Chris, *Shanghai Pierce, A Fair Likeness*, Norman, Oklahoma,
  University of Oklahoma Press, 1953.

Freeman, George Doud, *Midnight and Noonday*, Caldwell, Kansas, G. D. Freeman, 1892.

Gard, Wayne, *The Chisholm Trail*, Norman, Oklahoma,
  University of Oklahoma Press, 1954.

Greene, Jerome A., *Washita: The U. S. Army and the Southern Cheyennes, 1867-1869*,N
  Norman, Oklahoma, University of Oklahoma Press, 2004.

Haley, J. Evetts, *George W. Littlefield, Texan*, Norman, Oklahoma,
  University of Oklahoma Press, 1972.

Hardin, John Wesley, *The Life of John Wesley Hardin, As Written By Himself*,
  Norman, Oklahoma, University of Oklahoma Press, 1961.

Hollister, Ovando James, *The Mines of Colorado*, Springfield, Massachusetts ,
  Samuel Bowles & Co., 1867.

Hunter, J. Marvin, *Trail Drivers of Texas*, Austin, Texas, University of Texas Press, 1996.

Hutchinson, Clinton Carter, *Resources of Kansas: Fifteen Years Experience*,
  Published by The Author, 1871.

Hutton, Paul Andrew, *Phil Sheridan and His Army*, Lincoln, Nebraska,
  University of Nebraska Press, 1985.

Hunter, J. Marvin, *The Trail Drivers of Texas*, Austin, Texas,
  University of Texas Press, 1996.

Jelinek, George, *The Ellsworth Story, 90 Years of Ellsworth and Ellsworth County
  History*, Ellsworth, Kansas, The Messenger Press.

Kansas Pacific Railway Company, *Guide Map of the Great Texas Cattle Trail from
  Red River Crossing to the Old Reliable Kansas Pacific Railway*, Kansas City,
  Missouri, Ramsey, Millett, & Hudson, 1874.

Keim, De B. Randolph, *Sheridan's Troopers on the Borders*, Lincoln, Nebraska,
  University of Nebraska Press, 1985.

Kelly, Fanny, *Narrative of my Captivity Among the Sioux Indians*, Chicago, Illinois,
  R.R. Donnelley & Sons, Co., 1891.

Kime, Wayne R., *Colonel Richard Irving Dodge: The Life And Times of a Career
  Army Officer*, Norman, Oklahoma, University of Oklahoma Press, 2006.

Knight, Oliver, *Following The Indian Wars*, Norman, Oklahoma,
  University of Oklahoma Press, 1993.

Lee, Wayne C., and Howard C. Raynesford, *Trails of the Smoky Hill*, Caxton, Idaho,
  The Caxton Printers LTD, 1980.

Lyon, Charles J., *The Compendias History of Ellsworth County, Kansas,
  From Its Settlement to the Present Time*, Reporter Press, 1879,
  Reprint of First Edition, Prepared by Patricia Svaty, Ellsworth, Kansas, 1998.

McCoy, Joseph G., *Historic Sketches of the Cattle Trade of the West and Southwest*,
  Kansas City, Missouri, Ramsey, Millett & Hudson, 1874.

Miles, General Nelson A., *Personal Recollections and Observations of General Nelson
  A. Miles, Embracing a Brief View of the Civil War: Or, From New England to the*

213

Golden Gate, and the Story of His Indian Campaigns, with Comments on the Exploration, Development and Progress of Our Great Western Empire, Chicago, Illinois, The Werner Company, 1896.

Miller, Nyle H. and Joseph W. Snell, *Why The West Was Wild,* Norman, Oklahoma, University of Oklahoma Press, 2003.

Milner, Joe E. and Earle R. Forrest, *California Joe, Noted Scout and Indian Fighter,* Lincoln, Nebraska, University of Nebraska Press, 1987.

Otero, Miguel Antonio, *My Life on the Frontier, 1864-1882*, New York, New York, The Press of the Pioneers, Inc., 1935.

Ovando, James Hollister, *The Mines of Colorado*, Springfield, Massachusetts, Samuel Bowles & Co., 1867

Ripley, George, Charles Anderson Dana, *The American Cyclopaedia: A Popular Dictionary of General Knowledge,* New York, New York, Appleton & Company, 1874.

Roenigk, Adolph, *Pioneer History of Kansas*, 1933, Reprinted by the Lincoln County Historical Society, 1973.

Rosa, Joseph G., *They Called Him Wild Bill,* Norman, Norman, Oklahoma, University of Oklahoma Press, Second Edition, 1974.

Rosa, Joseph G. and Waldo E. Koop, *Rowdy Joe Lowe, Gambler with a Gun*, Norman, Oklahoma, University of Oklahoma Press, 1989.

Seitz, Don Carlos, *From Kaw Teepee to Capitol, The Life Story of Charles Curtis, Indian, Who Has Risen to High Estate,* New York, New York, Frederick A. Stokes Co., New York, 1928.

Stanley, Henry M., *My Early Travels and Adventures in America and Asia*, Charles Scribner's Sons, 1895.

Stevens, Walter Barlow, *Centennial History of Missouri*, St. Louis, Missouri, S. J. Clark Publishing Company, 1921.

Streeter, Floyd Benjamin, *Ben Thompson, Man With A Gun*, New York, New York, Frederick Fell, Inc. Publishers, 1957.

Talcott, Mary Kingsbury, Ed., *The Genealogy And Descendants Of Henry Kingsbury Of Ipswich And Haverhill, Mass, from collections made by Frederick John Kingsbury,* Hartford, Connecticut, Hartford Press: The Case, Lockwood & Brainard Company, 1905.

Tanner, Beccy, *Bear Grease, Builders and Bandits, The Men and Women of Wichita's Past,* Newton, Kansas, Mennonite Press, Inc., 1991.

Tilghman, Zoe A., *Marshal of the Last Frontier, Life and Services of William Matthew (Bill) Tilghman,* Glendale, California, The Arthur A. Clark Company, 1964.

Wellman, Paul, *The Trampling Herd, The Story of the Cattle Range in America*, Lincoln, Nebraska, University of Nebraska Press, 1988.

Whitman, Walt, edited by Arthur Stedman, *Selected Poems*, D. McKay, 1892.

Yarmer, Robert, *Zack Light*, Unpublished, Ellinwood, Kansas.

Miscellaneous

Annual Report, Western Union Telegraph Company, 1869

City of Ellsworth Tax Rolls, Ellsworth County Clerk's Office

Ellsworth City Police Book

Ellsworth County Commission Record Book

Ellsworth County Coroner's Inquest, November 8, 1873, Ellsworth County Court Records

Ellsworth County Court Records, November 8, 1873

Ellsworth Municipal Court Record, August 15, 1873

Ellsworth Vigilante Committee Document, 1869

Ellsworth Village Ordinances, 1870

Gray, Bruce Cody, Jr., Gray family story from his father B. C. Gray, Sr.

Inhabitants of Ellsworth, County of Ellsworth, State of Kansas, 1870 Census

L. O. Wight, Draftsman, *Plat of Ellsworth, Kansas*, Book A, Plat Books, Saline County Register of Deeds, May 4, 1867.

Minutes of the Ellsworth Board of Trustees

Personal Interview, Mrs. Mabel L. Bennett, Pagosa Springs, Colorado, 2001

Plat of Out Lots, Ellsworth County Register of Deeds

Records of the Ellsworth City Council

State of Kansas Vs Joseph Brennan, Ellsworth County Court Records

Wikipedia, Grand Duke Alexei Alexandrovich of Russia

Wikipedia, Nauch

INDEX

220

221

ABOUT THE AUTHOR

Known by one and all as "The Cowboy," Jim Gray is a 6th generation Kansan. His family has been in Kansas since it became a territory in 1854. His great-grandfather, George Gray, set up Gray's Ranch in central Kansas in 1883.

In 1996, Gray and partner Linda Kohls established the C.O.W.B.O.Y. (Cockeyed Old West Band Of Yahoos) Society to promote and preserve the Cowboy heritage of Kansas through The Kansas Cowboy, a bi-monthly (six issues a year) newspaper. The articles, researched and written by Gray, examine the frontier history of Kansas from Gray's own unique perspective on history. "I've always had an interest in things that have gone before. These Kansas plains have been witness to untold stories of joy and desperation. Many have been told over and over. Others have lapsed beyond recognition."

Desperate Seed puts flesh and blood onto the bones of stories that have been buried but not forgotten.

Printed in the United States
212557BV00002B/1/P

9 780982 274101